Between the Pews
*More than A Sabbath Day's Journey
From The Promised Land*

Between the Pews

*More than A Sabbath Day's Journey
From The Promised Land*

Sylvia Edmondson-Holt

Gotham Books

30 N Gould St.
Ste. 20820, Sheridan, WY 82801
https://gothambooksinc.com/

Phone: 1 (307) 464-7800

© 2025 *Sylvia Edmondson-Holt*. All rights reserved.

No part of this book may be reproduced, stored in a retrieval system, or transmitted by any means without the written permission of the author.

Published by Gotham Books (March 14, 2025)

ISBN: 979-8-3485-1775-5 (H)
ISBN: 979-8-3485-1773-1 (P)
ISBN: 979-8-3485-1774-8 (E)

Because of the dynamic nature of the Internet, any web addresses or links contained in this book may have changed since publication and may no longer be valid.

The views expressed in this work are solely those of the author and do not necessarily reflect the views of the publisher, and the publisher hereby disclaims any responsibility for them.

INTRODUCTION

My memoir was first published in 2016. I had a serious surgery in 2015. After that, I decided to retire from nursing, plus I was way past the regular retirement age. I was enjoying working from home, however. I also needed to finish my Memoir because of one story that kept bothering me. One of my favorite actors of all time, a professor at Tennessee State University, the late Barry Scott, would have put it like this: "It is a story that must be told." The story that triggered the memoir is tucked into the whole narrative. It couldn't be isolated from the entirety of the book.

Since COVID-19 our lives have been turned upside down. As a retired nurse I have had a great career and experience in washing my hands, and wearing a face mask, but this time, I wasn't getting paid for it.

Initially I heard about a shooting at a mall near Seattle, Washington. One of my twin granddaughters, Camille Sylvia Holt was living there at the time. Out of concern I called to see if she had heard about it. She immediately informed me that most people were worried about the Wuhan Flu thought to be coming from China.

I was out shopping but I went home forgetting about what I had been shopping for in the first place. When I turned my TV on to listen to the news, it was all I could hear about was a virus threatening its outrage and soon it became the "Worst Pandemic since the Spanish Flu Pandemic of 1912. COVID 19 was all you could hear about for months. It seems like overnight, people were being sent home to work remotely. Camille ended up back home in Pennsylvania with her parents and not soon after, her twin sister Candice Rebecca Holt was allowed to leave New York City to work remotely. Camille was allowed to work remotely as well. I retired in 2015 from the Veterans Affairs Hospital, having done Telehealth for the last 12 years of my career. The public sector hadn't grasped the concept, and it seemed like something new to most people. I had to give up on the Critical Care Nursing because of a prior ankle fracture. So, Telehealth was what I ended my career with.

I immediately got my vaccination and encouraged others to do the same. Then, the face mask became normal attire. People started making them and matching them to their clothing. Hand sanitizer swung from belts, stethoscopes, and purses. Hand sanitizer and masks were placed in front doorways to public buildings. Most of us began to isolate ourselves, and we were frightened. It became mandatory to stand six feet apart in stores. When I made my quarterly visit to my doctor he looked like a coal miner in a white lab coat and bubble head gear. He had new portable air purifiers in every room. Chairs were spread apart as much as the office space allowed. It ran as fast as a fast food line. No more waiting long to get to see the doctor. I liked that. We went as far off the deep end as a society of people can go. The blessings were today's technology. Technology allowed many people to work from home, get healthcare visits, and stream church and funerals online. The vaccines were ready in record time. We learned to wave at family and friends while staying six feet apart.

Because of my surgery, I had become accustomed to live streaming church services. I even confessed to one of my pastors,

Pastor Bryan Cowan, that occasionally I'd dozed off to sleep during the sermon, but the anointing of the "Holy Spirit woke me up just in time to grab onto the computer before the altar prayer was done." He said, "Amen, sister. I'm going to have to tell that one." We had a hearty laugh, and he promised not to call any name.

Seriously, the Pandemic left none of us untouched in some way. We lost family members and friends to the virus and some to natural causes. But through all the sadness and pain, we know that we are not alone on our journey. And we remember the voices of those gone before us.

I must pause to say that I was concerned about the Shooting at the mall near Seattle, but I quickly turned my attention to the global pandemic instead. Now the pandemic, "I pray, is under control" with the vaccines and other measures. But it saddens me to know we still have an epidemic in the United States, and that is gun violence. Gun violence is higher in the United States than in any other developed country in the world. It is like an uncontrollable virus. Yet, we have not come up with a solution to stamp out this epidemic. We are not an ignorant nation. We know that Gun violence can be better controlled because it is being controlled in other countries. Is the Second Amendment that important? If you don't have access to a gun, then you can't shoot it. I understand the "Right to Own and bear arms." I'm afraid nothing will be done soon. That's all I have to say about that, dear readers.

WHAT WAS I THINKING

Before the pandemic, I had been contemplating reinvesting in our first home, a charming 66-year-old brick house built in 1955. It had been our home for 25 years and a haven for several families and college students since 1988. My former rental manager had suggested adding another bathroom to increase its appeal to renters, but I hesitated, thinking it would be a waste of resources.

As I resumed managing the property, I witnessed the neighborhood transforming. Investors reached out to my sons and me, eager to purchase our sentimental possession. We were resolute: we wouldn't sell. I began to adopt an investor's mindset, responding to callers with, "I'm an investor too. Do you have any properties for sale?" I became rude, sarcastic, and very angry at how people think they have the right to disturb you about a property that is not for sale. One person called my son to inquire if I was in a Nursing Home. If they knew what I was about to do, it would have blown their minds, an elderly black woman about to tear down a perfectly good home in the middle of COVID-19. The more they called, the more I knew that we were not going to sell. My sons were having sentimental feelings about tearing down their childhood home.

Sometimes, sentimental value can hold us back. While it's essential to cherish memories, progress often requires letting go. I recognized that tearing down the old house would unlock more value. Bobby and I had purchased the property when we were just 22 and 20 years old, respectively. Our children had created countless happy memories. I knew I was dreaming. I was careful about who I shared this moment with because people will try to wake you up. When I approached the bank, I was treated like an investor. The rest is, "I accomplished one of the biggest of my dreams ever.

On the morning of the demolition, I parked across the street, observing from a distance. At the same time the pandemic was unfolding, threatening to disrupt my plans. Lumber prices, materials, appliances, and labor costs were rising. Yet, I know that time waits for no one. I thought about changing my mind a few times. But I knew if those other investors could do it I could too.

Embarking on this ambitious project proved to be a grounding force amidst the pandemic's chaos. It allowed me to focus on something beyond the virus's impact on our world. As I watched the old house come down, I felt a sense of transformation, knowing that something new and better would arise from the rubbish that was thrown about the ground. I also knew I could no longer change my mind. I told my contractor that I knew I would not be allowed on site during work hours. But "You had better believe I'm going to be in site." I stationed myself in site most days. My eldest son Terrell Sr. and I would examine the construction daily after the workers were gone.

We watched as our former neighbors' homes were sold, and even "The church across the street" was sold for the second time. Thank God the building is historical and cannot be torn down or altered on the outside. The Historical Commission had to approve the building design process for our homes. So smaller homes were demolished, and two or more were built back on the same lot if the Historical Commission approved. Despite the annoying calls, I repeatedly asked them, "Is there a for sale' sign on the property? Did I miss something? Well, then it is not for sale." I was still rude, sarcastic, and angry at the number of calls I received. However, the number of calls has not slowed down, and it makes me think, why do they want my property so much? Greed has taken over, and they will try any way to break you down and make you say "Yes." But we stuck on "No." They are still calling me, and I'm sure others are being harassed by greedy investors.

May I encourage you to keep dreaming? Go for it at any age. If God woke you up this morning, He has more for you to do.

Dedication

Mr. Alex Williams
Home Telehealth staff of TVHS
Promise Land Community Heritage Association.
The residents of Dickson County, Tennessee
The Masons and Eastern Star Association of Charlotte, Tennessee
Hampton High School Alumni Association, Dickson, Tennessee, and Class of 1962

Special Dedication

Mr. Harold Bell because Bobby considered you his best friend in the world from high school and on. Not just anybody had that privilege. Thank you for your friendship.

Mr. Dan Buckner, former mayor of Dickson, Tennessee. Mrs. Bettye Buckner and Reed. I simply cannot express how much we appreciated this family. Mother met and worked several years later in life for them. She loved you like family, and you gave that love back. She often talked about her friendship with Mrs. Ledbetter like a sister (a white family, for the reader who does not know).

Special Dedication and in Loving Memory

Mrs. Wilma Talley, my sister. My lifetime pal. She was my sister and best friend forever.

Dr. Ardis H. Edmondson-Holt, my niece. You left us too soon, but we believe that God knows best. We love and miss you.

The late Mr. Dennison and Mrs. Thelma Dennison. They owned Dennison's Motors, a car dealership and was the first sponsor of

Theodore Edmondson and the Promise Land Singers radio program. (Some readers might not know; these were white friends of my parents.)

The late Bro. Henry Ragan and Mrs. Nancy Ragan. Former owners of the Friendly Neighbor's Furniture Store, Dickson, Tennessee. This store is still open today.

Our family will never forget this family. They also sponsored the Promise Land Singers on the radio program. They remained friends with my mother until her death. When mother passed, Brother Regan wrote in her visitation book: "Lizzie, tell Theo hello." I can imagine what a time they are having together around the Great Throne of God. The day of Mother's funeral Brother Ragan had breakfast for our family at the Shoney's in Dickson. That was the kindest thing and exactly what we needed (white friends of my parents).

Very Special Dedication and in Loving Memory

Mr. Bobby Lane Holt and his children.

I respectfully dedicate my memoir to the Late Bobby Lane Holt because we met at the ages of fifteen and seventeen. He is naturally a large portion of my story and the father of my three sons. If in writing I have made any comment or statement about him that seemed negative in any way, I apologize. It was not meant to be. The truth sometimes is negative, but the positive is how we deal with it. I am thankful for many good memories. I am sorry that it could not have lasted forever. I believe he served his purpose while here.

Because he possessed excellent wisdom as a young man, our children are blessed for generations to come. To disrespect his memory would be a direct reflection on my own integrity. Without him, I wouldn't have you, my children and grandchildren. I gained a lot from the wisdom and knowledge he possessed that has made me a better person. I owe God first and then him the highest praise for protecting our family until we are like baby eagles—could fly alone.

We developed a compatible relationship to accommodate our children and grandchildren and to facilitate closure to our own. God has commanded us to love one another and to forgive each other as he so generously has forgiven us.

I know that it was well between us before his passing as our children witnessed. And in closing, I say, I want to remind his children: he was proud of you, and he loved all of you.

"Is it well? Yes. It is well. I thank God it is well with our spirits, his, and mine."

In loving memory of our babies lost at birth:

Our son Bobby Edmondson Holt (Bobby and Sylvia Holt) and our grandson Avery Duran Holt (Andre and Chiquilla Holt). We look forward to seeing our babies in heaven.

ILLUSION

Hold me not illusion
Let me have mind eye
That I may see what is true.
Move me not in waves;
Let me taste not, thy beauty
Empty me not. Leave me my pride.
You must not balance my fate
Let me make it through the gate
That I may be free of your wrath.

Terrell J. Holt Sr., 1981

Camille Holt
Union League Essay

My background shaped my journey toward embodying patriotism, limited government, and free enterprise. My immersion into free enterprise started with Pennsylvania Free Enterprise Week (PFEW) following my 9th - grade year at Abington Senior High. Guided by a teacher's recommendation, my twin sister and I delved into PFEW. In this Penn Tech College program, entrepreneurial minds imparted knowledge about stocks and enterprise to youth. Learning about the advantages of free enterprise ignited my desire to delve deeper into software start-ups and real estate. This curiosity led me to participate in Mobile App competitions, leading to my career at Microsoft.

My first-hand experience with the U.S. government started when Judge Doris Ribner invited me to the White House Leadership Development and Policy Hackathon in June 2015. Discussing technology and education with fellow students and government officials unveiled the imperative of maintaining an equilibrium between government oversight and business autonomy.

As a Bonner Scholar at Spelman College, I volunteered with the Center for Working Families in Atlanta from August 2016 to May 2017. Through collaborations with Atlanta veterans' organizations, the center facilitated tax preparation services, financial literacy workshops, employment certifications, and digital literacy courses. My contributions encompassed computer literacy sessions and scheduling tax services. This engagement, juxtaposed with my familial connection to my grandfather's military service, catalyzed a profound love of the U.S.

As I appreciated the Union League Legacy Foundations Civil War exhibit artifacts donated by many families' collections, it reminded me of Holt & Son's Venture's (residential rental company) contributions to the Promise Land Historical Society. My grandmother, Sylvia Holt, reverence for American history and legacy is showcased in her recent attainment of historic landmark status for our ancestral land. From generations of gospel music tradition to our commitment to preserving familial artifacts and contributing to historical societies, the significance of safeguarding heritage resonates deeply with me.

– Camille Holt

Candice Holt

Union League Essay

My love of country, appreciation of free enterprise, and limited government stems from my family and life experience. John Nesbitt, my great-great-great-great-grandfather, fought in the Civil War. As a veteran in the U.S Colored Troops of the Union Army he used his pension to buy land, build a house, and contribute to the formation of Promise Land in Dickson County Tennessee. My grandmother grew up on that land and inherited it. She ensured to pass along the rich history and contributions my ancestors made to this country. As a retired VA nurse she taught me to love and honor my country. I plan to uphold my family's legacy by helping my grandmother preserve the land and contribute to the Promise Land School Museum. Like the Union League, I too am proud and dedicated to the preservation of American history and culture.

I witnessed my grandmother expand her one story single family home into 8 bedroom townhomes. She now operates and maintains a multifamily rental business. Her financial mobility is allotted because the U.S. promotes free enterprise. Her success in the rental property business illuminated the power of free enterprise and financial mobility and has inspired me to follow in her footsteps.

In high school I actively volunteered with H2O For Life, a nonprofit that addresses the global water crisis. I lobbied for the Paul Simon Water for the World Act of 2014 in Washington D.C. I met Madeline Dean and other Congress members. I came into the trip doubtful and nervous, but left feeling inspired that I can positively impact my country. It is reassuring to know that America's limited government allows individuals to contribute and influence resource allocation to keep us free.

– Candice Holt

Table of Contents

Acknowledgment xxiii

Introduction of Mr. and Mrs. Theo Edmondson xxxv

Introduction   Every Child's Right xli

Chapter One   An Uneventful Occasion 1

Chapter Two   News Flash, February 1944 10

Chapter Three   The Christening 12

Chapter Four   Where Love Abounds 15

Chapter Five   The Pews of the Low Church 23

Chapter Six   One Sunday Dinner 27

Chapter Seven   The Greatest Carpenter (Sylvia) 34

Chapter Eight   The Greatest Entertainer 37

Chapter Nine   The Pews of Saint John (Sylvia) 41

Chapter Ten   Silver Dollar 47

Chapter Eleven   The Same Old Sack of Rags 50

Chapter Twelve   The Best Lessons 52

Chapter Thirteen   Lazy Days of Summer 62

Chapter Fourteen   The Charlotte Picnic 69

Chapter Fifteen   A Singing Ministry (The Jewel of the County): The All-Night Singing 83

Chapter Sixteen   Other Pews I've Been In 93

Chapter Seventeen   The Best Christmas Ever 96

Chapter Eighteen   A Season for All Things 107

Chapter Nineteen No Rhyme, No Reason.. 110
Chapter Twenty Soon One Morning 116
Chapter Twenty-One Will Time Heal All Wounds? 124
Chapter Twenty-Two Comes August / Back to School 131
Chapter Twenty-Three Dear Alma Mater 140
Chapter Twenty-Four What's next? 146
Chapter Twenty-Five A Full Fun House 153
Chapter Twenty-Six My Disability of Minority 161
Chapter Twenty-Seven Change Unstoppable 169
Chapter Twenty-Eight Flights of the White....................................... 176
Chapter Twenty-Nine Standing Up, Talking Back........................... 189
Chapter Thirty Can't Look Back... 197
Chapter Thirty-One A Juggler's Determination 207
Chapter Thirty-Two Red Dress / Black Dress.................................. 221
Chapter Thirty-Three Traveling Shoes 230
Chapter Thirty-Four Business Ventures: What about James Sr.? ... 235
Chapter Thirty-Five Spirit and Family 241
My Tribute Keep History Alive in the Museums 247
Rebellious 256

Acknowledgment

Special Thanks

Special thanks to my sister Helen M. Hughes for your generous support while we reminisced together during the time I was working on this project. We laughed at the fun times. We cried over the sad times. Most important, you listened to me all the time. Your diligence to ramble through your endless pile of pictures and memorabilia trying to find the right relic has been priceless. Thank you so much for your love and dedication to the preservation of our heritage.

Special thanks to my coworkers

Un agradecimiento especial a mi compañero de trabajo

Un agradecimiento especial a Natalie Rodríguez. Usted ha oído y leído muchas de mis historias. Su ánimo y fe en mí ha sido apreciada. La mayor parte de todo gracias por su amor y amistad.

Special thanks to Alex Williams. I appreciate all your help and encouragement as a friend and coworker. Your awesome wisdom and wonderful sense of humor will never be forgotten.

TO MY CHILDREN/GRANDCHILDREN:

Favorite Memories of My Sons:

Terrell Sr.

You have always been adventurous. Have you told me really? Have you told me about all the trips you and your best friend took in that little Dodge Dart while calling and telling Daddy and me, "We are across town at friend's house and spending the night." Donor finally confessed about the flat tire in Memphis when you guys had to sleep in the car overnight. I am sure there were other times and places you went. God protected you then, and he will continue. You enjoyed your adventures; that is all I care about.

When your daddy left the table at dinnertime, he'd say, "Boys, eat all your food." When he'd return, those plates were cleaned. Usually the dogs had enjoyed it before he got back. One time he looked out the back door to find turnip greens swinging from the rail on the porch. He loved to tell that story to his friends. Who didn't eat their turnip greens?

Andre

You have been a true delight as a child and in adulthood. You are the one who never got in trouble, except you hit a little girl in kindergarten. When the principal called me, I took up for you, letting him know I have taught you to protect yourself. Upon investigation, we found that the little girl had passed the first lick. He understood that I had not told you it was all right to fight anyone. But the little girl must be taught not to hit as well.

My most precious memory is when you were about three years old, we were trying to put up an artificial Christmas tree. You stated, "Well, let's just find the recipe (directions). Then we can do it."

You were always the early riser, and in the summer, you could be found in the backyard fishing in Lake Imagery (your imagination) before the rest of us were up.

I think you are the one who so generously told your six-year-old classmates about Old Santa Claus. You were not trying to ruin Christmas for them. But he was not in the same league as Jesus Christ.

Were those your turnip greens hanging on the rail? Or were they Terry's?

Kevin

You will always be my baby. Besides the many late breaking news reports when you called to report while I was at work, I have enjoyed being your mama. We played a lot of games with you because most of the neighborhood kids were older. Your daddy and I enjoyed playing Uno with you almost every night. And we knew you were hiding cards under the bed too. You won most games. I hope you know you can only do that with Mama and Daddy.

You loved running the vacuum as soon as you could walk, and you still are Mr. Cleanliness. Thanks for being the one who likes a clean house. Oh, I really could read Babar Babar the Elephant in the dark. You didn't want to turn the light off because you didn't want to go to sleep.

The best was when they did the news documentary on Overton High School. Your father didn't know you were driving his brand-new car to school until he saw you on the six o'clock news five days in a row.

Finally, Favorite Memories about My Grandchildren:

Some of my adventures and favorite memories of grandchildren are as follows:

Terrell Jr.
(Son of Toshiba Cato-Holt and Terrell Sr.)

I could write on Honnie alone. My favorite, when he told his mother and me, "Y'all stop laughing at my lady." We were making fun of someone in a car parked next to us. Our windows were down. Another time we were coming home from taking him to the doctor. We stopped at the big M. I was holding him and trying to eat a burger. I had mustard on my mouth. He looked at me and said, "Wipe your mouth boy. You look gross!"

I took you to Taco Bell. You ordered a large amount of tacos. I didn't think you would be able to eat all of that food. You were about three or four. I ordered less thinking, "I'll eat what he doesn't eat." When I started to reach into your stash, you screamed out in your loudest voice, "Grand mommy, if you wanted tacos, why didn't you order tacos?" People were looking at me like they were about to call DCHS. (Department of Children's Services) So embarrassed, I was about ready to crawl under the table.

I never figured out how Aunt Wilma cut your sandwiches. We threw out a ton of bread because we couldn't cut it like Aunt Wilma. Really, now what was up with that?

I am sure I have participated in most of your homemade scientific experiments. While you were attending Nashville School of Arts, I took you to school until you learned to drive. Precious memories of those times. I saw all your dance performances. I had the pleasure of accompanying you to Savannah College of Art and Design (SCAD). I was there for admission and when you received your degree (BFA) in fine arts.

Jaime
(Daughter of Kevin and Nikki Crowder)

I am sure I attended every play starting with *The Big Fat Spider* on down to the marching band both in high school and in college in most competitions and concerts. I was a big supporter of Jamie in Little Miss AKA at seven or eight years old. I worked at night for a long time. I was watching you after working all night. I fell asleep. Jaime, you woke me up and informed me, "Grand mommy, there is no one watching me. And I don't have time to watch myself." I woke up because when a fellow doesn't have time to watch himself, "there is no telling what they are about to get into."

Juan Diego and Jamie met in college; they are the parents of my only great-granddaughter at this writing (Ivy Maria Diego). I love him for the way he loves Jaime and Ivy Maria and the way they pray together at bedtime, time of trouble, and at odd times. Juan is my favorite grandson-in-law! He has blended into the family. Your whole family has bonded with our family.

Marlene and Domingo Diego, you are special, so don't ever forget that this grandma says, "Te amo," and I mean it. (Parents are Alberto and Dorayra Diego) Te amo.

Candice and Camille
(Twin daughters of Andre and Chiqullia Holt)

I was there for their birth. The two have kept me busy since. It has been a pleasure to experience an overnight stay at Franklin Institute in Philadelphia. After working all night, I flew in just in time to grab my sleeping bag and headed straight to the Museum for Girl Scout Sleepover with Candice and Camille (the Pennsylvania twins.) More recently in 2014, I was able to meet these girls in Washington DC to see them receive their congressional gold medals, a very prestigious award and one well deserved. I attended graduation from high school and accompanied them on admission day to Spelman College in Atlanta, Georgia.

I am enjoying you being just four hours away at Spelman and making my house home and the place you love to go on your school breaks. I love the way we get together with Grandma Rosie Ludwig, Aunts Adrian Lewis, Nedra Knox and cousin Phoenix Knox.

Being your Grand Mommy is such a pleasure. The most precious thing you have done for me was this statement, "We want to be just like you Grand Mommy." To me that is the highest honor you could give me.

Olivia and Aliyah Holt
(Twin daughters of Kevin and Tara Clay-Holt)

I was there at their birth. Most special occasion was the Girl Scout meeting when they told me, "Grandma, you have to come to our Girl Scout meeting. And you have to give a speech." Later, they sent a formal invitation. I love the way they told me what I had to do. They knew they could depend on me. I was one on a panel of speakers at their Girl Scout meeting; I felt so honored for their confidence in me to do such a job. It was awesome.

I have seen them play volleyball and martial arts and in band concerts and band performances. More recently, they have attended Candice and Camille's graduation with us and our trip to New York to visit Cousin Terrell Jr.

We enjoyed spring break 2016 in Atlanta with the Twins at Spelman. The tour of the campus was inspiring.

It is an indescribable pleasure to have both sets of twins together.

(My Ohio twins, you bring the bang to the party.)
There is never a dull moment.

Mikayla Marie Holt
(Daughter of Terrell Holt Sr. and Gina Batey)

She is so amazing she deserves a book by herself. She is the only girl with four brothers to help spoil her—Andre, Aaron, Paul, and Terrell Jr. She especially loves to visit her brother Terrell Jr. in New York City where she loves to tell him, "You got us lost. Yes, you did." She loves spending time in the library with her father learning and exploring beyond her grade level.

My youngest granddaughter is an amazing reader at the age of eight, she is reading at college level. She has received awards at school for her reading ability.

Mikayla is fast becoming an excellent dance performer through her studies at Malone Dance Academy. I have not missed a performance since she started dancing at age three. Mikayla has also performed with the children's choir at Faith Is the Victory Church, Nashville, Tennessee. Currently she is a member of Temple Church Children's choir and is a Brownie Scout for which she has received several awards.

Ivy Maria Diego, great-granddaughter
(Daughter of Jaime and Juan Diego)

She has been dancing since birth. She is also a student at Malone Dance Academy. Performing since two years old, I have not missed any of her recitals. Ivy practices diligently in and out of the studio. She has received awards for perfect attendance two years in a row.

Ivy has been selected to my personal Prayer Warriors Club. She is diligent to get the family together for prayer especially at her bedtime. She makes sure that everyone put their hands together. Then at the end she asks, "Now where is Jesus?" Making sure we know that he is in our hearts. She knows that he is in us. Ivy is three years old.

Special Grandsons:
(By choice)

Ivy Larue and Dominic James Dobson
(Sons of Nikki and Ivy Dobson)

Last but not least, I would like to mention my last two grandsons, Ivy Larue and Dominic Dobson, brothers of Jaime, sons of Nikki and Ivy Dobson. I cannot complete my memoirs without reminiscing the precious times we went to the rodeo and coming home with cow poop on our shoes. We often went movie hopping sometimes with Subway snacks tucked away in my purse. Often we would see at least two movies. I was always careful to go back to the ticket booth to purchase more tickets so as not to have them think that Grandma Ms. Sylvia would teach them to be dishonest. I usually fell asleep on the second movie.

Sorry, Larue, I think you were about four years old when we took you to Pennsylvania for New Year's Eve. You slept at the foot of the day bed while I had the head. New Year's Eve, you hopped into bed without first going to the bathroom. At exactly midnight, you woke me up with a warm stream of water on my feet. As a matter of fact, you woke up the whole house.

People who have been the greatest influence in my life:

My parents, Mr. and Mrs. Theodore Edmondson, my first and greatest teachers.

My aunts and uncles on both sides of the family: Aunt Allie, Uncle Lorry on mother's side.

Ms. Ollie Huddleston, my teacher from first through seventh grade, who taught me the basics to continue my education.

Ms. Etta Adams, a substitute teacher who taught me to be a lifetime learner and achiever and to continue my education one step at a time.

All my family who watched out for me and truly cared for me while I grew up in Promise Land: Aunt Ruby Robertson (Uncle Baxter), Aunt Betty Ruth (Uncle James Edmondson), Cousin Hattie Robertson-Hall (Mr. Hersey), Aunt Essie Gilbert (Uncle Robert), Cousin Tamer Lee (William Primm), Aunt Hattie (Uncle Rev. J.J. Bowens); they were good role models to all of us. Aunt Hattie was a classic first lady of any church her husband pastored.

Mama Anna Holt (mother of Reverends Dalton and Arlus Holt). My favorite of her expressions was simply, "Speak a**, because your month won't." Usually she would be sitting on the front porch. (She never said it loud enough for the offender to hear.)

Mrs. Rebecca Owens became my best friend forever after my son Andre married her granddaughter Chiquilla. We bonded and became more like blood sisters or another mother. She was a storyteller that would put the average one to shame. My favorite is of her riding down the Cumberland River (as a child) after delivering her father's lunch. She said, "I would sit on the back of the barge with my feet in the water while they moved down the river." "Could you swim?" I'd ask. "No, I expect someone was watching me. Daddy would always find me stored away."

Her stories were endless and always ended in "Now, I wouldn't advise anyone to do that today." Her stories were good for heartache or heartbreak. I spent many days and nights stretched out on her couch while listening to her adventures. She could have charged a fee because I always left feeling better.

Rev. and Mrs. King were so full of wisdom. (Former pastor of Bass Street Baptist Church) Reverend King shared a lifetime of equally interesting stories. If these stories did not have you feeling better, you might need to visit the nearest emergency or convenient care.

Introduction of Mr. and Mrs. Theo Edmondson

Yes, I am Mrs. Theodore Edmondson, born Elizabeth (Lizzie) Elnora Van Leer on May 7th 1910, in the Promise Land Community. Susie Van Leer (Mama), a single mother, raised my brother Lorry, my sister Allie, and me while she worked for some of the white families in the county of Dickson, Tennessee, washing and taking care of their children. Furbee, Niblett and Harris are the names I remember.

Earsley Nesbitt, my father, was a son of the early settlers of this community, John and Ellen Nesbitt. I have many fond memories of spending time with my grandpa John. I slept many a night snuggled up behind Grandma Ellen's back. John Nesbitt had gone off to war with his master in the Civil War. Civil War veterans and newly freed slaves—these men obtained this land soon after the war. On their farms, they raised crops from peas to corn and tobacco. Eventually, the community had a school, churches, and stores and was independently self-contained.

Mama didn't talk much about slavery, but I suppose she must have known a lot from her own parents. But later when I became an outspoken, "strong-headed" young lady, she used to warn me, "The white folks are going to white cap you, gal." I was never afraid. To this day, I don't know what that meant, and I don't care. I was as nice as anyone could be, but if anyone talked crazy, I let them know:

"That isn't going to work too well with me." I walked off and left a whole basket full of wet clothes because the young miss—the same age that I was—hollowed at me.

Her mama come calling me. "Lizzie, Lizzie! She's just nervous. She's feebleminded. She just had a baby." I turned around and told her, "Yes, ma'am, and I am as nervous as she is. But I'm not feebleminded though. Lord, she must have been crazy if she thinks she can talk to me like that. I can go home and wash my own clothes." I knew right then; I could have never been a slave. I kept on walking until I got home. That's when Mama would talk about that white-capping mess or whatever.

"But, Mama," I'd say, "I am not going to be treated like that by someone who doesn't have as much sense as I do. I don't care what color she is." I demanded respect, and I got it too.

I became a member of Saint John Methodist Church as soon as I became old enough and remained my whole life. As the church secretary / treasurer, I have worked diligently wherever and whenever I could.

I went to the Promise Land School across the field where Ms. Mae Etta Dansby was my teacher. She was a fine teacher, and I loved her dearly. On graduating from the eighth grade, I was qualified to teach school myself. Soon after graduation I had met and fallen in love with a young man by the name of Theodore Roosevelt Edmondson from Gilbert Town down the road below the Hickory Flat. He was named after Mr. Teddy Roosevelt, the twenty-sixth U.S. president, Theodore Roosevelt.

Lord, we courted for a while, going to the dances and picnics and to church in the community. It was a lot going on all over the community.

Soon after marrying, we started our family. We had ten children: five boys first and then five girls. Unfortunately, we lost three of our babies in infancy. Seven out of ten is still a huge blessing and a lot of mouths to feed. Lord, Lord, and we brought every one of them across that dusty road to the church to have them christened. We raised our children in the church. Every Sunday and every event they had, we were there.

Sometimes I worked, and most of the time I was busy having our babies. My husband Theo mostly worked building barns and sometimes houses. When that got slow, he did whatever was needed to keep us going. He was a little more tolerant of the white folks than I was. I'm telling you that because one day, he was working on a nearby farm plowing. The owner's mule had gotten loose, and he spent most of that day trying to catch the mule. He brought home his paycheck that week; she deducted one day for the day the mule got loose. When he gave me that check, I just started steaming. I was recovering from childbirth. I got out of my bed, tied my head up, and started walking toward that woman's house. I walked in without knocking, handed her that check, and told her, "Now if you can live with this, we can sure live without it. It was your fool mule that got loose." That was one way I got respect. I demanded it. I was mad. As Theo used to tell me, "Mad as a wet hen."

Brother Theodore Edmondson

I am Theodore Roosevelt Edmondson, born July 26th 1907, to James (Jim) Edmondson and Josie Armstrong-Gilbert-Edmondson. We had a very large family because each of my parents had been married before they got together. We had the Gilbert brothers and sisters from my mother's side and Edmondson siblings from my father's side and then the Edmondson brothers and sisters from Jim and Josie Edmondson's clan. Whew, talk about a blended family. But we were never taught the half-sibling thing. We were all just brothers and sisters.

My father was from African / Anglo-Saxon decent, but my mother was strongly from Native American heritage and might have been full-blooded Cherokee Indian.

I learned mostly what I needed to know from Daddy Jim, a skilled carpenter. When we were not farming, we were building. He didn't have much "formal education," but he taught me how to draw up plans or blueprints for building barns and houses. He could estimate down to a penny the amount of materials including nails before we began to work on a new building. He taught me what he knew, and the rest I picked up on my own. Off and on I went to Promise Land School. I would say more off than on to the third or fourth grade. When it comes to real business, my wife Lizzie takes over. I met her when we were young. She was the most beautiful girl I had ever seen.

Most of the time, I kept busy building barns or upkeep on homes for the white neighbors in the county. I did a little plowing and farming when the construction business got slow. My family has a history of singing while at labor. It keeps you sane and makes the time go by faster. I don't know at what point people started really listening to me sing. Shucks, I just enjoyed hearing myself. Cupping one hand around my mouth and one behind my ear, I'd listen to myself. A lot of lunch breaks and getting-off time, I had a small audience listening and sometimes joining in singing and having a good time. Back then, we didn't watch the clock too much. We just quit at a certain point or when we were tired or finished.

We'd prayed together and diligently went to church and taught our children right from wrong. We taught them that they are no better than anyone else. But most of all, we taught them that no one, white or colored, is better than them. I made sure they believed that. I taught them not to be jealous or envy anyone because God made us all just the way he wanted us to be and that nobody can't take that away from you. No matter who you are, God loves you, and you ought to love him back. I taught them that no matter what anyone say or call you; you'd better know who you are, and don't be affected by what anyone says about you.

As our boys began to mature of course, we encouraged them to move on up north where the opportunities were better, and hopefully they wouldn't have to experience a lot of the foolishness that went on in some of these other places in the South. Our oldest son was in the army for a few years, and the other two moved to Ohio and New York.

We had to teach our boys about the facts of life and staying in your place as a Negro or colored man because things were different when you extended your travels. We continued to raise our girls here in the South, and life has been good. God has been good.

Introduction
Every Child's Right

Every child, no matter what race or color, should be able to grow up in a place where they feel loved, protected, and a sense of belonging—a place where they can explore freely. Such a sterile or perfect environment might also be harmful. Growing up in such a place could leave you unprepared when it is time to venture outside the sterile box. You might need to build up immunity to a different environment.

Let me tell you a little bit about this place. The Promise Land is located in Dickson County, Tennessee. But to tell it all would be a lesson in history and an entirely separate book. You will find a historical description if you look online at promiselandtn.com. It was founded by African-American men and women after the Civil War. These men were former slaves who had fought in the Civil War with their masters. Nesbitt, Van Leer, Bowens, and Redden are names to be associated with the early settlement.

Arch and John Nesbitt were two brothers who donated land to build what would make Promise Land a thriving community. The Promise Land School and Saint John Methodist Church are still standing today. Religion and education was vital, and it remains the backbone of our African-American families.

Promise Land allowed people to grow up in the South without as much of the racial hatred and Jim Crow activity that most African-

Americans experienced during the Civil Rights Movement. These people were not sharecroppers; they were landowners who had created an environment conducive to what would be untouched by the cross burnings and lynching heard of in other places. This protective shield around them could not be torn down as long as, "they stayed in their places." Perhaps that was the key.

Chapter One

An Uneventful Occasion

What would I give to hear the crunch of his car tires and to see the dust flying up and then settling back down just as fast on that old gravel road? We raced through the field between our house and mamas trying to be the first to meet Daddy when he jumped out almost before the car came to a halt. That's when the excitement began. You could depend on him bringing everyone a treat no matter how much Mother fussed. He'd just smile and tease her until she couldn't fuss anymore.

"All, Lizzie, let them have some fun," he'd say while calling the children. "Come here, son," he'd say while pulling a nice red apple seemingly from James' or Doug's pockets. "See there, I told you all. Cousin Emma's been talking about someone picking her apples. Where did you get that apple, son?" Then he'd pull one treat after the other from behind someone's ear, or he might just go behind Bernice or Wilma's back and find a sugar daddy.

Little Brother (Lorry) was too old, and Helen was too young for these games, but they got a treat too. He'd keep that up until every child had a treat. Greeting Mother with a kiss, he'd reach for his guitar. Old Skippy stood wagging his tail waiting for a pat on the head. Life is so full of changes that we don't seem to notice as children. No matter how many times he did that trick, the children were still surprised. They loved it. You couldn't tell he'd worked all day.

While doing her morning chores, an annoying pain crossed her lower back, intermittently, a sign too familiar to ignore. When the last child left for school, the house was quiet at last. She hurried, wanting to finish before two-year-old Helen woke up. Looking out the front door, she noticed large snowflakes falling. Cold fresh air felt good against her face, but quickly she closed the door, keeping the warm air in. She had told Little Brother to warn Mama that she might need her to come to the house later.

It was extremely cold, with snow flurries. Not a lot was on the ground.

It's hard to predict the weather any time especially in winter. Thanks to the Warm Morning—plenty of wood and coal. The house would stay warm all day. If she needed it, there was enough wood piled behind the stove. There had been plenty on the land to be cut. She could hardly wait till spring.

Theo could start building their house. *This old house is too small,* she thought. Every crack had been stuffed with old rags and newspapers to keep the wind out. Still if the fire goes out in the Warm Morning, you'd have to thaw the water bucket before doing anything. Stoking the fire with coal, usually it would last all night. She heard the crunch of gravel as a car approached. There was hardly ever any traffic on the road. Dust settled back down as she looked out to see if Theo had returned. Mama and Cousin Emma were the closest neighbors. Fewer people lived there every year. Some were dying, but most were moving up north, one or two families at a time.

Grandma Susie lived a few yards beyond the field separating the two houses. Attending most of Lizzie's labors, she felt like she could do it alone. While not a midwife, she knew a lot about birthing babies. Clean rags of old sheets and white towels kept in the attic were waiting by the door. The ritual of boiling water preceded every birth she attended partly to keep the men folk out of the way and make them feel useful. The other part was to keep the dry air moist in winter while the mother labored so hard. A warm cloth spread on a protruding belly was sometimes comforting. After cutting the cord, Doc spanked breath into a dusty newborn before passing it to Mama for a warm soothing bath. Babies have to be cleaned up to show. When she finished the squalling, baby would be all rosy, calm, and ready to meet the world.

"Mother wants you at the house, Mama," Little Brother yelled. Rushing in, he went straight for biscuits from Mama's warmer above the stove. Promise Land School was almost directly in front of Grandma Susie's house. The Edmondson children had the luxury of breakfast, lunch, and dinner at either house. "Gone, child. You'll be late for school," she scolded him, knowing her feelings would be hurt if he didn't help himself. She cooked enough to have food for the grandchildren if they wanted it.

She put her coat and bonnet on and then grabbed the birthing rags. "Don't you be late for school, boy," she yelled as she headed out and across the field, passing the rest of the children on their way to school.

Large snowflakes were falling fast. So fast that as young Theo turned his rickety old battered jalopy off Main Street and headed north on Highway 48 toward Charlotte, his tire tracks were covered almost instantaneously. On Main Street, he had observed the ruins of an old building that had burned mysteriously on Sunday night. It had been home to a well-known dry goods store called Fussell's. A self-employed carpenter, he was always on the lookout for work, especially during the winter months when everything slowed down. It was doubtful that business would pick up before spring. He rode on.

A grass sack covered the rear window, blocking out the cold air. While flapping in the wind, it played a tune. He began to whistle and sing along with it while making his way through Charlotte. Suddenly he came to a halting stop at the bottom of the hill, leaving what some folks surreptitiously called Nigger Hill. He went into Baton's grocery store and spent his last quarter on candy and gum. He knew Lizzie would fuss because money was needed to pay the doctor. He cranked up the car again and started singing, "The Lord Will Make a Way Somehow."

Everything was packed in an old grass sack; he'd make it home if he had to carry it on his back. Sometimes he did. He bought only staples like flour, meal, sugar, and baking powder. Most food was grown and raised on the land.

Navigating Cunningham Hill ahead was the biggest obstacle in his path. If the snow didn't take over, he'd have a better chance. A set of tires with deeper threads would have helped too. He notified Dr. Bell. He was sure nothing would happen before he got back. This was their tenth child in eighteen years. Still he was nervous.

Approaching Saint Paul Road, he noticed the snow not sticking on the pavement. That was good.

Dr. Bell usually had Lizzie timed just right. Labor had started, no doubt. Had Theo reported her water broken, he would have made haste. Doc was a nice middle-aged white man who was kind enough to deliver both white and colored babies. Most folk didn't have much money. Doc didn't need to buy much food either, after a good season of delivering babies. A country ham and a few jars of jam were just as good as gold.

As he turned onto the old dirt road, he noticed that the snow had slacked up tremendously. He frequently had to visit rural areas like Promise Land. Good tires and chains were all he needed. Two medical bags and instruments were kept handy. He never knew when he would be flagged down by some nervous husbands or other frightened family members. No telling how many babies this makes. He'd lost count of the number he had delivered. White or colored, he was a blessing to the residents of Dickson County.

With so many mouths to feed, Lizzie had enough food put up. All summer she'd canned vegetables, fruits, and blackberries all arranged by color on the shelves. No one would go hungry in her house. Sometimes she helped other less fortunate during the winter months. She learned the art of preserving food from her mother Susie, Aunt Sarah, and Aunt Sallie. She could tell you exactly how many jars of green beans, field peas, peaches, pickles, jelly, and preserves she had, neatly setting in a row and covered with quilts to prevent freezing. The smokehouse held an abundance of salted meats, smoked hams, and sausages.

Now and again, that aching pain in her lower back returned; but unalarmed, she continued to clean. Two things she could not tolerate were a dirty house and an empty cupboard. The Warm Morning heater kept the whole house warm and was used to cook a pot of beans or stew during the winter.

As the day progressed, Theo returned home. The children returned from school. All chores were done. Everyone was fed and tucked into bed. The snow had stopped. Dr. Bell arrived at dusk. Lizzie's pain had gotten significantly closer. Mama, who had been in and out all day, made a fresh pot of coffee.

Expecting no complications, Doc explained to Theo, "It won't be much longer." No matter how many births he had attended, Theo got nervous near the end. They had done their routine of checking to see if the children were all asleep—a trick they carried on until the children were pretty big. Standing at the foot of the beds scratching his chin, he'd said, "Lizzie, I think they are sleep. What do you think?" The children lay real still trying not to giggle. Going from bed to bed on tip toes, finally he sighed, "Hum, I tell you what, Lizzie. Here is how we can tell." He paused, picked up somebody's hand, and said, "Watch this." Raising the arm high above the child's head, he let go and then let it fall. He whispered, "I tell you what. If she's asleep, she'll raise her arm like this." He raised his arm and waited. Pretty soon, usually the youngest child accommodated them by raising their arm, and the game was over. Everybody burst out laughing. Tipping out of the room, they pretended not to hear a sound.

The older children, all boys, had been born first. The eldest child named Theodore Jr. died at almost three years old. That is why Lorry was called Little Brother. Then came Douglas Lee, another boy stillborn, and James Arthur, the last boy.

The first girl was Susie Bernice and then Wilma Jean, a girl stillborn, and then Helen Marie was a premature baby. She was so small. "We had to hold her on a pillow," Lizzie often explained why Helen was treated so delicately.

Little Brother was holding Helen one day. When he dropped her, I screamed. Lord, have mercy. He has killed my baby. "It's not easy losing a baby." Theo added, "I had to make those three little coffins by myself. We were heartbroken each time."

The snow had stopped, but the wind was still howling; the temperature had to be dropping. Lizzie cooperated with each direction to push hard. Not wanting to wake the children, she held a wet cloth in her mouth with each pain while pushing as hard as she could. "Next time, should be it, Susie," he told Grandma Susie as she bought him another cup of coffee.

"How many this make for you, Susie?" he asked, smiling.

"Would have been ten," she whispered, not wanting Lizzie to hear. "We lost three," she said. "Well, seven out of ten isn't" bad he said. "Some have not been that blessed."

Finishing his second cup of coffee, he motioned for Grandma Susie to take it and get ready. Her water had broken about thirty minutes ago. One long hard push, and the baby was born without complications. It was the easiest labor she'd had. Doc whacked Sylvia a time or two before she squalled waking up the whole house.

Well, by no means was she going to be a conversation piece. Those sisters and brothers were sure going to love her though. A normal sized healthy baby girl with all ten fingers and ten toes and a little clump of curly brown hair pulsating on top of that big head where the fontanel bones appeared. She was welcome. She had dimples on her cheeks and knees. Her cheeks were so fat you couldn't tell whether she was frowning or smiling.

All babies are cute, especially the little colored babies. *Not so*, thought one grandma. She quickly wrote to her daughter, Theo's sister, Hattie, in Nashville to inform her of the uneventful occasion. She wrote, "Lizzie and Theo have a new baby girl. She is fine and healthy but not as pretty as Cassandra."

Well, now isn't that a slap in the face? Bad enough to get your butt whacked when you enter this world, but when your own grandma doesn't think you are too cute, that is a pretty appalling blow below the belly button. Shame on you, Grandma Josie.

....

Chapter Two

News Flash, February 1944

It was a bitter cold night in a rural, very sparsely populated community called the Promise Land. On February 22nd 1944, a child was born where love is the most abundant commodity. She shall be called Beautiful, Precious, Princess, Glorious, Blessed, and Wonderful Child.

Our nation was busy watching the Second World War etch its way to an end. It was two years after the bombing of Pearl Harbor. As millions of American men and thousands of women dedicated their services, a small rural county in middle Tennessee played no less a part.

The County Salvage Committee was calling for waste fats and paper to support the war effort, since contributions in previous months had been less than five hundred pounds. War Bonds chairman urged citizens to buy extra bonds by February 29th since the county remained short on the fourth war loan. South Central Bell limited telephone calls to five minutes because of the war busy days and nights.

A local Motor Company advertised, "Wartime drivers find Studebaker, the ideal economy car." City dry cleaners began calling for customers to return clothes hangers because of the war conditions. The hatchery guaranteed an increase in egg production while raising fewer chickens by buying their pulllorum-tested chickens. Greyhound introduced a fifty-one-seat coach as the latest in highway travel. Retina was highly recommended for relief of distress from nervousness and sluggish elimination, while Black Draught was first choice of thousands as a laxative to keep one going regular and smoothly.

For entertainment, *Hers to Hold* and *Thank Your Lucky Stars* were showing at the Roxy Theater. WLAC was 1510 on the radio dial boasting fifty thousand watts and located in Nashville, Tennessee.

Franklin D. Roosevelt served his fourth and last term as president of the United States with Harry S. Truman as vice president. Sadly, a local Negro was accused of slaying a prominent Negro doctor. Dr. Theodore Blake was the only Negro doctor in the county and for forty miles around. He maintained an office and home on North Mulberry Street. He was well thought of by both white and colored. The man who was accused served several years for a crime he didn't do. I was told by a relative that "at the point of death, a white man owned up to the murder, and the Negro was freed."

Chapter Three

The Christening

Easter Sunday morning, 1944, Lizzie bathed and oiled her new baby girl, getting ready for church service. Discovering the little clump of hair missing from her baby's big round head, she screamed, "Oh my god, oh my god! What's done happened to my baby?"

With shaving cream on his face Theo ran into the room. "What is it, Lizzie?" He yelled. "What is it?"

"Susie Bernice, Wilma Jean, you all come here. Lord, have mercy," she said, wringing her hands. She kept screaming, while Sylvia cooed. "Who done cut my baby's hair?" she wailed almost out of breath. "Who cut my baby's hair?"

Sylvia started crying, excited by the commotion. Holding the scissors behind her back and the clump of hair in her left hand, Wilma sheepishly said, "I didn't do it, Mother. I didn't do it. Honest. Honest." She pleaded, standing at the door. "I mean I didn't mean to do it," she whined while standing in the doorway. Bernice and Helen just looked at Wilma trying to look innocent. James waited at the door behind Wilma, glad it wasn't him on the witness stand this time. Lord knows he had been in Wilma's shoes many times.

Twelve-year-old Douglas, known to do his own preaching while dressing, could be heard from the boy's room. (He stuttered when he talked.) "And, ah, yes, yes, yes. He, ah, delivered Dan, Dan, Daniel, um, hum, from that old, old lion's, lion's den." Hacking, he stomped and repeated, "Yes, he, he did. Yes, he, he did. I say, yes, yes. He delivered old, old Jo-Jo-Jonah from the belly of, of the whale—" Raising his voice another octave, he continued, "Um, hum, yes, yes, yes, he will."

Little Brother (Lorry), the lone spectator, advised the young preacher, "Yes, he will." Lorry joined in, while the young preacher pranced. "Boy you better get them clothes on. Else, Daddy's going to deliver you."

Trying to console everyone and make his wife happy, he took the little ribbon meant to be worn in Sylvia's hair. He tied it loosely around her fat ankle and explained, "It will ward off evil spirits."

He reminded her, "Baby Doll, it will grow back and more." After planting a soapy kiss on all his baby dolls, he went back to finish shaving. He listened to see if the sermon was finished in the boy's room. "Amen. All right, boys. Get them clothes on," he yelled, encouraging the boys to make haste. He'd help the boys finish dressing.

Lizzie took the fistful of hair from Wilma. She put it in her keepsake box on the dresser. Before Sylvia could be christened, she got her first haircut.

Finally, the whole family crossed the road in their usual formation: Lizzie and Sylvia (the baby), Little Brother (Lorry), Douglas, James, Susie Bernice (sister), Wilma, and Theo carrying Helen. Skippy followed them to the church door where he'd wait until service was over. Producing a biscuit, Theo dusted their shoes again and pitched it to the dog. Before it met the ground, Skippy gobbled it up.

Later that morning, the Edmondson, Bowens, Van Leer, and Gilbert families proudly gathered around the altar at Saint John Church. She wore a traditional long white dress. Sprinkled with holy water, she was christened, Sylvia Elnora Edmondson, a ritual in which her parents, grandparents, uncles, aunts, and the entire community promised to nurture and raise her as God would have them to. Quickly they covered her bald head so she wouldn't catch her death a cold. The next eighteen years, she would be shaped by the master clay molders of the community, between the churches, school, her parents, and grandparents.

Luke 18:16: But Jesus called them unto him, and said, suffer little children to come unto me, and forbid them not: for of such is the kingdom of God (KJV).

Chapter Four
Where Love Abounds

The Edmondson brothers and sisters were too eager to join in helping take care of the new baby. They didn't want her to grow up. To this day, you might hear them refer to her as "my baby sister," as if she was still swaddled. Grandma Josie's letter found over forty years later proved that beauty is in the eye of the beholder.

Sylvia cannot remember Grandma Josie or Grandpa Jim (Theo's parents). All that adorable baby fat, she lost when she started walking. Folks thought it was fashionable to be plump. People started asking her, "Are you an Edmondson?" "You are not an Edmondson, are you?" Poor Sylvia started telling them, "No," and kept on walking. I think it was because she was so skinny. The other sisters were not fat but "pleasingly" plump. She was so boney that water collected in her collar bones when she washed her hair.

She was healthy, except she tended to be troubled with her tonsils a lot. Lizzie said, "I think her tonsils must have rotted out." Another time she was sick. Her daddy took her to see Dr. Somers. He looked at her tiny little frame, shook his head, and said, "Theo, there isn't a thing I can do for her. Nothing. You just take her back home. Let her get plenty of rest. Let her eat anything she wants. Give her lean meat and anything sweet she wants."

Theo hung his head sadly. He dreaded telling her mother. How would he give the news to her siblings? Expecting his eight-year-old daughter not to live much longer, he returned home. Shaking his head, he told her mother what the doctor had said. They made sure she rested. They wouldn't let her pick up a broom or hit a lick at a snake.

Lizzie cooked all her favorite foods. Sylvia was a real picky eater. They encouraged her to eat and rest like the doctor said, trying to make her last days happy. They made her bed downstairs in the dining room. She'd shown no changes in about two weeks.

One day, mysteriously, a lady knocked on the door. The lady was alone and on foot. Nobody knows from whence she came or where she went. She laid hands on Sylvia and prayed in some language nobody understood. As soon as the lady left, Sylvia, well, jumped out of bed. She was well from that day. They never saw the lady again.

Mark 5:41–42: I say unto thee, Damsel arise. And straightway the damsel arose (KJV).

She took a lot of teasing from other people outside the immediate family. They called her Skinny Minnie, Boney Maroni, Olive Oil, and a few more names that she can't even remember. *Possibly most of them meant no harm*, she thought. There is no excuse for ignorance. That child's self-esteem had to be affected some kind of way. Encouraged by her parents, she became an achiever in her own right. Many children are not that fortunate. She never had any doubt that her family loved her. That's all it took. *Why was it any of their business?* The child often thought. People didn't think then, and they still don't think how they can affect children by being inconsiderate. Why were they so interested in Sylvia's DNA? It was mostly old ladies with floppy hats being nosey and wanting to know Brother and Sister Edmondson's family.

Once her mother explained it to her. "It's because of Daddy," she said. He was well known for his melodious voice and had made a name for Himself and the family. "People just want to know our children." But still Sylvia wanted to ask why it was any of their business who she was. She felt she had more right to ask them that question. But at that time, the community was in charge of raising the children. No doubt if she came off with a remark like that, it might be her last remark because Sister Edmondson did not play that. So she just kept saying no. In her mind, she was thinking, *why do you see me with the Edmondson's all the time i*f I am *not one?* She thought, *no. I'll just say no.*

Before she can remember, her mother's sister Allie had moved away. Aunt Allie, they called her, was twelve years older than Lizzie. Without Allie and Lorry (Lizzie's brother), the entire Edmondson story would have been much different. Because of their generosity, love, and wisdom, the family enjoyed many things the average person in their area—black or white—might not have been able to have and enjoy.

Aunt Allie was tall and slender like today's model. Her skin was like dark chocolate and smooth without a hint that there was ever a blemish. Her nose was narrow and nicely pointed between two small round deep-set brown eyes. Her eyes were so deep that they gave you the impression she was always vigilant; nothing caught her off guard.

Now and then she had a star like twinkle in her eyes as if they had changed direction automatically. You could tell she was thinking seriously about something.

Her hair was black and of medium length. She wore it parted on the side while curls and waves framed her defined high cheek boned face. Her speech was articulate with correct pronunciation and grammar. She was a great supporter of the arts and education. Often, she spoke to her nieces and nephews about learning all they could. Her favorite statement was "There is no need for anyone living in or around Nashville, Tennessee, not to get an education." She was aware of Nashville's historical institutions like Fisk and Tennessee A&I that provided education for people of color. She wasted no time gossiping.

Sylvia was too young to seriously understand the value of this strong African-American lady. Born in 1898, she was the eldest of her siblings. There must have been volumes of interesting stories that would rival any story ever told. She must have had information from experiences while growing up in the South to her destination in the extreme north in Buffalo, New York, and beyond the Canadian borders. She could have taught a class on good etiquette and good housekeeping as well.

Allie never learned to read or write, which is one reason she was so passionate about education. She worked for a white family as a young girl. She thought migrating to Buffalo, New York, with this family was an excellent opportunity to help "Mama, Lizzie, and herself." She often explained, "I would rather take them with me.

Mama is too old and set in her ways to survive, and Lizzie is not going to leave Mama. I wouldn't want to leave Mama alone either."

Allie sent clothes by the box full. Each season brought new clothes for Lizzie and the children. Most children did well to have one winter coat. She made sure each child had at least two. The smallest girls had little snow suits and boots to protect them in the winter. Christmas, she sent the biggest boxes with toys, clothes, fruit, nuts, and candies.

After Lizzie and Theo started their family, Allie and Lorry seemed to dedicate their lives to helping them raise their family. Neither of them ever married or had children.

Around 1952, she brought a busload of members from her church in Buffalo to Promise Land. They stayed with the Edmondson's and other members of the community. They performed while being in Tennessee. They highly respected her. She was a very intelligent and high-class woman. One can only imagine what she would have done had she been able to read and write. Many of the members had not been down south. They fell in love with Promise Land, like most people do.

Lorry, Lizzie's brother, was a little lighter skinned, a milk chocolate flawless skin, a medium built, and tall. Born in Tennessee, he migrated to Indianapolis, Indiana. He came home one time and bought the land. After receiving the deed, he said, "I went and handed it to my sister and mama. Theo is the best carpenter in Dickson County. He will see that the houses are built." Lorry told his mama, "I don't want you all depending on anybody else. This land is yours."

He dressed very well with suit and necktie. His shoes were always shining despite the dust in Promise Land. Neither he nor Aunt Allie were selfish people, no telling how much they sacrificed to lavish our family with the gifts that they gave: expensive china, silverware, linen tablecloths, fur coats, shoes, and purses to match. Allie sent it all except a TV. For some reason, Lizzie would not let her send one. She did accept the piano for the children to take music lessons. The land still belongs to the Edmondson descendants. What would they have done without Aunt Allie and Uncle Lorry? No greater love than this.

The family dog was in the family as long as Sylvia can remember. Without him, how would they dispose of garbage, especially Sylvia's picking's over? She was so picky. *She's liable to pitch a whole pork chop out that door,* Skippy thought, while sitting with ears pointed forward listening for the back door to swing open. He was good protection since he ran away all kinds of would-be intruders from the wild. The fox alone would have eradicated that henhouse too had it not been for him. He even followed them to church. Who else would eat that dusty biscuit after Theo shined everybody's shoes at the church doors? He was a sooner. No pedigree. Long beige and white hair made him look kind of like a terrier.

One of his favorite pastimes was chasing cars. Promise Land traffic was slow most times on that dusty road. Skippy and some buddies went up to the highway seeking more fun one night. When cars passed, they ran as fast as they could trying to catch them.

Once, the night before Thanksgiving, they were chasing cars. Skippy got hit. He was accustomed to rolling over and playing dead. But this time, he barked, "I thought I was dead."

Skippy's food was waiting for him. No one had seen him. That was unusual.

When Theo got home and Skippy was missing, he thought, Oh my. That something I just hit might have been old Skippy. It was too dark to see what it was.

He went back to the highway, and sure enough, there was Skippy lying on the side of the road. They brought him home. He was hurt, but he survived. That was the biggest Thanksgiving the family ever had including "Skippy Edmondson." He didn't have to wait on scraps that day.

Helen and Sylvia fixed his plate before anyone ate. He was too sick to eat for a while. In a few days, he was fully recovered with no limp.

Grandma Josie and Grandpa Jim were Theo's parents. There are a lot more of them than on Lizzie's side. Grandma Josie's first husband Mark Gilbert died. Likewise with Jim, his wife died. She married James (Jim) Edmondson. She and Jim both had children before they married each other.

Hopefully the reader will not be confused while I try to drop a few names in place for family. Mark Gilbert and Josie had Jewell, Robert, Ruby, and Hattie. James (Jim) and Silvia Edmondson had Birdine, Sylvonia, Nissie, and Slayden. Josie and Jim added Peonie, Nack (O.C.) James, Theodore (Theo) and Thomas (Tom). That is about a dozen or more between them. I never heard anyone refer to step or half brother or sister. They were simply brothers and sisters. That alone is proof enough that there was a lot of love in the family. Some of the brothers and sisters who didn't have children helped raise the children of their siblings. What I am trying to say is the whole clan supported each other.

We are lovers of music. Most can play the guitar or piano, and everyone can sing and dance. All are still good at storytelling. Family get-togethers were a time to sing, dance, eat, and enjoy the fellowship. It was a festival. Music is still in the genes—amateur and professional.

Chapter Five

The Pews of the Low Church

"Yaw sur, Brother Edmondson, you can't live a Hoss (horse) and die a mule," the reverend bellowed out as he ended one of his famous fire-and-brimstone sermons based on living right versus going to hell if you were just so unfortunate to die while being a sinner. Sitting still was hard to do.

Sylvia kept herself entertained sitting on the floor by her mother's feet imagining she's outside running up and down the road between Grandma Susie's house and theirs. That final statement was her clue that church was about to be over.

She stretched her skinny little arms and rubbed her mother's silk-stockinged legs while she played with a torn cardboard fan that was advertising a local white funeral home. It had the picture of a pretty little white girl on the front of it. She imagined that little girl's face being the prettiest, smooth brown color just like her own. It was the same color as the milk chocolate icing on the cake made for Sunday dinner. Her hair was dark brown, almost black. It was parted and plaited in three sections. One plait stuck up in the top of her head and had a bright red ribbon on it tied in a large bow. The other two plaits on each side of her head had matching bows. *She looked just like me,* she thought. That little girl came to life while Sylvia stared at it.

When the usher came down the middle aisle collecting those fans, that little girl's face returned as pale as a ghost, and her hair hung in ugly long blond curls. During the summer before church ended, the ushers came by collecting those precious instruments to save for next service.

I don't mind giving Pinky up, Sylvia thought because she's so out of place and could never fit into her daydreaming. That explained why she always had to rush and change back to the way she was. The ushers placed the fans in a neat stack on the backseat next to the door to wait for the next service at the Low Church in Promise Land. Sylvia took one last glance at her as they passed by on the way out. And just as sure as the sun rises, there she was in a pretty dress with her ugly blond hair arranged in long dangling curls.

"Yaw sur, Brother Edmondson," the preacher bellowed out again, as though he was talking to no one but Theo. "You sho can't live a Hoss and die a mule."

"Wonder why he singled my daddy out. Why, Bro. Theo Edmondson was one of the most respected and most righteous men in the community." She heard her mother say more than once that he was just as good as any preacher. *She ought to know,* Sylvia thought. Unto this day, you haven't heard anything about him swearing, cussing, drinking, or chewing. That was all addressed in the orations of the second and fourth Sunday sermons delivered by the right Reverend Bradley, pastor of the Mount Olive, African Methodist Episcopal Church (AME) or simply the Low Church down the road from the Methodist Church. It worked out fine because the Saint

John preacher preached on the first and third Sundays up the road. Everybody went to both churches.

At the age of three or four, she never concerned herself with much more than being comfortable while sitting there for however long it took for the service to be over, and then they could be on their way back home where Sunday dinner was waiting to be devoured by whoever might come along.

After church, folks would stand around under the oak trees shading the front of the church to talk for a spell. While fanning with handkerchiefs or their hats, the ladies would review accounts of the blessings of the Lord the past week and exchange little bits of gossip in between those holy and righteous "I don't mean no harm, and you know I am not one to gossip" statements that preceded each little tidbit of gossip.

Sylvia plopped down on the feet of her mother. She'd rare back on Lizzie's hefty legs while playing with the grass or a pile of rocks and tugging impatiently at her coat tail until the last "Yes, Lord" or "Child, you don't mean it."

The men had their own form of business to talk about, usually where some work could be found. Any little news of what was going on in the county was welcome. A little bit of politics was thrown in to keep it interesting and make them feel important and manly. The men who had served in the military returned to Promise Land to live for only a short length of time. Those who had not served in the military, like Uncle James, Uncle Robert, Uncle Baxter, and Theo continued to live and be satisfied in the Promise Land.

Every now and then, you might hear a little talk of unrest; but for the most part, Promise Land was a thriving peaceful community of colored landowners who were proud people. Some of the men worked at farming and odd jobs. Everything seemed to equal out, and everyone stayed in his place. There usually was no trouble because everyone, whether white or Negro, "knew his place." It seemed to be an unspoken law.

The community had two churches: the (Low) Church Mount Olive and the Saint John Church. The two churches were supported by the entire community including the sinners. It would have been hard to live in Promise Land with the Methodist Church as your front door and the AME Church for your back door and not eventually get saved. The only "white congregation" was Saint Paul that sat at the corner of a dry creek and Promise Land Road. Now the billboard reads, "Sons of the Confederate Veterans." At the bottom of the billboard it reads, "Heritage, not Hate." Interesting! This is a friendly group who I have seen participating in the annual Promise Land Festival.

John 3:16: For God so loved the world, that he gave his only begotten Son, that whosoever believeth in him should not perish, but have everlasting life (KJ).

Chapter Six
One Sunday Dinner

Disclaimer: This story was one told to me while we were growing up. I do not know if it is all true or not. Parts from my memory I tell it here because we enjoyed hearing it many times.

Most of the time, the men waited to see which one of the wives had prepared food to feed the preacher before putting their hats on and marching away somewhat relieved that it wasn't their turn. More times than not, the good preacher would follow us home where he would continue to deliver the "Good news of the Gospel." First, we would all gather around the table where the preacher would deliver a pretty lengthy prayer over the cooks who had prepared the food and each member of the family present or not.

After the blessing of the food, each person would have to say a memorized Bible verse. Usually my eldest sister Bernice or someone would get tickled during the prayer, and Mother would have to roll her eyes at all of us. It almost never failed that someone would try to be funny.

Since I was the baby, I always got to go first with my Bible verse. I'd raise my head and say, "God is love," as loud as I could. One of the others would chime in, "Jesus wept," in a soft voice, while Mother smiled and Daddy's chest stuck out with pride. Then another one mumbled almost inaudibly, "Moses crept." Still another would mumble, "Peter crawled" and another, "But John beat 'em all."

Since the good reverend's mind was more stayed on that big platter of chicken, he didn't seem to hear or care what verses that were just quoted. Mother at least would let it slide until later. We would exercise our faith in God and Daddy that he would be able to talk her out of killing all of us just to get the right one. He had had to intervene on many occasions, catching a lick aimed at one of us children when he leaped in the way to save someone's naughty hide from her switch. He would say, "All Lizzie, they are just children." After a while, we would all bust out laughing because he was as big a kid as any of us.

After the blessings, we children would be excused until the adults finished eating. We were never hungry, just impatient, while we waited on Daddy to quite passing that dish of fried chicken, all the while hoping that he didn't get carried away with that bowl of dumplings.

The reverend was a small-framed man like my daddy, but he was well known for the "heaping mountain of food that he could put away."

My daddy used to explain it like this: "He eats so much it makes him po to carry it." My theory was this: He must have spoken to that mountain and said be thou removed and be cast down and just like that, that food would be gone. I used to wonder how he could eat so much fried chicken, dumplings, candied yams, turnip greens, white beans, macaroni and cheese, pickles, and relishes. The Lord only knows how many pieces of corn bread and then top it off with peach cobbler and homemade ice cream or pound cake with caramel icing and a big bowl of peaches, all the while flushing it down with half a gallon of tea. I used to imagine that he only ate every two weeks, and he reminded me of a story about Grandpa Jim's old horse.

Grandpa Jim (whom I never knew) had an old horse, and I am told he got loose and ate from the corn bin all night and all day. Daddy said, "That old horse ate so much until his hooves came off." I kept waiting on something similar to happen to the reverend.

Well, the reverend never even took his shoes off, just loosened his suspenders and laid back in the big easy chair in the living room picking his teeth, grinning, and bragging about the delicious meal and how "Sister Edmondson sho nuf done put her foot in that pot a white beans." He must have thought he was so special, but every Sunday and special occasions, whether we had company or not, my mother cooked like that, and she served us on her real china plates with a large bright red rose pattern with the rims trimmed in twenty-four-karat gold. She'd use one of her linen tablecloths with napkins to match and use her real silverware, all of which Aunt Allie had sent from Buffalo New York. I am not kidding you; we probably ate better and with more class than the average family in the county, white or colored.

Fortunately, we had no lack of food in our house because Daddy always planted a garden and raised hogs and chickens. Mother canned and pickled everything and anything that she could put into a jar. But the average family feeding the reverend every other Sunday would have been set back a few meals, and their kids would have been hungry in the outcome.

After everybody had eaten, Mother and the elder girls, Bernice and Wilma, would clear the table and wash the dishes. Helen and I would feed Old Skippy (the family dog). The boys, Douglas and James, probably went courting or something after dinner. My eldest brother Lorry (named after my mother's brother), to my knowledge, left home shortly after I was born to work in Nashville at Tennessee A&I (the college for Negroes). He stayed with my daddy's baby brother Uncle Tom (Thomas Edmondson) and Aunt Dorothy (Mother's half-sister). They had no children at that time. Much later, Regina (my cousin) was born to them.

Oh, but they didn't get to go that easy. No, not before the stuffed reverend had called them aside and had given them a few more words of wisdom and advice. It went like this: "Come here, sons." He'd start out. Doug and James would step up like two good little wooden soldiers. "You know time is a changing, sons. Yes, sur, times sho is a changing." He would continue, looking like he was in deep thought. He rolled his eyes back as if looking inside himself. "You know we used to depend on trying to raise a good crop of cotton or, or, uh, tobacco and working for ah, ah, the white man." He'd open his eyes as he placed special emphasis on the "ah, ah, white man." Then he would pause again and take a deep breath, wiping the froth from around his mouth with the back of his hand before going on.

Looking over the top rim of his glasses, he'd say, "Yes, hit was a day when we had to depend on our hands for ever' thing." Then he'd reach in his back pocket, pull out a large white handkerchief with the letters that looked like GOD on it, and proudly wave it around for a while like he really was God. Then he would glance right and left to see if his audience was still captivated. Nodding his head, he'd continue, "Now we have machines to do a lot a things. Ah, don't ya see? And so now you know, boys, hits dun come a time when you better learn something else besides how to plow Old Beck (somebody's mule)." Then he'd bob his head up and down before making the final impression on the Edmondson boys.

"Ain't that right, Brother Edmondson?" And all in the same breath he'd finish. "Now you boys go on and mind yo momma and, ah, ah, and yo Daddy," he'd say, putting special emphasis on *momma* and *daddy*. "Now, y'all know why, don't you?" He'd finish looking over his glasses.

"Yes, sir," they would say simultaneously, partly because they were anxious to get going and partly because if he happened to ask them to quote Exodus 20:12, they'd come closer to getting it right together than solo.

At the first site of one of the elder girls, he would say, "Daughter, how about fetching Brother Pastor a good cold drink of water. Sister Edmondson, if I can get my hat, I'm ah go on in." And with that, he'd seem to disappear until the fourth Sunday.

About the time Reverend Pastor stepped out the door and got to his car, Old Skippy gave out a hell of yelp and came running around the house like forty going north and south. But by that time, the reverend was near about to the Hickory Flat, and the only evidence was that streak of reddish brown dust circling back down on the dirt road in front of our house. Daddy sat down on the porch scratching his head, wondering, "What was the matter with that crazy dog?"

My daddy loved my mother's cooking, and as soon as the preacher left, he'd jump straight up to hurry before the man of the cloth might return. "Lizzie, I want that chicken gizzard," he'd say. There is a part of the chicken organs that seems not to be good for nothing except to throw away, but my daddy loved that chicken gizzard. Mother would save that gizzard and cook it last and then set it out on the back porch to cool for him to have after the preacher left.

"Bernice," she'd call, "go out on the back porch and get your daddy that chicken gizzard." Bernice, being the eldest girl, was often asked to do things that the rest of us couldn't do, and she loved waiting on our daddy.

We all thought we were his favorite.

"It's not out here, Mother," Bernice reported.

"Child, stop playing," Mother warned her. "Your daddy's waiting on the front porch, waiting for you to bring him his chicken gizzard. Girl, if you ate that gizzard, I'm going to whoop you."

About that time, poor Old Skippy came out of the woods wagging his tail and tongue laid out as big as a new red potato, wet from head to toe. There was not much guessing what had happened to him since he took off about as fast as the reverend had sped away. He couldn't retract his tongue for a week. He was a much better dog however. He must have felt the fire and brimstone of that hot chicken gizzard and repented of his sins and then evidently self-baptized himself in the Hollow Spring. From that day on, Old Skippy never stole another chicken gizzard. Daddy was sure disappointed but relieved that the family dog hadn't gotten rabies like some were known to do.

Exodus 20:12: "Honor thy father and thy mother: that thy days may be long upon the land which the LORD thy God giveth thee" (KJV).

Chapter Seven
The Greatest Carpenter (Sylvia)

My first memory of home is the house that Daddy built on the property Mother's brother Uncle Lorry gave to her and Mama. It was a modest box-style structure with four rooms downstairs and two upstairs. Downstairs were the living room, dining room, kitchen, Mother and Daddy's bedroom. Their room had a door opening to the kitchen and one that opened to the living room. The stairway rose between the two bedrooms upstairs. The chimney came through the floor of one bedroom.

There was a nice sized front porch and a brick walk leading to the road ending at the mailbox. Assorted evergreen trees and shrubbery defined the front yard. A large back porch stretched full length across the back of the house and had a small room closed in that we used as a bathing room in the summertime. In the winter, we had to move that activity to the kitchen to keep warm. The larger side of the porch housed the old wringer washing machine. Daddy's carpenter tools and a variety of other things were stored there. Brick siding covered the exterior. There was no inside plumbing. A neatly grayed two-seater outhouse sat a respectable distance from the back of the house. (Only the higher class had one of these.)

Two large cedar trees a few feet from the back porch held a clothesline stretched between them. Beyond the trees was the smokehouse that held the huge smoked hams, salted meats, Mother's empty canning jars, and discarded clothing that we called rags. The hog pen and chicken house located farther out in the field held an array of squealing pigs, clucking chickens, and a big red rooster that nobody messed with because he was bad to the bone and didn't mind showing out.

The vegetable garden was between our house and Mama's with a few peach trees and one large apple tree in the middle. Sometimes tobacco and corn were raised in the fields farther out. Honeysuckle, hollyhock, wild rambling roses, pussy willow bushes, and locust trees were abundant and abounding on the property which gave it a pleasant and heavenly scent in all seasons.

Daddy built a small replica of our house, pitched it high up on a cedar pole, and planted it a few feet from the side of our house. That is where the purple martins lived. During the summer months, they put on quite a show dipping and diving swooping in and out of our front porch.

Mama was elderly by the time I remember her. The elder children have shared their memory of her with me. Wilma and James remembered walking to Charlotte with her to buy groceries. She had her list memorized. When she got to the store, she'd stand back with her purse under her arm informing the owner what she needed. There was no self-service. The owner had to get items for you.

They told how Mama would call out to Mr. Lonnie (a white gentleman). "Mr. Lonnie, I want some white soup beans, two pounds of meal, two pounds of sugar and flour," she called out as Mr. Lonnie put everything on the counter. Finally, she'd end it by saying, "And a piece of yo old white butt." They'd burst out laughing every time knowing what she meant (a piece of pork meat used to cook vegetables). It just sounded so funny to them. She always bought that old white butt—that boiling meat taken from the hind parts of the hog. She kept a supply of Horehound candies for medicinal purposes. They'd walk back home, or someone would give them a ride. She usually cooked enough to feed the grandchildren at any time.

Chapter Eight
The Greatest Entertainer

Most summer evenings after dinner, our whole family gathered on the front porch listening to Daddy play his guitar, singing and telling funny stories. He was the first comedian I ever knew. We didn't have a television then; nor did we need one. Aunt Allie wanted to send us a TV from Buffalo, New York. For some reason, my mother would not allow her to send it. We never knew why because we all liked TV.

Sometimes we went to Uncle Peonie's house up near the highway and watched TV with him, Aunt Mable, and Carrie Pearl (cousin). After working hard all day, Daddy was still ready to entertain the family. We gathered on the front porch, while Mother looked on to keep us in order. He sang songs from the Grand Ole Opry which we listened to on the radio every Saturday night. He started out telling us about things that happened to him while he was working that day.

One of my favorites is the one about a very well-known white lady, Ms. Mae Billie, a pretty good old soul I am told. She always fixed him lunch and would sit down at the kitchen table to eat with him. "Well, what was so funny about that?" we'd ask.

"Everything was all right," he said, "until Ms. Mae Billie got me a glass of milk. She had milked it that morning from her own cows. That milk was good and cold too, and right away, I turned that glass up and started gulping it down. Just as I lowered the glass, I saw a great big old fly swimming around."

Lord, we children were busting our guts. Mother was looking pretty disgusted by then. Bernice let out a scream, "Oh no, Daddy. What did you do? You didn't drink it? Oh no, no, did you?" She was gagging as if she was about to consume it herself. She's so full of drama.

"Ah, naught," he said. "But I didn't want to embarrass her or hurt her feelings—bless her heart—by not drinking the rest of the milk."

Bernice kept jumping around. The rest of us waited to see what happened to that poor old fly.

He cleared his throat and crossed his eyes and picked up his glass off the porch and demonstrated how he kept his eyes on that fly trying not to drink him down until all the milk was gone. He'd blow in the milk, and then he'd sip. Blow and sip all the while with his eyes crossed.

Mother was about to finish with all of us and about ready to send the whole lot to bed. Someone said, "Hey, Daddy, you better stop before the rooster crows. While you got your eyes crossed, they'll stay that way." The more we laughed, the longer he kept his eyes crossed until finally we became frightened that his eyes were really fixated. Suddenly he'd pull himself out of it just before that big red rooster strutted across the yard. Was that the truth or not?

To this day, we don't know, but it sure was some good entertainment. And we had an old Rhode Island Red rooster who would have been glad to accommodate him on keeping his eyes crossed. Daddy said, "When I went back to work, that old fly was about to make it to the top of the glass." It was a rerun sitcom and most-requested story.

Daddy never smoked or drank liquor. He loved to tell us this one, how he tried to smoke a cigarette. He was a grown man but slipped behind the hen house to try a Camel that one of his brother's gave him. It made him so sick he had to have the boy's help him back into the house. He compared himself to Shadrach, Meshach, and Abednego. But unlike the three Hebrew children, he said, "I did smell like smoke. Your mother was mad as a wet hen and didn't want to let me in the house." Mother would be rolling her eyes at him by then. "Look at her, children. Look how pretty she is. When I first met your mother, she was so pretty and sweet I could have eaten her up." Then he'd laugh, cover his face sheepishly, and say, "Sometimes I wish I had." He'd bust out laughing.

He was somewhat a pretty good magician too. Whenever our little boy cousins came around, he would ask them, "Come here, boy. Where did you get that egg in your pocket?" Little cousins, like Thomas, Jimmy, Mickey, Billy, or Joseph (Joe) would say, "I don't have no egg in my pocket, Uncle Thee" (their way of saying Theo). Then they would walk up to him and were completely outdone when he'd pull an egg out of their pocket. I cannot adequately describe the surprised look and sometimes anger on their faces. So funny. That egg never got broken either. I don't know how he did it.

Sometimes Mother scolded him, saying, "Those children are going to lose respect for you." Then the kids started saying, "See there, Uncle Thee, that's why I don't have no respect for you." But they kept falling for the stolen egg. They really loved it.

Chapter Nine
The Pews of Saint John (Sylvia)

If you live across the road from the church, you are involved in every event. Unless you were dead, you were there every time the doors swung open. Amen. There was Uncle Boss Redden who rang the big church bell that hung in the yard. It was heard all over the community.

We called Uncle Boss's wife Aunt E. They swung those doors open first for Sunday school and church on Sunday, prayer meeting and Bible study, and anything else in between. Ms. Betty Cunningham, Uncle Noeie, and Mr. Lev, members of the Low Church, also supported Saint John and were among the early to arrive.

We got up pretty early on Sundays. Everyone had to have breakfast. Four girls with bushy hair had to be combed and water waved. Almost every Sunday when Mother got to the last head, Jehovah Witnesses knocked on the door. She was always nice and didn't talk against them like some people do even today. Sometimes people laughed and talked about "those old Jehovah's Witnesses made me late."

I started not to open the door. I don't mind talking to them until they start calling God Jehovah. Had they studied their Bibles, they would have known that Jehovah is God. Later I learned that what they were saying was "those old God Witnesses." I sure wouldn't want to say that. People sometimes dislike people because they don't know them.

Mother and Daddy were polite. They taught us to respect people no matter what their belief is. Ignorance is not an excuse. Little did I know the Edmondson family was always on showcase? My mother and daddy took great pride in how we looked. Appearance was as serious as worshiping. When all of us struck out to church on Sunday, it was a sight to behold.

Mother was the church secretary for as long as I can remember.

Unofficially, Daddy was head of the praise and worship department. Aunt Ruby (Daddy's sister) played the piano. We sang from the Methodist hymnal songs like "Holy, Holy," "Jesus, Keep Me near the Cross," "Savior, More Than Life to Me." And on communion Sunday, we'd sing "There Is a Fountain Filled with Blood."

Holy Communion was served on the first Sunday. Aunt Essie and Aunt Betty Ruth usually were the ladies in charge to help the pastor. They prepared the unleavened bread representing the body. It was stored in a silver serving dish covered with a white linen cloth. Grape juice was served in tiny glasses, representing the blood. After each member received the bread and wine, the pastor read Matthew 26:26–28 (Luke 22:19–20, ESV): "Take, eat; this is my body …" "Then he'd say, "Drink, this is my blood of the covenant …" He finished, saying, "As often as you take it, take it in remembrance of Jesus Christ." The communion stewards took the tiny glasses to be cleaned and used again.

Rev. and Mrs. Hawkins were the first pastors I remember. The faithful couple came from Nashville to Promise Land for the worship service. Methodist preachers seemed a bit tamer than the ones at the Baptist Church. They seemed to have a set of rituals or a little more organization in conducting the service.

Reverend Hawkins was a very light-skinned man and had hair like a white man. His wife, we called Sister Hawkins, was dark like my mother. She was tall but very slim. Both had beautiful white hair.

I liked the style of service because it didn't interrupt my four-year-old daydreaming. He wore a fancy white or black robe which made him look more holy to me. He marched from the back of the church holding his Bible neatly across his small framed chest while the choir sang, "Holy, Holy" in its entirety.

Holy, holy, holy! Lord God Almighty! Early in the morning our song shall rise to thee. Holy, holy, holy! Merciful and mighty, God in three persons, blessed Trinity!

Amen.

I stood quietly beside Mother on the second row of seats. Reverend Hawkins raised his arms showing off the wide sleeves of his robe that reminded me of an angel. As the choir ended that first hymn, he'd say, "The Lord is in his holy temple. Let all the earth keep silent before him." You could hear a feather fall.

After reciting the Apostle's Creed in unison, he motioned for the choir and congregation to be seated. Even as a child, I could sense the presence of the Lord in those services.

After a few more hymns and scriptures read, Daddy was called on to lead the congregation in prayer. I remember it like it was yesterday. My daddy prayed a very simple prayer. He bowed down on one knee by the front pew, and this is his prayer:

"Dear Lord, our Heavenly Father, this is your humble servant bowing down here on bended knees. Bowing here not for shape, form, or fashion. And neither for an outside show to this unfriendly world."

The congregation filled in an, "Amen" or "Yes, Lord" while some of the men would growl and hum, "Um, hum, well."

He continued, "Lord, I thank you that you woke me up this morning in my right mind and with the right activity of my limbs and the right constitution of my body. I thank you, Lord, that my bed wasn't my cooling board. Lord, I ask you to heal the sick in Jesus name. I ask you to feed the hungry. Clothe those who are in need of clothing. Bless the widows and operands."

By that time, the church was pretty heated up and the spirit was flowing. Uncle Boss or Cousin Emma would wave a handkerchief and wipe off the sweat from their brow. And finally, he brought it to a close just as smooth as he had started.

"And now, Lord, when we are done bowing down here in spots and places, I ask that you will give us all a home in your Kingdom, Lord, where every day will be Sunday, and sweet Sabbath day will have no end. Every day will be howdy, howdy and never good-bye. All these blessings we ask in Jesus precious name. Amen."

After Daddy's prayer, I was ready to take my favorite place on the floor by Mother's feet. Reverend Hawkins's sermons were somewhat shorter and to the point, but with no less fire and brimstone. He didn't mind letting a sinner know where sinners go.

Like all preachers, he was committed to the great commission and was continuously calling for some sinners to come home. As the choir began to sing, "Come Home, Come Home, Ye Who Are Weary, Come Home," I watched from beneath the pew to see if anyone got saved. I secretly eyed some who I thought needed to come up. But they didn't. Reverend Hawkins stretched out his hand and offered the sinners a chance to come to the altar. The choir began to hum, and the preacher described how easy it is to just give yourself to Jesus. "No need to hang over hell on a spider's web," he begged. "Come to Jesus. Come to Jesus." He repeated as the choir switched songs and began to sing "Come to Jesus, Come to Jesus, Come Just as You Are."

He continued to plead as he walked from one side of the pulpit to the other. "Come just as you are. Don't take another chance of hanging over hell," he called. "No need to hang over hell on a spider's web." Then the choir began to sing "Just as I Am without One Plea."

I sat quietly by my mother's silk-stockinged legs. Just then, Mother began to pat her feet, and her legs moved up and down. I noticed and caught hold of a snag in her beautiful stockings. She never noticed me hanging onto that tiny silk thread. But the faster she moved her legs, the longer that silk thread grew until I could imagine that string being the very web that Reverend Hawkins was talking about.

He continued to plead, "You don't need to leave here today if you don't know Jesus. Won't you come?" You could hear people all over the church saying amen and helping him to encourage the sinners to come on in.

I watched as he continued to stroll back and forth across the pulpit. Firmly I held to that silk thread like I couldn't let go. Mother kept bouncing her legs up and down, up and down to the rhythm of the songs being sung. That silk thread got longer and longer. My heart began to pound inside my little chest. I was afraid to let it go. My eyes opened wider as I imagined myself swinging back and forth, back and forth.

I imagined a few of the community's well-known sinners swinging out there too on that silk stocking string like a trapeze artist in the Ringling Brothers Barnum and Bailey Circus. And that day, I thought I am going to ask my mother if I am a sinner. I don't want to be swinging out over no hot fire.

Chapter Ten
Silver Dollar

Nobody got saved. I forgot all about that sermon after Mother discovered the big run up the side of her silk-stockinged leg. I was just plain hungry and could hardly wait to eat. I didn't eat much. When I was hungry, nothing else mattered. I was a picky eater, but Mother never noticed. She knew she cooked and put it on the table, and it usually was all consumed.

The pastor and his wife were having dinner with Brother and Sister Edmondson again. We gathered around the table as usual, and a delicious meal was spread before us—fit for a king—but I just didn't feel like letting the grown folks eat while I waited for them to finish.

After the prayer, we said our Bible verses and then were excused so the adults could eat. I don't know where that practice came from. All I could think about was that "I am hungry. I haven't eaten since breakfast."

Bernice and Wilma helped Mother wait on the guest, while Helen and I ran around in the living room. Between the dining and living rooms was a large doorway opening. I stationed myself there watching Wilma and Bernice prance back and forth carrying food and iced tea to the table. I listened while the grown-ups talked about the Lord and the church while they ate. *They can talk about them in the living room*, I thought.

I took it as long as I could. They seem to be talking about the same thing and taking too long. "Shoot." I tapped Helen on the shoulder. "I wish they would hurry up and get through eating so we can eat." Helen never liked to agree with me on anything. She acted like she was deaf and dumb. Unfortunately, I don't think too well when "I'm starving." I had to repeat what I said. I repeated it louder. I said, "I wish they would hurry and get through eating. Shoot, I'm hungry." Everyone, including the preacher and his wife, heard me.

Daddy tried to look serious and Reverend and Sister Hawkins laughed out loud. Reverend Hawkins reached his hands out to me and said softly, "Come here, Silver Dollar." I had a quick come-to-Jesus moment.

I thought, Man, I know I'm going to get it now.

I couldn't imagine hanging over hell being much worse than that evil eye Mother was giving me. I'm not so sure Daddy can help me out of this one. He looked so serious. The preacher opened up his arms and said, "Come here, Silver Dollar." I took the pastor's hand and let him lead me to sit down between him and Sister Hawkins. Sister Hawkins offered in her softest voice, "Are you hungry, Silver Dollar?"

I took a deep breath, and in my sweetest voice, I covered my eyes and said, "Yes, ma'am." I sat between them for as long as I could without much appetite anymore. As usual I picked at my food. And ever since that wonderful day, I have been saved. Thank you, Jesus.

Miraculously, Mother didn't send me on to glory. I am so thankful he has kept me here to tell this story. From that day on, they called me Silver Dollar. The practice of having the children eat last was done away within our house forever and ever. As soon as possible, I sneaked Old Skippy that piece of chicken on my plate. I wasn't so hungry after all. Amen. He was waiting with his ears pointed forward. He was expecting the door to open at any time. Nobody got saved that Sunday, but I sure thought I was going to be lost.

Chapter Eleven
The Same Old Sack of Rags

After the mailman came, there wasn't much traffic on that old dirt-and-gravel road we lived on. So when a car did go by, we pretty much stopped and paid attention to who it was, usually waving in the meantime.

Most of the time, it was some white folks. There were some tractors and also people on horseback traveling on the Promise Land road. Occasionally, some white man would stop and knock on the door looking for Mother or Daddy. One old man had the habit of asking, "Is yo Mammy here?" Wilma and I would always say, "I'm sorry, there is no one here by that name." He stood there looking stupid and scratching his head yelling. He kept saying, "Yo mammy. Yo mammy. Lizzie." Then finally we would say, "Oh, you mean Mrs. Edmondson." Then Mother heard all the racket and came to the door. He would say, "Lizzie, they don't know who they mammy is." She smiled, with her gold tooth showing. "No, they call me Mother." Then he got on with his business for being there.

We called him the ragman because he bought used clothing and rags. Wilma and I went down to the smokehouse where we kept a grass sack of rags ready to sell to that silly old man. We brought it around to the front of the house. He had his truck parked in the middle of the road with a scale hanging from the back that he used to weigh the rags. Then he paid us by the pound.

Mother went about her business and let Wilma and I handle that business. Mr. Tom, we called him, would pick up the sack and weigh it, and then he would pay us whatever it was worth (only he knew what). Then he would say, "Tell yo mammy thank ya." He got back in his truck, and just before he pulled off, we pulled our sack of rags off the back of that old truck and say, "We'll teach you to call somebody mammy."

Mother knew we were being smart with him, but she didn't care. She explained that he just didn't know any better. He came around about once a month asking for "yo mammy." And the whole scene was repeated. The next time he came by, we had put a brick in the grass sack to make it weigh heavier. We pulled that same old sack of rags out to the road for the last time and waited on Mr. Tom to weigh it and give us our money. He weighed it and with a puzzled look gave us twice as much money as usual. He got back in that old truck, looked back, and said, "Tell y'all mammy thank ya."

When he pulled off, we waved good-bye to that grass sack of rags for the last time. I don't think that foolish old man ever was the wiser. I am sure that Mother never knew how many times we sold that one sack of rags. She sure would have skinned us alive. I don't remember a store being in Promise Land at that time. I don't even know what we did with the money.

Chapter Twelve

The Best Lessons

The Promise Land School sat between two tobacco fields almost in perfect alignment with Saint John Church. Both buildings were painted white. The school was an L-shaped structure and had two rooms. The land for both buildings was donated by my great-grandparents (Mother's grandparents) John and Ellen Nesbitt.

The school of two large rooms were utilized, one for class all grades and one for kitchen or storage. The first room was furnished with school desks, benches, and a desk for the teacher. Large blackboards hung neatly on the wall stocked with white and yellow chalk and dusty worn-out erasers.

A large pot-bellied stove sat a safe distance near the front of the room, close enough for everyone to stay warm and far away enough for everyone not to get burned. At the extreme front of the room, a stage ran all the way across the room elevated about one step high. This was our entire fine arts department. There you could find an old art easel, a few well-used crayons, and a display of some of the students' artistic work. During inclement weather, the American flag stood on stage next to a very out-of-tuned piano.

That old stage holds fond memories of the speech and drama department. Many people got their start on that stage. For example, my cousin Roebuck (Dr. Sokoto Fulani), author of *The Ethos of Promise*

Land. I spoke to him to refresh my memory on how he spent his time performing on that stage. He recalls having an excellent memory of his speeches. "When it came time for me to perform, I had what I call an eye-knee desertion. My heart got me up but my eyes and knees let me down every time," he explained.

Memory was not the problem, he confessed. "I was excited being around all my favorite girlfriends, Wilma Jean, Wilma Louise (Spooky), Corina, Della Bee, and Helen. We went in groups to the kitchen of our two-room school to practice. What self-respecting eight-year-old man is going to miss the opportunity to be surrounded by these beautiful ladies of around the same age and older? You see, we practiced two weeks ahead of time. My coaches were my sister Mary (Bootsie) and Beverly."

He continued, "In retrospect, my excitement lead me into a no-win situation. The night of the performance, I realized I'm alone trying to look up and not straight at the audiences, as I was told. I froze, and all I could do was cry. Sister and Bubba tried to help by yelling, 'Go on, you can do it.' They kept telling me."

After reciting the poem (Danny Gray), he recalled about his little pony still in his memory since 1948. He stated, "I foolishly accepted those speeches just to be around the girls. I am not sure it was worth the humiliation of being called Cry Baby after being yanked speechless off the stage by my older sister Minnie or brothers Lemuel and Bob."

Dr. Fulani, a retired United Methodist minister, is frequently the featured speaker at the annual First Sunday in June Homecoming Celebration. He and Sister Beesigye are great supporters of the community and events.

Another cousin (all country people are cousins), the late Lorenzy Robertson, learned to perform the works of James Weldon Johnson, "God's Trombone." He performed that several times both in the school and at several churches. Seasonal plays were performed each year by the whole school which by the time I came along might have been less than twenty children.

I loved it when we had school plays, and sometimes the men got together and had what they called a womanless wedding. It was a lot of fun because some of the men had to dress like women. The bride was always the funniest one (usually Uncle James) and was a bit taller than the groom. Today it is called Drag Queens. That was a time when sexual orientation was not an issue. Straight meant, well, straight. And if you were gay, it meant happy and gay. And, Lord, we all were happy and gay. We were one big happy family. We are still full of love for one another. Who are we to judge anyone?

The front room was completed with roughly made bookshelves that lined one corner filled with secondhand books, newspapers, and magazines (all handed down after our kind white neighbors had used them.) That, we proudly called the library.

Children went to school in Promise Land almost as soon as they could walk. There have been stories told of the many great teachers who have taught at our beloved Promise Land School, such as Mrs. Mae Etta Dansby who taught my mother; Mr. Jared O. Dixon, founder of the Cabin Kids, for which Aunt Betty Ruth was a part of; and Mrs. Fannie Nesbitt-Horner to name a few. Fortunately, I had the same teacher for the first seven or eight years of my elementary education and will have to give credit where my thought process and memory allows.

Everything I needed to know academically that would prepare me for college and a successful life, I learned in the Promise Land School from Miss Ollie Huddleston. She was the principal, the teacher of every subject, the guidance counselor, the coach and head of the athletics department, the secretary, the school nurse, the special education teacher (because whether you walked, rode the bus, or however you got there, you were included). She had something to teach every child. She truly believed that no child should be left behind. And last but not the least, she was the custodian and chief of the department of sanitation and environmental services. In other words, Miss Ollie made the fire and kept it roaring, called the roll and kept ongoing. With no running water, she still made sure that everyone washed their hands after going to the outside toilets and before eating lunch.

School was fun, and I never heard of her calling 911. She created a safe environment for all who came. The only assistants she had were the older children in the school.

Now a word on bringing a gun to school. If you did, you had better be aiming to kill that rattlesnake and copperhead hanging around in the back field. There was no chance of anyone hurting Miss Ollie or her students. The woman should be made a saint for all that. She did all that while walking one mile and a half both ways to catch a ride with the county postman to and from Dickson, Tennessee.

No doubt, we were some of the smartest children in the county because when it was time to play, we played. But when recess was over, it was over—time to get the books out and learn the three R's: reading, riting, and rithmetic (reading, writing, and arithmetic). It's too bad that we didn't know how to appreciate her as children.

We know kids will be kids. I admit I was among those who tried to see what I could get away with. When recess was over, my favorite cousin Thomas and I tended to keep on playing. Despite what Miss Ollie had to say, we continued our little fun and games of throwing spit balls, pinching, and making faces at each other—when she was not looking of course. She might have had eyes in the back of her head, but her side vision was not keen enough to catch the naughty ones all the time. Thomas and I kept on having a heck of a lot of fun both in school and out. We liked school a whole lot. Miss Ollie started acting like she didn't even see us.

We decided that fun was the most important thing to kids like us, and homework didn't mean anything to us. We continued to go to school and forgot all about learning. We could read Mack and Muff, Dick and Jane without even looking at the pages. (That's before Hooked on Phonics) We kept on creating new and more secret games to play during our regular learning time. Everything went really well until Thomas got bold enough to pull my hair and sneak up and plant a big old kiss on my cheek. You already guessed it. I turned around and slapped the tar outta him before he could get back in his seat. Poor ole Miss Ollie started treating us like we were invisible. She just kept on teaching those who were trying to learn. She must have thought, *if that lick doesn't stop him, nothing will.*

You could hear that slap in the next room. I know Thomas wanted to cry. Poor thing. He was thinking how to get me back. He would never hit back his little girl cousin. Or would he?

Whenever she did act like she saw us, we'd pick up our primer and start reading out loud. "See Dick and Jane. See Dick run. See Jane run. Run, run, run." The way we could see it, we were way ahead of most of the children from around the county as we compared our knowledge at the annual Field's Day in Dickson.

Hampton High was the only high school for colored children in the county, and some surrounding counties had to come to Dickson to get a high school education. The county's elementary schools gathered at the high school for a day of fun and activities before school was out for the summer months. We thought we were geniuses compared to a lot of them. What we didn't realize was that, while Miss Ollie might have been concerned about other children, she wasn't comparing us to anyone else. She was more serious about our education than we were. She was planning on doing something about it.

It was almost the end of the year. I don't remember how old we were. Most children started school young in Promise Land. Thomas and I continued to scheme and play games of follow the leader.

Whatever he did, I'd try it too. Sometimes Billy (William Gilbert) tried to follow the leader, but he was almost a year younger. We thought he was just a baby next to us.

Christmas break was fast approaching, and everyone was excited about that. However, Ms. Ollie held one more PTA meeting before she let us out of school. Surprise, surprise. She mentioned how much fun Thomas and I were having in school. She announced, "If they don't behave and get their lesson, I will have to let them repeat the same grade. They need to pay attention and bring in their homework."

Wow, what kind of news was that to be spreading at the end of the year? All the adults, whether they were parents or not, went to the PTA meetings. So now the whole community, including their hogs and dogs, knew that Thomas and I were possibly failing whatever grade it was and would have to repeat the same grade or pass on condition. Our parents let us slide through the Christmas holiday before they actually said anything. They didn't want to spoil Christmas for everyone.

Uncle James and Daddy were brothers. They were always trying to make everyone laugh and have fun. There was never a dull moment with the two of them around. The day they got together to discuss our indiscretions finally came. But no one seemed to be smiling now. Mother was the disciplinarian at our house. Daddy used to tell her, "Ah, Lizzie, don't be so mealy mouthed," meaning lighten up and smile and give us a break. "Won't you?" No one was smiling, except Thomas and me. Looks like all the adults had a mouthful of meal now.

I have never seen Daddy and Uncle James look so serious. The children looked on as though they saw a ghost. They thought Thomas and I would soon be dead meat. Helen and Hattie Ruth (cousin) were secretly hoping we were going to get a beating. We had gotten on everybody's nerves, I am sure. Some of the children were trying to learn.

Finally, we were put on trial, and the questions began. Miss Ollie was going to have to let us repeat the same grade if we didn't start paying attention and stop cutting up in school. She had made it very clear what had been going on, and she'd tried everything she could to motivate us, except separating us, and she didn't intend to do that. "They have to learn to obey in the classroom," she said. It turned out, she saw everything we had been doing. So the question was: "Do you all want to fail and have to repeat the same grade next year?" our parents asked.

Before I could get my tongue untied, Thomas had already spoken up and said, "I don't care." And like the "follow the leader" that I was, I repeated after him. "I, I don't care either." *Dang Thomas's time. Why don't he shut up sometimes?* I thought. It only took me one second to realize that I really did care, but it was too late. Just like that; it was over, and they all said in unison, "OK." That was it?

Miss Ollie said, "It is too late to even pass on condition."

We would fail if we kept up the foolishness we were up to. We knew some kids who had passed on condition, and we labeled them dumb and made fun of them. We never thought that could happen to us.

They explained that we had made our own decisions and what we planned for our future. As far as we were concerned, why should we worry about the future when the present was so much fun? So we fell right back into the same old habits, and we did have fun the rest of the school term. Shucks, we were celebrities in our own right. People, young and old, talked from one end of the community to the other. From the Rodney Owens Road to the Redden Crossing and for miles around, rumors spread about us for standing up and saying we didn't care.

Some thought, it was kind of odd that we didn't get beaten with the Hickory switch that was so popular in that day. Besides, who would have thought that ole Miss Ollie would want to do that to us? Since she was the only teacher, she was going to have us all the way through the eighth grade. What were we thinking?

Finally, the last day of school rolled around, and everyone was collecting personal things. The report cards were passed out. I must have been dreaming or something. Our fame came to a sudden halt when Thomas and I got our report cards. Big fat F's all the way across the card. Where the next grade would have been, it read FAILED TO PASS, all in caps. I sure didn't want Billy or Hattie Ruth to catch up with us. Bad enough to be the same grade as Thomas. Now Hattie Ruth and Billy will catch up with us. I really did care.

I was speechless as the other children's teasing set in. Again, Thomas saved the day by saying, "I'd rather fail than to pass on condition." I soon repeated after him. We were teased and humiliated so bad that summer. I must have repeated that phase a million times.

I can't remember anything else that summer. I don't remember what our parents had to say. That summer to this day is a complete blur because all I remember is that phrase. They had taught us the most valuable lesson that we would ever learn. From that day on, I would spend the rest of my life trying not to fail or pass on condition. It was the longest hot summer ever.

Chapter Thirteen
Lazy Days of Summer

We enjoyed the lazy days of summer with our siblings and cousins. Most of the cousins lived in the community. Promise Land Road runs through the middle of the community. The Gilbert Cousins, Beverly (Bell), Joe, Della, William (Billy), Serina, Linda, and Rita (our baby) were on one end of the stretch and our house on the other. We kept the road hot between houses.

Billy, Thomas, Hattie, and I were all going to be in the same grade now. It wasn't so bad after all; we could always sneak a peek at their papers. Hattie Ruth was pretty smart. Now Billy, I am not sure, he could get into just as much as the rest of us. We were always up to something. That was the fun of being cousins in the same school and same room. Poor Miss Ollie had her hands full with Sylvia, Thomas, and sometimes Billy.

Some of our cousins were city slickers who came down from Nashville on holidays and during the summer months when we enjoyed the fruits of our labors. Everything was homegrown (organic vegetables and fruit, free-range chickens, eggs, pork chops, and country ham slices) so big it had to be cut in four pieces to fit in the cast iron skillet. In other words, food was good and most of the time plentiful in our house. But those cousins seemed to flock to the house where the most children already were. I wonder how Uncle James and

Aunt Betty Ruth fed and kept all those children clean, not to mention where everyone slept.

They had seven of their own and seemed like that many more came to visit during the summer. Those City slickers were the children and grandchildren of my aunt Hattie and uncle Rev. Jesse Bowens who had migrated about fifty miles to the largest city (Nashville, Tennessee) seeking better opportunities for their family. That was way before "busing for racial equality became a subject."

Bath time for them was held outside under an old oak tree in the front yard next to the path leading to the closest spring. They had one of those old oblong metal tubs. They would fill it up with water and dip every last one of those young'uns in the same water until it was as muddy as the puddle around the outside of the tub.

Aunt Betty Ruth was a gracious hostess. She seemed to work from sun up to sundown trying to keep all of them clean, fed, and unharmed. I never heard of her complaining though. We would have the best time up and down Promise Land road all day. I don't know how our parents kept up with us. Sometimes we gathered in the old wood lot/picnic ground (now Bowens Memorial Park) where Cousin John Wesley Edmondson and some of the men in the neighborhood had fashioned a real fun playground.

We rode the Flying Jenny (something similar to the merry-go-round), the see-saw, and the swings made out of old car tires, ropes, and chains.

The girls found a way to have an imaginary playhouse made with a few leftover bricks and concrete blocks. We'd find a clump of tall grass and pretend to be fixing hair. Don't tell me you never heard of that. There is no fun like making mud cakes and pies. My cousin Cassandra and I made the best.

One day, we found some ice cream salt leftover from a picnic perhaps. We mixed that lumpy salt with mud and water. We began to mix these ingredients with our hands. You would think we had made honey. The sweet bees tore us up. We took out running while slapping at the bees. When we got to the house with mud and salt from head to toe, of course you know who (yep, Helen) wouldn't let us in. She had cleaned the house up and wanted it to stay that way until Mother got home. She made Cassandra and me stay out all day.

Often, no one wanted to be bothered with us. We didn't care. Mercifully, she gave us a drink of water now and then and something to eat. Luckily, we found water in the rain barrel and was able to wash that mess off before being stung severely. It was so hot that day. Being wet kept us cool the rest of the day.

After that, Cassandra talked me into going into the tobacco field to "sucker tobacco." Did I say she was the ringleader of most of the stuff we got into? Between her, Thomas and Billy, little "Miss Intelligent" didn't have a chance. Now the first taste of that sticky leaf was enough to let us know we didn't want no parts of that "sucking tobacco." I, being the country cousin, should have known better. That big fat green juicy worm with the black horns was no fun to look at either. We took a stick and completely demolished one beautiful, healthy big burley tobacco plant.

With a scream, you could hear us all the way to the Hickory Flat. We hightailed it outta there, leaving that giant-sized worm rolling around in anguish. That was the end of our tobacco farming days forever. The tobacco crop was planted on our land by a white farmer. Hopefully, he wouldn't notice the torn-to-pieces plant. Daddy didn't have time to grow tobacco.

When we got real bored, we would get together with other cousins and go up on the highway (the paved Road 48) and count cars or better play "the next one is my car." We would always try to get back home before dark because we couldn't see the ground, and we would be afraid of stepping on a snake.

Uncle Peonies (Daddy's brother) and Aunt Mable were the only ones in the neighborhood who had a TV. They lived almost to the highway. We would stop in and watch TV with them and Carrie Pearl (cousin). Usually we stayed too late. Then we would take high steps like majorettes all the way home. Down the hill, up the hill, and for about a mile, we sprinted home.

School was out in May, but the real summer didn't seem to get started until after the first Sunday in June. People came home for the church homecoming but not like they did for the picnic. I remember we looked forward to Uncle Jewel and our cousin Bobbie Jane; they'd never missed the homecoming. Bobbie Jane was one of our most beautiful cousins. She was Aunt Essie and Uncle Robert's eldest daughter who lived in Saint Louis, Missouri.

The highlights of the summer was a series of family reunions, church homecomings, and literally dinners on the ground. From the first week in June, celebrations got started and lasted all the way through September. Each community had its own agenda arranged so that other communities could come and support them.

Promise Land Homecoming is held the first Sunday in June. Native son Rev. Jessie James Bowen was born and raised in Promise Land and had preached his very first sermon at the Saint John Church. He was a pastor in the Methodist Church Conference. Whatever church he was pastoring came with him to Promise Land.

These events called for the latest fashions affordable and available. Most people got new outfits. Helen and I were dressed alike, and Wilma and Sister Bernice dressed alike, down to the shoes and socks. Mother must have wanted us to be twins. Or was she making her own statement? She was proud of us all and especially the girls. What Aunt Allie hadn't sent, Mother would top it off in Dickson at Fussell's or Baker's Mercantile.

The more uncomfortable you felt, the more dressed up you were. Our dresses were usually a bright spring or pastel solid colors or flowers. The material these outfits were made of were hot anytime. They had layers of organza over taffeta and lace added to bodice with a fitted waistline atop full skirts and sashes that tied in back. Shoes were always black patent to match any other outfit. Little white gloves were sometimes worn in June. A bow ribbon (matching the dress) was worn on all three plaits of water-waved hair.

Some of the little boys were made to wear homemade long-sleeved suit coats with no collars. They barely made it through morning service with the whole outfit on. We'd shed one piece at a time like strip poker, until the day was over.

Dinner was served between services. People ate so much they were sleepy during the second service. They were just drunk on food and the spirit. I never heard of diabetes back then, but somebody's blood sugar must have been sky high.

One of Uncle Jessie's sermons title, "The World Is Topsy-Turvy Today," I heard him preach that subject several times; and if that didn't wake up both sinners and Christian brothers and sisters, they had more of a problem than one sermon could fix. He could preach that same subject today and tomorrow and still be right on time. It seems strange how those words—I heard him say over half a century ago—have stayed in my mind, and the subject still is so current.

By the end of the day, everyone was completely worn out from all the festivities.

After our brothers migrated north, the Edmondson girls started spending their summers in Columbus, Ohio, with James (Mary) and Douglas (Betty), or we took turns going to see Little Brother Lorry (Margaret) in Chicago but not until after the homecoming.

In 2000, my cousins Jewel Bennett, Bobbie Bowens, and Ruth Inez Jordan teamed with other Promise Landers to realize a longtime dream come true. The Promise Land Community Club was organized by former and present residents of the community. Their dream has formed a strong club dedicated to the preservation and restoration of the first African-American community in Dickson County, Tennessee. This event, under the leadership of Ms. Serina Gilbert, has grown and become a favorite for people who are interested in the rich history and culture of the post-Civil War and the Civil Rights era. Mrs. Helen M. Hughes served as first president for many years. She is still a member and avid collector of memorabilia from the past.

The Promise Land School Building has been restored and is now on the National Register of Historic Places as of 2007. In 2010, a Civil War Trails marker was placed on site in front of the school. I would recommend for you to take time and look up promiselandtn.com for more and accurate information. I strongly recommend the PLCHA for membership, and it is just a wonderful place to visit. It is in association with the Clement Railroad Museum in Dickson, Tennessee, and the buildings are open for tours.

In 2014, the Traveling Civil Rights exhibit from Smithsonian Institute of Washington DC was on display at the PLLC festival. The festival has turned into a weekend event starting on Thursday and ending on Sunday. Y'all come to see us.

Chapter Fourteen
The Charlotte Picnic

Last but not least of the summer events was the Charlotte Picnic. People fall out of the ski it seems from everywhere. Literally. People save all year from one end of the globe to the other just to come to that famous Charlotte Picnic held in Charlotte, Tennessee, the third Friday in August. I mean even today from overseas, no matter how far away they are, they come home for that picnic.

People came to the Charlotte picnic like it is a federal holiday. It is a mystery to me even to this day how people revere the Charlotte Picnic like it is holiday. Started by a group of men and women called the Masons and Eastern Stars, the picnic is held annually on the third Friday in August in the County Seat of Dickson County in the small town of Charlotte Tennessee. It actually kicks off on Thursday.

My earliest memory is that gigantic man made hole in the ground with a very strong wire netting or fencing stretched across it and held together with wooden stakes at intervals. It reminded me of the volcanos that we studied about in school. Instead of blowing up steam, smoke, and a mix of hot lava rocks, it produced a dish of succulent greasy pork meat drenched in the reddest, hottest sauce that would soak the bun, the waxed paper, and the brown paper bag. Like those volcanic eruptions, there was no stopping that barbecue and hot sauce until it was all consumed, and it ran its course through the mouths and down the elbows of those who loved it so much.

Who does not remember Uncle General? Sorry, I don't know why, but he was uncle to all who knew him (Henry Sherron). Not just anyone was allowed near that pit though. Then you might wonder how I know so much about it. I am telling you what I heard and what I observed and have heard from someone else who ought to know.

There was a gentleman known to everyone as Uncle General. I knew him since childhood, and as I up grew, he never seemed to change. He was ageless. Uncle General, for all that I know, is still the master barbecue chef of times. I can see him right now.

Uncle General had not a blemish on his face. His skin was as smooth as a lump of coal and almost as black. By contrast, his hair was a mixture of white and black, just enough that in sunlight, it reminded you of a piece of fine silver freshly polished. It was kinky curly, and he had a full beard to match. He stood tall and erect, and I would say he was of a well-built medium statue (as much as one could tell) dressed in those classical bibbed overalls. He also wore a clean white bibbed apron.

Overalls was the traditional attire worn by the vast majority of the men. The only variation was a suit coat worn on Sunday. If it was a real special occasion like their funeral or someone else's, a bow tie or necktie was added.

The preparation of the barbecue had to take shape precisely at the right time. The pit had to be just right to receive the load of whole hogs brought in. They would be stretched out in five points with heads up. There must have been a dozen or more whole hogs on that pit with their heads held high.

Beside this huge hole of smoking coals was a large pile of smoldering hickory logs being reduced to cinders? These hot coals would be added to the pit periodically by the master barbecue chef throughout the night. This process kept the meat at an unfluctuating temperature until it was ready to fall off its smoky bones.

However, those old hogs were still in their skin, which held them together until the directions were given to the meat carvers of the Free Mason Club staff to pull, cut, and chop in preparation for the sales of the main attraction. Nothing would be left, not even the skin, which many thought was the best part. Having been cooked to such perfection, so tender and crisp, it was a pleasure to eat by both young and old regardless of the condition of the oral cavity. From toothless little babies to the toothless older population everyone loved that skin.

Uncle General was quiet. He was a man of few words and even fewer as he watched over those hogs sizzling with their open mouths, grinning, eyes becoming wider open, and the greasy tears dripping down their big fat jowls, causing flames to flare up that demanded attention. These flames were put out with precision so as to not get aches on or to burn the meat. From that pile of logs burning, he would add more coals to the fire and gently turn each hog. This procedure would go on like clockwork from Thursday afternoon until picnic day early Friday morning. He carefully watched over that meat all night until it was ready. The once pink skin became evenly the color of dark brown sugar.

When he felt that the meat was just right, he and some of the other committee workers would transfer a whole hog to the chopping block to be pulled chopped and rendered ready to be consumed on a first-come-first-serve basis. What had taken roughly twenty-four hours to prepare would be reduced to a greasy red stain in less than four.

Both white and colored citizens came from miles away to stand in line waiting to purchase their share of the long-awaited Charlotte Picnic barbecue by the pound or by the sandwich. The only sign of it ever being was the delicious odor that lingered and permeated the perimeter of the picnic grounds for days or even months.

Poor Uncle General looking broken from being up all night rested on a bench in his now greasy red sauce-stained apron, his face dripping greasy sweat down to his beard. There was no sign that he ever slept or ate during the function.

Nearby was the table where the empty hot sauce pots sat with their red mops hanging neatly over the rims completely drained of all evidence? People really loved that meat.

You might remember Rev. C.D. Jenkins. It takes many followers to host such a great function, and all are equally as important as the leader. To name them all, it would be impossible. But one of these leaders was a well-known and well-respected minister who seemed to be the head of the whole function from start to finish. He was known for performing Last Rites or Masonic Rituals whenever a Mason or

Eastern Star passed on to their heavenly rewards. It was rumored that he read these ceremonies from a blank sheet of paper while strutting up and down the aisles of the building. He was a very articulate and eloquent speaker and excellent preacher by the name of Rev. C. D. Jenkins. He was always referred to by his whole name, Rev. C. D. Jenkins by his younger admirers, and C.D. Jenkins by his peers.

Rev. C. D. Jenkins was not a very tall man as I remember. He was pretty heavyset or rotund as a matter of fact and enormously energetic. He had a way with facial expressions that even a deaf man could understand his vocalizations. When he walked, his short stout legs seemed to stretch an extra foot and retract as he planted each oversized slightly turned-up shoe one in front of the other with a thud so that he arrived at his destination with record speed and agility for a man of his BMI (body mass index). Whether inside a building or out on the grounds when he moved, things got out of the way with a shake and vibrate. It seemed like his every step and every word was done on purpose.

A suit and tie was his main attire. He always wore a long-sleeved dress shirt with necktie, a belt, and suspenders no matter the season. On picnic day, he'd have his sleeves rolled to just above the elbow and black ribbons or bands to keep them in place, which also marked him as distinguished. He wore an apron capable of holding a large amount of cash that was generated from the sales of concessions of the day.

As he moved over the picnic grounds, his money apron grew in size and depths. Not being a part of these organizations, I have never had a report of the intake, but the economy of Dickson County must receive a healthy boost from this yearly affair.

I decided to contact Elder Ruby Perkins to check the accuracy of my remembrance of her father whom I visualized as a very important man. She told me, "The way that rumor (the blank sheet of paper) got started was because the secretary forgot to write up the resolution for a member's funeral. The funeral had already started. Nothing had been written down. He told her, 'Just go and get me a piece of paper.' When it was time to read, he held the blank sheet and started walking up and down the aisle, speaking as if reading." She said when they asked Daddy for the resolution to keep on file, he said, "I don't know what you want with it. There ain't nothing on that paper."

He kept up the practice. It worked for him. He graduated from Fisk University and was the first black chaplain of the Tennessee State Penitentiary. He organized the Prison Aires a singing group of inmates. He also marched with Dr. Martin Luther King Jr. in the March on Washington. Elder Perkins (an Eastern Star) also shared that her father's full name was George Claiborne David Jenkins. Rev. Dr. C. D. Jenkins was the grand master of the Masonic Lodge and a presiding elder in the AME Church for twenty-one years. I am thankful to her for sharing this information.

Plenty of food was prepared and sold by the Lodge members. Each family arrived with their own picnic baskets and preparations. Food was spread out like the basket dinners on the ground: fried chicken, coon, possum and sweet potatoes, country ham, coleslaw, baked sweet potatoes, turnip greens, green beans, white beans, poke salad, collard greens, cabbage with carrots and little new potatoes still in their skin, roasted corn on the cob and creamed corn, cornbread, homemade yeast rolls and biscuits with preserves and honey, homemade pickled cucumbers, peppers, onions, squash, and watermelon rind. Everyone made their favorite cobblers, cakes, and pies. Some had drinks in bottles, bucket, and jars.

As hot as it is in August, the Eastern Stars Organization managed to freeze some ice cream. Everyone enjoyed that sweet milky confection including the June bugs, honeybees, sweat bees, and every other kind of bug that could be present on a sweltering August day in the South.

Who Was There? (The Fashion Runway at the Picnic)

The picnic ground was and still is a narrow strip of land with a road dividing it down the middle. It might be a paved road now, but it was gravel and mostly dust in the early days. This road was the main thoroughfare of the picnic area. Some of every kind of fashion and for every season can be seen. It's fashion week in Dickson County showing up and turning up on the Charlotte Picnic Runway.

It was a time that the colored people up north, out east, and out west came home to show off to their Southern kinfolks. But the colored people of the South would not be outdone. The statement on both sides of the Mason and Dixon Line or from either the gold rush or coal miners was to emphasize prosperity. People wore their finest and strutted up and down that road from beginning to the end of the day. One lady who was thought to be more blessed than others was said to have worn a full length mink coat one year in August.

People came on horseback, back of pickup trucks, on foot, fancy cars, and by any means necessary. There was a continuous hustle and flow of pedestrians on that dusty road. But now and then, they had to step aside to allow those most prosperous participants to have the right of way. They cruised slowly through the crowd in a brand-new Cadillac or Lincoln Continental. Some sported a long unlit cigar or expensive pipe jutting out from the corner of their mouth, leaving space to show off a gold tooth or two when they smiled.

Cousin Jiggs Primm was one, with plenty of beautiful gold teeth, money, fine clothes, and a car to match. He'd pick up a load as he drove by, announcing, "Outta here. Outta here," before burning rubber, never did say where he was headed. If you were lucky, you might get to ride in that fancy car.

Another such gentleman was Uncle Babe Nesbitt (his real name). He was a direct descendant of the original settlers of the Promise Land Community and was probably sitting on some old money. He was the modern-day Harriet Tubman of his time. He had migrated all the way across the Ohio River to Columbus, Ohio, and had afforded many a person and whole families a ticket to the hopeful, more opportune Northern shore. He would drive down the road in his dust-proof shiny yellow Cadillac. Rolling slowly, trying not to get it dusty, to have time to bow and chat along the way. There was no shame in his game. His was a statement not to be matched. He came to show off and made no secret of it. He would cruise the whole weekend all over the county. He wanted to be seen by both black and especially by the whites.

People loved to ask him, "Who have you seen since you came down here, Uncle?" There was one white gentleman I will just call Mr. Billy. People would say, "Uncle Babe, have you seen Mr. Billy since you've been down here?"

Uncle would stop his car, straighten his bow tie, adjust his hat, remove that expensive pipe, and clear his throat. There could be no doubt of what he was about to say. His response was. "Well, now, now you know I don't care a thing about seeing Mr. Billy." Pausing, he'd nod his head while looking over the rim of his glasses. He'd say, "Uh, I just want to make *sho* Mr. Billy sees me."

You never knew if he had seen Mr. Billy or not. But it was with special emphasis on how important it was for this gentleman to see him. People loved to hear him say it, and he loved to oblige them.

I think Mr. Billy had been dead for years, and people were asking, "Uncle, have you seen him?"

Another attendee was Uncle Babe's brother, known to most of us as Uncle Lerce (Earsley Nesbitt, a descent of original settlers). He would sit in a full-vested suit and shoes to match, leaning back in an old cane-backed chair passing out money (old money) to us little picnic goers for ice cream and whatever a dime would buy. He seemed to take great pleasure in handing out these shiny new dimes. He lived in Columbus, Ohio.

I don't know how he arrived at the picnic. I never saw him in a car. Nevertheless, he dressed sharp as anyone with dust proof shoes to match. Turns out he was really our grandpa (father like Abraham), but we still called him uncle. Had I saved all my dimes, I would have roughly about two dollars by now.

The Friendly FEUD/PTSD (Story Told to Sylvia: True or False?)

People were highly concentrated on that picnic ground of no more than ten acres in size. Blankets, quilts, and chairs would move according to the direction of the sun until there was nowhere else to go. People rested on benches nailed between trees while fanning, wiping sweat, and trying to stay hydrated throughout the day. Young mothers nursed their new babies while juggling an older toddler on their knee. Some children napped while older ones walked along the runway beside an older sibling or adult relative.

With such a high concentration of people and the atmospheric pressure on the rise in the midst of a heat wave, you can expect someone is going to become disagreeable and irritable. And so occasionally, the event would end with a friendly feud. Well, here, it is just about two hours before dark sets in. Unfortunately, two well-known families are about to bring it on. I don't know if I really remember the event or just remember my family telling and retelling the story until it became so real that it created a post-traumatic stress disorder (PTSD) that you couldn't imagine.

The story is that there was an altercation kind of similar to this. No one remembers what the friendly feud was about. I am not sure it actually happened. It is a story that has been around, and it won't go away. It might have consisted of a little name-calling, some tumbling and rolling around in the dust, and a little bit of fist flying around in midair. The older, more civilized, level-headed relatives of the opposing sides would be begging and holding the younger, more rambunctious opponents, while they bounced around kicking up more dust than fuss not as eager as they made out to be let go and get the heck beat out of them. So it was more noise than anything and other people trying to see and get out of the way.

During all the commotion, I came up missing. I am sure that it must have seemed like longer that it really was for my weeping, distraught family who claimed to love me so much. Lately, I begin to wonder how the baby of this beloved family could have been lost. All those sisters and brothers, mother, father, and grandmother—how could I have been lost?

I was found safe, however, when the feud was settled. I was sitting in a big old rocking chair on "Mrs. Low's porch." She was an elderly lady whose house was right at the edge of the picnic ground entrance.

Every year, that story grew in size until in my mind it became a major war zone and practically ruined "la fiesta" for me. I never complained because it was not going to do any good anyway. But I couldn't wait until I was old enough to stay home and not go to the biggest event of the year—the Charlotte Picnic.

In 2010, I decided to take my now grown children to the picnic. We went about midafternoon when it was beginning to cool down. I explained to my family the situation of why I never liked to go to the picnic. As children, I only took them a few times. They agreed to go.

We arrived and parked the Suburban and the car. We began our stroll down the runway, stopping to greet people whom we knew. I observed nothing much had changed. The road is now paved. A few royal blue porta toilets were a welcome verse the original. The trees were seemingly larger, but the benches were still nailed to them where people sat. The crowd seemed to be having a good time just sitting and walking around talking.

My three-year-old granddaughter Mikayla enjoyed sitting on her father's feet playing with a collection of rocks that she had gathered. She reminded me of the times that I too rested on my mother or father's feet at these occasions.

The family was able to get some of the food that had been prepared by the picnic staff. There was no barbecue left but plenty of fried fish, hamburgers, and hot dogs. There were vendors with arts and crafts for sale. Later that night, there was gospel singing on the stage that had been set up.

My sons, no doubt, enjoyed the affair. We left with them wondering why I had such a fear of the Charlotte Picnic. Andre said, "Well, you know it was just people connecting and enjoying the fellowship." I say, "To God be the glory for the taming of the crew."

In existence for over one hundred years, let the Masons / Eastern Stars live forever. I salute the Charlotte Picnic, its founders, and those people who continue to make the affair the largest, most popular gathering in the county of Dickson, Tennessee.

Again in 2014, I decided to attend the picnic late in the afternoon. It was almost dark when I arrived. I had picked up a flyer from the high school reunion on Thursday night. It stated that it was the One Hundred Eleventh Annual Charlotte Picnic hosting a Gospel Explosion Throw down.

The lineup featured the Dynamic Dixie Travelers, Revelation, Union Choir of Dickson, Emanuel Church Choir, Charlotte Community Choir, (Mr. Ben Vaughn, director), New Day Church Dancers, Mr. John Primm (solo performer), The Robertson Brothers (Hubert and Hersey Jr. or June), Harold Corlew (saxophone), and the Mount Olive Baptist Church of Waverly Tennessee.

When I arrived, the Dixie Travelers were well into their performance backed by the band. One of their lead singers, Vernon Holt, was stomping and singing, "It ain't no party like a Holy Ghost party and Holy Ghost party done started. It ain't no party like a Holy Ghost party and the Holy Ghost party done started."

As he potentially stomped a hole in the ground, the audience joined in with this chant, and things escalated. Small children danced and pranced before the Lord. Men and women clapped, and some chanted with uplifted hands and worshiped the Almighty God.

At breaks between singings, a local pastor would give out door prizes using Bible trivia. At the end of the flyer, it stated, "Proceeds will support the community needs and educational scholarships for high school graduates. For more information, call 615-789-4514. Sponsored by Lone Star Lodge No. 15, Maurice Haggins, Grand Marshal" (most worshipper master).

And again, I say, "To our God be the glory. He is awesome and worthy to be praised."

Chapter Fifteen

A Singing Ministry (The Jewel of the County): The All-Night Singing

Daddy kept himself occupied and entertained while working. Other people who heard him enjoyed listening. They enjoyed him so much until they ask to come to Promise Land to hear him sing. Some wanted to sing with him. He started out at the house with a few people while Bernice played the piano, he played the guitar. It was an informal gathering. Soon it outgrew the house. Some of his white friends wanted to sponsor him on the radio. Dennison Motors (a car dealership) and the Friendly Neighbor's Furniture Store (Bro. Henry Regan, owner).

Soon they had to move it to the church. Theodore Edmondson and the Promise Land singers became the jewel of the community and county. Mother was the manager and mistress of ceremony for the singers.

The group consisted of Brother Edmondson; two daughters, Susie Bernice and Wilma Jean; nieces, Beverly Gilbert, Mary Nesbitt, and Ethel Pearl Robertson. These young ladies were teenagers.

Bernice, who started music lessons at the age of twelve, soon became the pianist for the group. Theodore Edmondson was not a preacher, but I'll tell anyone that he was just as good as one and better than some—Mother's favorite testimony. He gave sermons in song. People tried to talk him into singing the blues, but he refused.

Daddy was a medium-framed but well-built man. He was taller than Mother; I would say medium height. His skin was light like caramel icing. Daddy didn't have much facial hair, but he shaved daily. He'd sneak a little of Mother's face powder on performance night. That was to put just a little on his nose to keep it from shining.

All the Edmondson and Gilbert brothers had beautiful wavy black hair. Daddy wore a part on one side. He was a handsome man.

Promise Land soon became the place to be on Friday night. The radio announcers traveled to Promise Land and set up their equipment. The first thirty minutes of the program was taped and was carried back to Nashville to be played on radio the next day.

The theme song was "Jesus, Keep Me near the Cross." During commercial break, they hummed this song to give the announcer's time to advertise those fine cars at Dennison Motors, or the nice furniture at the Friendly Neighbor's Store located in Dickson, Tennessee.

Three of my Daddy's brothers lived in the Promise Land Community. Uncle Peonie worked away from home a lot but was present as much as possible. He and Aunt Mabel had no children but were second parents to all their nieces and nephews. Two of my favorites were Uncle Robert (wife, Aunt Essie) and Uncle James (wife, Aunt Betty Ruth). They were always on hand and ready to be available whenever and wherever and by any means necessary all around the community. They just, like Daddy, were real big practical jokers and loved to see people have fun.

Uncle Robert loved to whisper in your ear and say something to make us laugh during church. He wouldn't crack a smile. We would have to hold back on laughing or risk getting in trouble with the mothers of the congregation.

After the first program, Uncle Robert (I was told by Aunt Essie) suggested in his own comical way, "Well, shoot. Why don't we just sing all night?" He might have been joking, but the show was on. People came from everywhere after working all week to relax and bask in the most peaceful place on earth it seemed. The "All-Night Singing" became a show stopper and regular earlier version of showcasing raw American's talent.

Mother, the manager and MC of the programs, was sure to put minds at ease as she announced her intentions to allow anyone and everyone to showcase their talent. Some had it, and some didn't. But she put everyone's mind at ease as she began in her rich and smoothest voice. She loved to sing, but she knew where her greatest anointing was. She used it to perfection.

Mother was a full-figured woman. After having had ten children, she was still in good shape, and she knew it. She had a small waistline and wide hips with natural voluptuous breast that not even a plastic surgeon can fashion today. She wore the best-in-foundation garments, and a lot of her clothes came from New York by way of her sister, Aunt Allie. She was a dark chocolate by all standards that needed no makeup. She was proud to be black before black was even cool. She had medium-length black hair that she routinely kept dressed by the best beautician in Dickson County, Cousin Vera Van Leer (wife of mother's cousin Elsie Van Leer).

"Kind friends," she'd say. "We are about to begin the program. I want you all to know that first and foremost, you are welcome here tonight."

And as Mrs. Nan Breedlove (the first pianist for the singers) played, the group hummed softly, "Jesus, Keep Me near the Cross."

She continued, "I was glad when they said unto me, 'Let us go into the house of the Lord.' Amen. Now I don't need to remind you that we are here to praise the Lord tonight." She raised her hand and voice at the same time and proclaimed, "I don't know about you all, but I came to bless his holy name."

She really knew how to kindle the fire, and people were all ready to take it to a higher level by the time she finished the introduction. She adjusted her glasses and paused as people continued to stream into the building.

Faithful Uncle James and Uncle Robert were very good at keeping the crowd moving as they seated white families to the right and made sure everyone was comfortable. The church filled to capacity while many milled about outside where refreshments could be obtained. The doors were left open during the warm months so people could hear and observe as well.

Before the program started, she gathered a register of names and arranged the program accordingly. The first thirty minutes was dedicated to the radio broadcast. As she signaled the broadcast team to get in place ready to record, she announced, "Now, friends, we are ready to praise the Lord. And let me remind you," She said with emphasis, "if you put something into this program, I guarantee you that you will get something out of it. I can assure you that there are no big I's and little U's here tonight." She reassured each registered or unregistered guest that after the first thirty minutes, it was free for all.

Sometimes the special guest like the Golden Harps or the Prisonairs would have an opportunity to sing during the taping. But people really wanted to hear Brother Edmondson. Daddy sang songs like "Peace in the Valley" and "Jesus Will Be Waiting at the End for Me" while folks were walking the benches shouting and rolling on the floor. He proclaimed to our God, "Lord, you know we are not here for shape, form, or fashion. And neither for an outside show to this unfriendly world. For we know, Lord, that one day we're going to meet you on the other side of the River Jordan. Where every day will be Sunday. It will be howdy, howdy, and never good-bye."

The ladies threw hats, handkerchiefs, fans, and just about anything that could fly. Sister Augusta Holt shouted, "You better shut up now."

Oh Lord my God, just as I thought the spirit was about to calm down, Mother starts announcing the presence of a young lady by the name of Little Miss Annie Lou Harris rendering a solo. As she made her way to the choir stand, people stopped still and waited as she took her place beside the piano.

Sister Breedlove was well acquainted with the songs she sang since she was a member of the Bowman Chapel Methodist Church in Dickson. She was in her teens. She was a short pleasingly plump young lady (since skinny was not in).

As she began to sing "Walk around Heaven," she'd tell who all was going to be there, talking about loved ones who'd gone on. Then finally she'd end it with the same smooth angelic voice. Lord, even the sinners stopped going straight to hell and listened to that young lady sing. Little children like me stopped playing and listened. She stood there effortlessly and produced the sweetest voice that anyone ever heard. She was amazing and a blessing to the listeners. If you never heard her sing, you sure did miss a threat. She was a natural hit. My Lord, she tore that church up. Calmly she returned to her seat as if nothing ever happened. That's anointed God given talent. Praise the Lord.

The program took place in the Methodist Church, but it was nondenominational on Friday nights. I am sure that Jehovah's Witness, Church of Christ, Church of God in Christ, the Baptist, Methodist, AME, CME, and a few sinners and backsliders came out to hear Theo Edmondson and the Promise Land singers, the soul food of the times. People who only heard him on radio thought he was a heavyset man. I have heard many people tell him, "Brother Edmondson, I thought you were a larger man." His voice was larger than he. There was no division, and people didn't care what color the songs came from. The Body of Christ, anointed and appointed, showed up and showed out.

Bro. Henry Ragen (a white friend) was also a Church of Christ minister. He and Daddy equally loved to sing and loved to discuss the Bible. Although I was a child, I do remember that there was no division in the church denominations that I could see on Friday night. Everyone came to Promise Land on Friday night to get their spiritual food and to minister to each other.

On Friday nights in the Promise Land Community, everyone seemed to be color-blind. Both sinners and Christians came to enjoy whatever the Lord had in store for them. Everyone went away blessed, relaxed, and feeling absolutely rejuvenated after the "All-Night Singing." Music has no boundaries and is still a medium for bringing people together.

Groups came in from other towns and from locals. It was just one big "You Want to Sing" talent festival. Anyone who had the nerve got a chance to try their talent at singing. Most of them could, but you always have a few that would be better at taking up the offering, ushering, reciting a poem or something else. Some folks thought they could sing and would try anyway. There were some pretty good professional dancers and shouters who attended.

Rev. James (Pit) Satterfield could wear out that guitar of his in such a fashion that even the Methodist and Church of Christ folks wanted to dance. Rev. Satterfield was the pastor of a Church of God in Christ, (COGIC) in Dickson, Tennessee, and they believed in dancing. Let him start out with "Glory, Glory, Hallelujah," "Since I Lay My Burdens Down," and the ushers knew it was time to make room, for someone was going to pitch it to the wind, let their hair down, and you could almost see the shackles being broken from their feet. Did they ever dance? Yeah, the church house rocked.

The Golden Harps were a group who came from Nashville. This was a group of young men, Self-Sharp on the Guitar, singers Robert Britt and Walter Sellers, the local groups from Dickson churches and surrounding counties to name a few. Mr. Sam Hannah, Mr. Jippy Evans, and the Worley Furnace Church members came.

From my memory, I don't think the Dixie Travelers had formerly been organized, but I am sure that the original members were part of the group of people who came from Worley Furnace to sing and preach in Promise Land. Rev. Joe Evans, pastor of Worley Furnace Church, was a well-known fire-and-brimstone preacher. Many good preachers and singers came out of his congregation.

The Holt brothers, to name a few, became well-known preachers and pastors (Dalton and Arlus). The Horner brothers also came out of Reverend Evans's congregation (Hershel and Louis.) These were ministers who didn't mind sweating. Their sermons left them dehydrated, no doubt.

It was common to see a minister wearing an overcoat and scarf around his neck in the hottest month of the year. This was to keep them warm since they would be soaking wet from perspiration. There was no need for anyone living in Dickson County, black or white, not to be saved.

From one end of the county to the other, people lived and breathed, walked and talked about the Gospel of Jesus Christ. There used to be a tradition of the Four Gospels Program where four ministers would take one of the four books (Matthew, Mark, Luke, and John) and design their sermon on that book. That was a real treat, and you were bound to get Gospel-colic by the end of the program.

I was a child, but I had ears to hear and eyes to see. I will tell you from what I heard and saw. My memory serves me well. "Those superfine, smooth-talking, dark- and milk-chocolate-skinned, well-dressed, well-built brothers from the radio station were a pretty good drawing card too! They were being admired by all races of female observers.

They might have gotten more attention than even I was able to distinguish, being so young and very naive. I imagine a lot went over my head. I do remember one incident though. The residents of Promise Land were known to be the greatest host and hostess. You were sure to have a good time no matter what the occasion.

My uncle James was known to be the host with the most. If you were around him, you were guaranteed to have a good time. He saw to it that people were comfortable in and out of the sanctuary. Our doors were never locked. I am sure people got a little tired and needed a break, especially the workers of the night's show. For a time, there was just as much activity at the Edmondson's residence as it was across the road at the church.

One night after hours, we returned home to the sound of Mr. Sam Cook crooning some kind of love song on the radio or record player. Well, if that wasn't enough when Mother and I stepped up in the door, lo and behold, there were some smooth-talking, well-dressed brothers embracing a couple of white ladies and such another slow dragging they were doing. Well, they were surprised to say the least.

I really don't remember their names or what Mother had to say. I expect that we are all better off that my memory so suddenly fails me. I do know that she was not about to let that practice last another moment. I am suspicious that it had been going on for a while. Poor Uncle James (the host with the most) was so disappointed, and all he could say was "Ah nah, baby sis. You just ruined the 'All-Night Singing.'" Truth be told she might have saved the "All-Night Singing" and a few good brothers from hanging around from a tree limb—if you get my drift.

I don't know if Dickson County would have been open to Jumpin' Jimmy's Dance Hall in the early fifties, since we all had heard the sad, sad story of poor little Emmett Till. I understand why Mother and Daddy were not going to have that. Daddy was standing behind Mother all the way on that. He didn't believe in mixing secular with Gospel. And as for the rest of the story, they were not about to let any of that happen in Promise Land.

Chapter Sixteen
Other Pews I've Been In

In the prime of Daddy's singing career, we visited numerous churches both black and white congregations and all denominations. One church I remember in Nashville Tennessee, was Bass Street Baptist. I have no idea who the pastor was at that time. This was one of the most spirit-filled of the churches that we went to. The place to a little child (six or seven years old) like me was like a battlefield.

There was one elderly gentleman who had the strangest way of shouting. He reminded me of a bull in a rodeo. When Daddy was singing, he would just stand and stomp his foot as though he was about to attack something. Half the ushers would gather around my daddy, and the other half would link arms around the stomper. He would stomp and blow, stomp and blow when the spirit hit him. He would carry on until it let go or until Daddy ended the song.

On the ride home, Mother would always explain that the ushers had to hold that man off my daddy, or Brother Stomper Man would grab Brother Edmondson and shake him to death. I was always glad when we got my daddy out of there. I mean no disrespect to anyone. I am remembering what I heard and saw and telling it the best way I know how. I was fully prayed up every time we went to Bass Street Baptist Church so that Brother Stomper wouldn't shake my poor daddy to death.

The church is still open today. The last pastor I knew was the late Reverend King.

At WSOK (now WVOL), we met other people in the broadcasting industry. One such persons were Rev. Dr. Morgan Babb and Sis. Lucille Barbee. They continued on the air for years after my father as well-respected personalities and gospel trailblazers. They were known for their singing and preaching as well. These people should have their own books published because they were very colorful and talented characters.

We listened to all kinds of music on the radio from other great singer. Rev. C. L. Franklin, Bro. Joe Mays, the Fairfield Four, and other Gospel greats. On Saturday nights, the Grand Ole Opry was a staple with songs by Ernest Tubb, Red Foley, and Little Jimmy Dickens from the countryside. We loved Sam Cooke and Nat King Cole's smooth voices. Elvis Presley was also a great hit and conversation piece because of his "Wiggle."

Since music had no color, we didn't care what color the body it came from. The Promise Land singers had the opportunity to sing on TV at least once or twice.

My sister Helen and I were too young to be a part of the Promise Land singers. Occasionally they let me sing a solo. My song was, "Christ is all." I was never afraid to be on stage, but I'd hope to end the song before any one, "Got Happy," We had girls and boys groups from the church. These groups would sing on the programs at Saint John but did not travel with the group.

Between the Pews

It was not unusual to see a lot of action at the Worley Furnace Baptist church. They had many good singers and preachers. At any given moment the preacher might jump up and stand on the podium in the heat of his sermon. My pew experiences went from one extreme to another.

My sister Bernice remembers going to several churches of white congregations both in Kentucky and Tennessee where she remembers people shouting dancing and rolling on the floor. "I had never seen white holy rollers before." She said.

Almost every Sunday night, we would be traveling home late at night after the singers had performed somewhere out of town. I must have been around six to eight years old, and that was quite a bit of activity I had to endure since Mother, Daddy, and my elder sisters were on stage, and the brother's out courting. I will have to admit that at times it could be a bit frightening. I soon learned to duck, dodge, and stay out of the way of the well-known jumpers, bench walkers, and such.

Chapter Seventeen
The Best Christmas Ever

We never made a big deal out of personal birthdays. But we celebrated every holiday and special day from Memorial Day (we called it Decoration Day) on down to April Fools' Day. No day can compete with Christmas though.

The best Christmas ever was fast approaching, my brother Lorry and wife Margaret were coming home with my first niece Estrellita (Star Baby) James and Mary (his wife) would come with Cynthia and Ardis. My brother Douglas was still single and was living in Columbus, Ohio, with James and his family.

I was so excited to know that my little nieces were coming home. It meant that I would have someone else to play with since I was still a child myself. Yearly, everyone in the Edmondson family would be home for the holiday.

The first day that school let out for Christmas was the day that Wilma and I would go out into the woods and look for the perfect Christmas tree. Since all the brothers had moved away, Wilma and I did a lot of stuff that the boys might have done had they been still at home.

We would cut the tree down and drag it home. Then we would fill up a large bucket with water and rocks from the road to hold it down and keep it green. Now you can buy artificial snow, but nothing makes it smell more like Christmas than that fresh Tide washing powder scent. We would dump a whole box of the magic powder in a large bowl with just the right amount of water and sugar.

Helen and I took turns beating that mixture until it had the right consistency to cling to the tree and stick like real snow. Before the tree could be put up, we would make sure the floor was clean, waxed, and shined with a fresh coat of Johnson's paste wax. Nothing spells clean more than the combination set off by the mixing aromas of a freshly cut cedar, Johnson's wax, and Tide washing powder / snow. Bernice as usual made sure the silverware was freshly polished.

We would pull out the decorations that were lovingly saved year after year while waiting on the fake snow to dry and take hold. Some of the decorations were homemade, and some were store bought. The house already had that fruity smell because Aunt Allie would not waste any time sending that great big box from Buffalo New York. That box was Old Santa Claus himself, as far as I was concerned.

I don't remember ever having a lot of faith in the "real Santa." People just pushed it down the little children's throat so much. Asking then, "Do you know who Santa Claus is?" And in the same breath, they would tell you, "If you do, you won't get anything for Christmas."

Well, what kind of a dummy do you think was going to come out and say, "Yes, sir, I know who he is." So for years, I just went along with the program of getting that letter from Santa, written by my left-handed sister Wilma and leaving the milk and cookies or big piece of jam cake for the jolly old elf. And I bet Wilma and James ate that. They even advocated the reindeer on the roof top and down through the chimney with lots of toys.

The fact that I was smarter than a fifth grader did not dampen the joy and lovely time during the holiday. Besides folks, not many of us were owners of a big old fireplace with chimney. I am thankful they didn't try to tell me that big fat belly squeezed do the stove pipe. So now let's get real.

First, we wrapped the red ribbons around the tree followed by throwing on the individual pieces of silver tinsel. Then came the bells made out of milk bottle caps and then followed by the angels, those heavenly messengers cut out of cardboard and flocked with cotton balls with their hands clasped in prayer. A large silver star was placed on top of the tree, a symbol of the one that lead the Three Wise Men.

We got caught up in the worldly activity of the season but never downplayed the true meaning of the season. There was much to be said in the school plays and church activities as to the real meaning of the holiday. That was before the Black Friday frenzy you hear of nowadays. Thanksgiving was celebrated and enjoyed as a stand-alone holiday. And then came Christmas.

The usual fall and winter activities went on with cold weather and even a bit of snow, but not even the coldest, dreariest day could match the bright sunshine that Star, Cynthia, and Ardis would bring to our home that year for Christmas.

Star Baby was the eldest of the granddaughters and the only child since unfortunately we had lost her little brother Lorry Jr. just about a year before. He had what the doctors described as an enlarged heart and had died at the age of around two. That had been a devastating time for the whole family. Our Grandmother Susie (Mama) had what doctors described as hardening of the arteries and had suffered for a few years with her mind "going and coming" (today's Alzheimer's disease). She had accidentally burned herself that same year and never recovered.

My emotions were mixed because somewhere deep in my soul, I felt more joy than sadness when Mama died because of the pain and suffering I saw her endure. As a child, I didn't understand what I felt. But it felt good knowing that we would be together for Christmas, a happy occasion again.

The baking started a few weeks before to get everything ready for the season. It was a tradition to have cake and coffee / tea and / or homemade eggnog for anyone who happened to drop in during that time. Mother had pulled out her jam, (homemade jam), coconut and chocolate cake recipes. The yellow cake with caramel icing recipe was in her head. The pecan pie recipe was located on the dark brown Karo syrup bottle, and she had bought plenty of those ingredients at Dillingham's Grocery store in Charlotte weeks ago.

Everyone would help crack open the pecans and grate the fresh coconut in preparations for her to use at the right moment that the recipe called for. Daddy would sit nearby and keep the Warm Morning stove loaded with wood or coal while playing his guitar or working on his latest invention—a pair of shoes that would grip right through the ice and snow and allow him to remain upright while doing his outside chores like bringing in wood, slopping the hogs and such. (This invention was abandoned soon after Daddy busted his chops on the first big patch of icy snow.)

Daddy was not to be trusted with the pecans and coconuts because too much would come up missing, and Mother accused him of being the culprit. It was best to keep him occupied singing because he could not chew and sing at the same time.

We loved Mother's cooking, and to watch her in the kitchen was a show all by itself. She would have made some kind of a TV cooking show. She didn't own all those fancy kind of chef's tools, gadgets, utensils, etc., available today. All she had was herself, the stove and us. That was enough. She could separate a yolk from the egg white with one hand never getting the shell in the mixture.

Then while those pies were baking, she beat the heck out of the egg whites using every muscle in her body until that clear runny substance turned white and peaked like snow on a mountaintop. She would turn the bowl upside down and dare the meringue to move. That's how she knew it was time to add the appropriate amount of sugar before piling it onto the already baked pies. With a quick turn, she'd start the next dish while the meringue turned a nice golden brown. Nothing ever burned or stuck to the pan. Pies done; now it's time to start the seven-layer jam cake and cook the caramel icing that would cover both the yellow and jam cakes.

Mrs. Theo Edmondson could put an electric mixer to shame with her bare hands. She threw her whole body into motion hips, and everything in gear, her rhythm could have been set to music during the mixing of the batter that would end up with just the right texture and moisture that you will never get out of cake mix box.

She let us kids help cook the caramel icing. We tested it by dropping a few drops into a cold glass of ice water to see if it formed a ball. If it did, that meant it had cooked long enough and was ready to cool and be spread on the cakes.

Helen and I saved jar tops and would scrape the batter bowl to get enough batter to make a tiny little replica of the big cake which we would share with Daddy. That became our routine and kept us from being too restless for the big cakes.

Our brothers and their families arrived just two days before Christmas from Columbus and Chicago. They came with plenty of presents. The wrapped gifts added more to the beauty of that big old cedar tree with its star barely missing the ceiling of the house.

Right away, Ardis stole my daddy's heart as she seemed to be mesmerized in all the lights. He had put the finishing touch on the place by stringing the outside lights over the front porch, and the two evergreen trees on either side of the porch were all lighted up to. Ardis pointed out the front window at the lights strung outside. With her fat little brown baby hands, she clapped and padded around the room laughing. She was so excited over all the decorations. Her hair was short, curly, and red, framing her face with matching fat rosy cheeks. "Light, light." She pointed as her eyes lighted up with joy. That one word stole our hearts. Those lights shone brighter in Promise Land than all the many lights she must have seen back in Columbus.

Star Baby and Cynthia stood looking on equally as excited and cute. They were like living dolls to us. They were our three little princesses, more than enough to make my Christmas merry and bright. We worked late most nights leading up to that time, but on Christmas Eve, all children had to go to bed early for Santa Claus to leave his gifts. I always got some dishes, a new ball with Jacks, coloring books, paper dolls—my favorite—and a new baby doll because somehow I managed to wash the old ones until their skin rolled right off and exposed the cotton stuffing within.

All tucked in bed, Christmas Eve was harder than ever to fall asleep with my three little nieces being there. My brothers had left home almost before I can remember. I loved my brother's wives Mary (James) and Margaret, (Lorry) and they were equally as fond of me. We were one big loving family. The joy of waking up early Christmas morning outweighed the going to bed early, and it seems like before you knew it, you could smell the fresh Folgers coffee brewing as Mother and Daddy were waking us up because Old Santa had been there.

Oh no, no. We did not get up and run straight to the tree and start tearing into presents like you might see on TV commercials. No we started out with songs and prayer. We all gathered around in the living room and sang Christmas carols while Bernice played the piano and Daddy his guitar. Then Daddy would pray his signature prayer, starting with, "I thank you that you woke me up this morning and that my bed was not my cooling board." All the things that we take for granted he thanked God for. The best thing about waking up is "waking up with family."

Mother had already prepared breakfast of country ham, red-eye gravy, sausage and bacon, fried potatoes, rice, and those homemade biscuits that would be served with homemade pear or peach preserves and blackberry jam. We were allowed to eat at leisure while enjoying the three girls playing with their gifts.

I shared my new doll and dishes with my little nieces and tried on new clothes that my aunt and brothers had given me.

Star Baby, the eldest of the girls, had a beautiful, smooth caramel skin with curly, sandy red hair framing her plump little face. She was a little busybody who ended up in my daddy's lap with a comb. She loved combing Granddaddy's nappy head. She'd say, "Hold still, Granddaddy. Let me comb your nappy head." He loved her combing it. He'd act like he was trying to hold still while telling her, "Star Baby that hurts. Your hand is too heavy."

They had to compare hands. They took turns putting their hands in Granddaddy's to see who had the biggest hand. There was always a fuss over Star Baby's hands being bigger than Granddaddy's. Cynthia and Ardis would put their hand in his and try to pull back before he closed his. It was fun to try and get away before he closed his hand. They carried on like that the whole time they were home. With Daddy around, these kids didn't need any toys.

Daddy talked about the grandbabies for weeks after they were gone. It was a scene that I wish would have never ended. Helen and I played house and church with the three girls in attendance. Helen and I argued over who would play the (imaginary) piano. Ardis could never sit still long enough to play church. Church ended in us chasing her around holding on to her little dress tail. Poor Cynthia, overtaken by the commotion, would fall over laughing at us chasing Ardis, as if we were putting on a show for her only.

Cynthia had the cutest little round button nose. Her eyes were so deep. When she laughed, they seemed to disappear. These scenes ran back to back, like your favorite sitcom.

The adults didn't care how much racket the children made. Margaret (Lorry's wife) could always be found sitting some place quietly while reading. I don't know how she could concentrate with all that going on.

Mary (James' wife) loved listening to all the chatter and storytelling. She was like us; she enjoyed laughing. Doug was not married at that time. Life was perfect.

Douglas had saved his gift for Daddy until last. With a big smile on his face, he brought a large flat box out and placed it on Daddy's lap. "What is it? What is it?" Daddy repeated while ripping the wrapping paper to shreds. Finally, he stood up and held the most handsome suit you could imagine.

Douglas stuttered when he talked and was also hard of hearing. He was a man of few words, you might say. But that wide ear-to-ear grin that showed up when he saw how Daddy loved that new suit was enough to tell you he was so proud of himself.

Out of all the gifts that day, I don't think anyone was more thrilled and pleased than Daddy was. Joking, he promised to wear that suit proudly and never take it off. Douglas had completely dressed my Daddy head to toe with shirt, tie, cuff links, including the shoes and socks. Douglas Lee Edmondson beamed with pleasure, proving that it is more blessed to give than to receive. That was the best Christmas of my whole entire life. The whole Edmondson family was home for Christmas—that was the best gift.

Dinner was served in its usual fashion with Mother's best china, silverware, and linen tablecloths adorning the dining room table. People came and went throughout the day with greetings of Merry Christmas and Happy New Year until bed time. I was around ten or eleven and really too old to keep on with that Santa Claus business.

All good things must come to an end. I was always sad when my brothers and their families left to go home. I cried every time. A few days after Christmas, our house was back to normal as we began putting things back in place. We prepared for school to start the next week. We gladly went back to school with tales of what we got for Christmas. We would sing out like a chant and ended our list in "and fruits, and nuts, and candy."

It was rumored that some children added things to the list that they didn't really get. I realize that not everyone had an Aunt Allie in Buffalo and Uncle Lorry in Indianapolis to be sure that Christmas was filled with the kind of material things that we had. I am glad that Mother and Daddy didn't totally let us get carried away in the gifts and commercialism of the season. Just being together as a family means more than all those things. We are so blessed and should be more thankful. The whole community was about the true meaning our gift from God; his Son Jesus Christ was enough.

Come summer, we would be going to Chicago, but I still cried when my brothers and families left. Bernice and Wilma started spending their summers in Chicago with Brother Lorry and Margaret. He met her while working at Tennessee A&I. After their marriage, he was drafted in the army, stationed at Fort Campbell for a while, and then lived in Buffalo New York, briefly. Douglas lived with them for a while. We alternated summers between the brothers.

I was eight years old when my first niece was born. The first time we went to Chicago was by train. Margaret was a stay-at-home mom. She was our first sister-in-law. We loved each other, no doubt. She had polio as a child, which left her with a slight limp, just enough to make her walk cute. Her skin was lighter than milk chocolate, smoothie with a few freckles on her cheeks. A big smile, she was a beautiful woman. Her hair was long, naturally curly and sandy red. She wore a beautiful shade of red lipstick. She took excellent care of us while we were there and introduced us to homemade pizza.

She and my brother were blessed with three children. First was Estrellita Ann (Star Baby). (Lorry Jr. passed at two years old.) Later, they had Fydencia Ann (Twinkle) and Theodore Dehart (Sparky).

Chapter Eighteen
A Season for All Things

March marks the end of winter, but sometimes it can bring the coldest and most unpredictable weather. Some used to say, "It comes in like a lion and out like a lamb" or vice versa. March of 1957 was unusually wet for some reason. People say "April showers bring May flowers." But that's just a bunch of rhyming. That year, it looked like March showers had taken over. There was a small branch that ran behind our house that was usually just a ridge of dry dust until the rainy season.

Except for the Nesbitt Spring, the Hollow Spring, and a few private wells and cisterns, the water supply in Promise Land was not that great; and often, we hauled it in rather than pack it in buckets. Most of the time, our pond out in the back field was nothing but a very large mud puddle. Now it was overflowing its banks and flooding the ditch behind our house, turning it into a branch. That branch was flowing like Little Barton's Creek and teaming with bullfrogs croaking.

Birds could be heard chirping gaily at the break of dawn. Everything was coming to life again after the long cold winter. Dogwood trees and buttercups were the first bloomers of the spring.

Everything seemed to shine so bright right after the large sinister clouds fell from the sky in rain. It was like God was sending us a sign, and no one could interpret it. No one knew the meaning of the strange things that seemed to be happening.

Daddy's guitar that sat in the corner of the living room next to the sofa would sometimes make noises like someone was strumming it, but no one was touching it. The strangest thing was that dead bird that Daddy and I found on the roadside between the church and the school house. It caused quite a discussion since no one had ever seen one like it in or around Promise Land before. It was a brownish color, had a long neck and long skinny legs with webbed feet. Clearly, it must have been a water fowl usually found around large bodies of water. Surely we had seen something like it on Lake Michigan when we visited my brother in Chicago.

But the mystery was how and why it was there in Promise Land where the largest body of water was Rodney Owen's pond. It was so far away from its usual habitat, we thought. We didn't have a habit of believing in superstitions, omen, Friday the thirteenth, or any such thing as that. However, no one seemed to think that that bird might have been migrating and just fell dead out of the sky. Sometimes it is more fun to keep the wonderment going by not rationalizing. Why Daddy's guitar would make those strumming sounds remained a mystery.

I had turned thirteen almost a month before. As skinny as I was, I had started wearing a bra. I seemed to be late developing, unlike most of the little-colored / black girls. My sisters and cousins seemed to carry on that gene thought to be unique to our race as full figured, fat, and fine.

I was playing catch up in the growing-up department. That is why the young people teased me, calling me Skinny Minnie, Boney Maroni; and nosey old ladies would say to me, "You are not an Edmondson, are you?" To which I would say, "No," and kept on walking.

I basically ignored the children because God made me strong enough to deal with the "fame" of my father and the teasing that came with being skinny or different. My parents somehow instilled in me that "you don't have to be like anyone else."

I was proud of my intelligence and to be who God had made me to be. So sometimes when the children would keep on teasing, I would just tell them, "I am just too intelligent." Then my name became "Miss Intelligent." Whatever! (Bullying, they call it today.)

Chapter Nineteen
No Rhyme, No Reason

Time flies when you are having fun. School lets out in May, and the summer kicked off with the celebration of Theodore Edmondson and the Promise Land Singers Anniversary. Nothing much had changed in the time period that I had observed. I was not an avid listener or too well informed on world events of the social or political arena. Without a TV, the six o'clock news was not a routine thing at our house. Most of my news came from school and the adults conversations which did not include me. However, I had ears to hear and a good-sized memory to store what I heard.

Disturbing news was not very well spread in my circle of friends. My parents surely weren't going to spread any. Adults talked around children as if they are little deaf-mutes. Then the child is left to figure on their own what they just heard.

There were rumors that our beloved Promise Land School was in danger of being closed because of the low enrollment. Most children had grown up or moved away in the migration north. I never worried much about anything seriously.

It is part of the joy of being a child and living in a well-protected environment called the Promise Land under the wings of so many who loved me. Mother and Daddy, plus Aunt Ruby—, Aunt Essie, Aunt Betty Ruth, Tamar Lee, and Cousin Hattie, they taught us how to pray and about the love of Jesus. Uncle James, Uncle Robert, Uncle Peonie, our local ones did anything to make you laugh.

Uncle Tom lived in Nashville, but he was next to Daddy in being the biggest clown. Aunt Dorothy would look at him and shake her head. "Oh, Tom," she'd say. She was out done trying to stop him. She was as much fun to watch marveling over some of his shenanigans. With all that love and laughter, who had time to be sad?

The most frightening thing was when we saw (cousin) William Primm riding his horse. We'd run to the house with him right on our heels. Thus, my fear of horses today. It was funny too because we'd always outrun that horse.

I knew my daddy sometimes had sick spells when he took something called digitalis and that awful-smelling stuff called Asafetida. It was an awful-smelling dark brown hunk of stuff that looked like chewing tobacco. Mother kept it in an old fruit canning jar beside their bed where he could easily find it. You could smell it all over the house as soon as the top was removed.

Sometimes I heard them talking about his illness. He would have to stop singing because his heart was so bad that the doctor said, "Theo, you will die if you don't stop singing." Nobody expected that he would stop singing. Daddy just laughed and said, "Well, if I can't sing, I would rather be dead." You can believe that.

Every weekend, you could bet Theodore Edmondson and the Promise Land Singers would be preforming somewhere local or even out of state. Most Sunday nights after a performance, I curled up in one of my sister's lap wrapped in my cozy little blankets where I'd fall asleep listening to the sound of the motor of that old 49 Ford Daddy drove. I would be sleeping so good that I hated it when we got home, and I had to wake up and go into the house. It was harder in the winter when the fire would have gone out in the house and the whole place would be like an ice box. Even the bed sheets were ice cold.

Saturday, March 30, 1957, my father, for some reason, decided to spend time teaching my sister Helen and me a few things. My sister Bernice was in Nashville at A&I, now known as TSU, attending college. Wilma and Mother perhaps spent the day at the beauty shop and shopping in the little town of Dickson. We were the two youngest children. All my brothers had by that time migrated to the Northern states of Ohio, Illinois, and New York, as it was the tradition to leave the South.

My eldest brother, Lorry, was a businessman. He owned a TV repair shop and a barbecue rib restaurant in Chicago. James worked for the Board of Parks in Columbus, Ohio, and Douglas worked for Buckeye Steel. They were doing well. All in the family were well.

My daddy loved to sing the gospel, but he made his living as a carpenter by trade. He had built housed but his specialty was in building barns. This trade he was born with and learned from his father.

That Saturday, Daddy took my sister Helen and me riding all over the county showing us the houses and barns that he had built over the years. These were well-built structures that you can still see standing today over half a century later. I used to sit in Daddy's lap and stir the steering wheel while he put his foot on the accelerator. But that day, he let me sit in the seat of the car and drive all by myself. No permit was needed at that time that I know of.

Like my sister Wilma, I was headed toward being the next driver in the family. As soon as I was old enough, Daddy would take me to get my license. I don't remember Helen driving or even if she wanted to. I could hardly wait until the next time.

We reminisced and talked about the strangeness of the season.

My sister Helen recently shared this story: "I remember Daddy being sick and we tried to help Mother watch him. One day while Mother was cleaning the house, he decided to go outside to be out of the way." He possibly didn't need to smell the cleaning agents? She continued. "He finally laid down in the car and I was playing nearby. I would peep in to see how he was doing. I looked up and suddenly a large beautiful snowy white horse appeared in the field behind our house. Its mane was long and flowing almost like a silk veil. I had never seen anything like it. It stayed grazing and prancing around in a circle. Just as suddenly as it appeared it took off running and disappeared into the woods. I never told anyone about it until this day." What did that mean? Was that a sign of something?

What was Daddy trying to tell us? Many people told ghost stories and played games and played tricks on each other. Daddy had his own stories that he told about walking home in the dark as a young man, when he and mother were courting. There were stories about hot spots and strange things happening on the road near the graveyard. But the most fun for us was the one so soon coming, and that was All Fools' Day or April Fools' Day when you would walk up to someone and claim to see a bug in their hair or a snake or mouse on the ground near them. If the person being tricked fell for it, you could have the last words, and that was April fool.

It was so much fun for the boys to fool the girls. They would go round and round looking, kicking, and beating themselves up only to hear someone go "April fool."

Sunday, March 31, 1957, was not unlike all those other busy Sundays beginning across the road at Saint John Church in Promise Land where we would praise the Lord in songs as the preacher marched in from the back of the church in his long black-and-red robe. He would enter the pulpit with arms raised like an angel and say in his most reverenced voice, "The Lord is in his Holy Temple, let all the earth keep silent before him."

You could hear a cotton ball fall it was so quiet. After the entire Apostles' Creed was repeated in unison, he would order us to be seated by lowering his arms. And that was the order of every Sunday morning worship carried out in the little Methodist Church that sat across the road from our house.

Mother, the manager of my Daddy's singing group, kept a tight schedule, still even though the girls were either away in college or married and moved away. Daddy was scheduled to sing that night at Saint James Church in Dickson, which was just about ten miles away.

After resting and having dinner, we loaded into the car to make our final church service for the weekend.

As usual, the spirit was high at Saint James that night. All the saints and sinners as well had shown up to hear that awesome and melodious voice that no one could seem to get enough of. He sang all the favorites like "Peace in the Valley" and "Jesus Will Be Waiting at the End."

The church was full as usual when Brother Edmondson was scheduled to sing. Mother encouraged the people as she announce each song. "Kind friends," she'd say. "If you put something into this program, I guarantee you that you will get something out of it. Amen."

"Amen." The saints and sinners would join in.

After the service was over, people stood around a little while and talked. Some came around to shake hands and proclaim, "Brother Edmondson, you sure sung your heart out tonight." And with a love offering, a few pats on the back, we headed home to the Promise Land Community to start our week over again.

Chapter Twenty
Soon One Morning

Tomorrow was a new day, a new week, and a new month all rolled up in one. On the trip home, I thought about what trick my favorite cousin Thomas would try to pull on me and how I could retaliate. Mother got us all settled down for the night as quickly as possible since we had to get up and go to school in the morning. It really had been a wonderful weekend with Daddy showing us the works of his hands and especially letting me drive all by myself. He would do anything to make us happy.

Lights out, and everyone covered head to toe, and the house grew quiet and still. With the girls upstairs and Mother and Daddy downstairs in their bed, everyone drifted off to slumber land.

It must have been only three or four hours later that Mother woke us up again with a loud cry, "Lord, have mercy. Children, you all get up. Come downstairs. Get up and come down. Your daddy is dead." She was crying and wringing her hands. I couldn't wake him up. He was lying on his back and was snoring so loud it woke me up. I kept trying to tell him to turn over. "Theo, turn over. He is gone. I couldn't wake him." (Today it is called sleep apnea.)

Someone had called Uncle James who lived up the road, and he was there, more torn up than Mother. He was standing over the bed trying to die himself, crying, "Lord, why couldn't you have taken me? Not my brother, Lord. I wish it had been me."

Mother had to gain her composure to quieten him down. At first I thought, *God, I must be dreaming. It is April first.* But no one could be that cruel and joke about someone being dead. How could this be? He seemed all right and so happy when we went to bed. We had a perfect weekend as usually our weekends were.

I moved slowly down the stairs and sat beside my oldest sister on the sofa facing Mother and Daddy's room. The bedroom door was open, and we could see him lying there motionless as we waited on the next procedure to take place. Uncle Robert and other family members came to assist and bring comfort as much as was possible.

We are all going to be laughing hysterically at any minute. I kept turning over the thought in my mind. Suddenly we saw his foot move. Bernice screamed, "Mother, he just moved his foot. Look. He did." Some adult explained it to be something called rigor mortis setting in.

"He had also lost control of his bladder. And was lying in a pool of water," I heard Mother say. I knew my dad would never do such a thing if he could help it.

Our house was so full of people. Where did all these people come from? It was usual for us to have a lot of people streaming in and out of our house laughing, singing, dancing, and just having a good time. We lived in the center of the community, and Mother and

Daddy loved to have people come and go. Our doors were never locked, and you never knew "who's coming to breakfast or dinner."

Daddy was a real entertainer. But the atmosphere was so different this time. People whispered and looked too serious at one another as they paraded in and out like there was a secret or not wanting to wake the dead.

Finally, the coroner arrived to pronounce my father deceased. And soon one morning, death came creeping in the room my father's room. His bed became his cooling board, a prayer I heard him pray often as he would give thanks to the Lord our God.

Mother and Uncle James cleaned Daddy up and put fresh pajamas on him before the undertakers came to take his body to the funeral home in Dickson. That was the hard part seeing them take my father's still body away, while it was barely a hint of daylight in the sky.

The sun rose as usual, and the birds chirped as well, but not a sound would ever be heard again from my sweet, fun-loving father. Cars as usual could be heard as they crunched the gravel on the dusty road, leaving clouds of dust as they disappeared in the distance. But never again would my loving father start up that old 49 Ford with the letters, "Theo Edmondson and the Promise Land Singers" adorning each side.

For as long as I could remember, every evening, we'd heard the tires crunch gravel while running to meet him as he approached the driveway to our house. He would jump out almost before that old Ford could stop. With treats for everyone and stories to tell, you could not tell he had worked all day and might have been tired. I felt so hopeless knowing that my daddy, the comedian, the entertainer, my rock, my shield, my hope was gone, never to return to this place again. He is gone; he was dead at the age of forty-nine.

Daylight finally came, and I must have fallen asleep again during all this quiet storm surrounding me. I woke up again to realize what was going on. My thirteen-year-old aching heart had felt so grown up a few days ago. Beneath my skinny little frame, I had never felt such deep, sad, brokenhearted pain before. I wanted to be my daddy's "Baby doll." Again. I wanted to hear him sing and play the guitar. I didn't want to wake up and face reality. I thought this cannot be happening to me. I can only imagine how my mother felt. What would we do without him?

My parent's bedroom was cleared completely out as if we were moving. The next time I saw my father, he was dressed in the new brown tweed suit complete with shirt, necktie, cufflinks, and tie pen to match. These had been gifts that my brother Douglas had given him the last Christmas the whole family was together. He had jokingly told Douglas, "I will wear it forever." Or was he joking?

The casket was placed in front of the window facing the living room exactly where the bed had been when he took his last breath. He was surrounded by flowers, so many flowers that our house smelled like a flower shop. The family Bible and a guest register were placed on a table by the door. Cards poured in all week, some by mail and some by person to person. Letters came from Tennessee Politicians, the Honorable Governor Frank G. Clement, and Sen. Ross Bass, both natives of Dickson County and white friends of my father. Daddy had sung at a campaign for the governor, I remembered.

Flowers, cards, and food were everywhere. Lots of food and the continuous aroma of coffee filled the air. No one seemed to be sleeping. Cards and letters of condolences flowed like water from the Hollow Spring. Nothing could fill the empty, lonely hole left in my soul. It seemed impossible to recover from the feeling I had. How can anyone eat at a time like this?

Mother, as usual, prepared our clothes and dressed us in the finest that she could afford for the funeral. Helen and I were dressed alike in matching grown-up-looking suits. It was the first time I ever wore a straight skirt.

I knew that the chance of a prank on April Fools' Day was long since over and gone. But somehow the thought kept entering my mind. Gloom filled my heart and overwhelmed me. I felt light-headed as if I was going to float away, but no one noticed. I imagined I was standing, shaking my daddy while he was shooing me away to be quiet to act like he really was dead. I shook that casket so hard. Only I saw that Daddy was playing a joke on us. This would be the biggest joke yet.

The whole family was here. I watched while my father smiled at me trying to keep from laughing. Soon, April fool had to end. He would declare this nightmare over. April fool would be over. I blinked away hot tears. These daydreams had to stop. It felt good not facing reality. I knew I had to stop.

While the undertaker (funeral director) arranged the silk overlay and pillows preparing to close the casket, I tried to stay focused. Pallbearers positioned themselves to roll the casket through the front door of our house. I struggled to stay focused, thinking, "He will never enter these doors again."

Reality hurts too badly. I had been pretending. I was waiting for someone to say April fool. And this gloom would turn to laughter.

Flashback, Easter 1944 (My Christening): Our family crossed the road in our usual formation to worship. April 5, 1957, in only thirteen years, was the final crossing of the whole Edmondson family. This time, Daddy led the way. His coffin was carried by the Willing Workers Men's Club. We crossed the road for the occasion of my father's funeral. Our beloved pet Skippy had gone before my father in death four years before.

The whole family marched behind the casket, holding my father's body as the pianist played, "Nearer My God to Thee." Finally, the casket was rolled into place, and the family seated. The church was running over with people, both white and black, coming to pay their last respects to my father. Many people had to stand inside and outside; people crowded around. He was loved so much and respected by everyone for miles around.

The choir and songs ended, and then started the funeral that lasted too long a time but too short a time. Cousin Vera Van Leer sung my favorite of her songs, "Standing on Life's Pure Jordan."

Rev. James (Pit) Satterfield showed out on his guitar, playing, "Yes, Christ is all." Mrs. Nan Breedlove and Mrs. Imogene Springer took turns on the piano. Mrs. Beatrice Pendergrass and Mrs. Lizzie Gleeves were also on program. The more they sang, and the more kind words they spoke, the more they buried me deeper into despondency. I felt like no one was attentive to how I felt. I wanted to run. But I had nowhere to go. Would anyone notice that I was gone?

I felt guilty for wanting to grow up a few days ago. I was too young to lose my father. He was too young to leave me. Everyone was crying, except my three nieces—too young to know—and my sister Helen who seemed to be everyone's greatest concern because she showed no emotions at all.

My youngest niece Ardis was getting a bit restless and scrumming around in her seat. She was lucky not to understand what was really going on. I started praying for relief to be able to pull out of this deep, dark feeling overtaking me when Ardis broke out singing. She was singing her favorite cartoon rhythm," Mickey Mouse." She sung it for no telling how long, and no one could stop her.

People all over the church began to chuckle until Ardis was done. The atmosphere was completely changed as ladies and gentlemen pulled out their handkerchiefs to dry eyes and blow noses. Some were trying not to laugh. The funeral continued with more songs and acknowledgments. At least I had something to laugh about.

My knowledge of her childish love of that cartoon would sustain me in the days to come. Every time I felt grief overtaking me, I would remember her singing that song in the middle of my daddy's funeral. I think my daddy somehow was looking down from heaven, and he knew I needed to laugh. That was his way of saying, "Look, guys, life is too short to spend it in sadness. Life is serious. But we still have to laugh. Enjoy it. Laughter is like a medicine. Seek it. Look until you find it in all situations. Even at a funeral, find something to laugh about."

At that moment, I knew time and with so many fond memories I would be all right. I had lots of stories true and false but all funny to help me heal. God will wipe all tears away.

Chapter Twenty-One
Will Time Heal All Wounds?

Time passes, and healing must begin. Remembering how bad I felt for the family of Cousin Hersey Robertson who had died about a month before Daddy, I thought I knew how it felt to lose someone so close. My cousin Birdie Christine was the same age as me, and I felt so sorry for her at that time. But until it happened to me, I really didn't have a clue what the Robertson family was going through.

Mother did her best to continue life as usual for the sake of us girls. We were always going someplace on the weekend. Wilma took over the driving since she was the only one who knew how to drive and had a driver's license. Our cousin Ruth Inez Jordan became a lifesaver to our family. She practically moved to Promise Land and stayed with us during our most difficult time. She managed to keep us laughing when we felt more like crying. A great storyteller and a beautician by trade, she knew how to pamper us and Mother. I will forever be grateful and thankful to God for putting her in that place to help fill the void.

Her husband, we called him Uncle Babe Jordan, never complained. As an adult, I can appreciate more what they did for us. She loved my father as much as we did. She knew the value of laughter and used her God-given skill to keep us going in our gloomiest and darkest hour.

We never slowed down. We worked and went to school during the week, and Friday nights or early Saturday morning would find us on the road to somewhere. Nashville to Ohio, my poor sister Wilma, still a teenager herself, became the driver for the family. Bernice was the eldest, but she had not started driving.

Despite the fact that Daddy had worked hard both privately and a few public jobs, no help was found financially in the way of Social Security for us. Something technical like he lost the first Social Security card, and instead of him getting a new one with same number, he actually had two different numbers and something about not enough credit.

Mother was not one to beg, so she didn't waste any time over that, and she did what she had to do. Mother didn't discuss it with me, but little bits leaked out, and over time, I realized that she was working and doing the best that she could to keep us going. I remember one white man named Mr. Errington would take Helen and me to buy shoes once or twice a year. He might have been employed by the Board of Education. That was it as far as I remember.

Aunt Allie still helped some, but she was aging and might have been on limited funds. I tried not to ever complain about anything. I know my mother missed Daddy more than any of us could. So who was I to complain about how she had to save money for the necessities of keeping up a lifestyle she had become accustomed to? Aunt Allie still sent her clothes, fur stoles and coats, shoes, and purses. No doubt they were top-of-the-line fashion. So when she took us girls to Sears and Roebuck or the local Fussell's and Baker's mercantile stores in Dickson, I tried to show my appreciation for whatever she picked out.

We still traveled the same roads as before my father's death, and we were well recognized and respected visiting these places.

It was hard for me to not see my father on stage singing, but I supposed it was therapeutic for Mother to continue to experience the love and recognition of the people who had supported and loved Daddy so much. One of her favorite places was at church where the shouting, bench walking, and stomping were still going strong. Usually, I was so overwhelmed that all I could do was cry softly and hope I could find something in these services like a child singing or something to make me laugh.

I welcomed those who couldn't hold a tune in a bucket on stage to give me some relief. If you try hard enough, you can find something to laugh about. Mother frowned on that kind of carrying-on, but to me it was a relief from the sadness I felt being in such familiar places without my daddy.

Some people cry when they are happy. But I can assure you that those were tears of the deep void that was left in my life from the loss of my father. It was a long time before I could get through a church service without crying for him.

I grieved longer than I should have. At that time, I was not encouraged to talk about my feelings. As if the silence would somehow help you to heal. Therapeutically, I wish I had had an opportunity to share my feelings with someone. We had one record of the first anniversary of Theo Edmondson and the Promise Land Singers that was given to us by my aunt Allie. We listened to it only once after his death. I wish that we had listened more and that we might have learned to appreciate it. It was destroyed when my mother's house burned in the mid-1980s. I believe that we should have used it to help deal with the grief. I sure wish I could have saved it for the generations to come.

Our first event after his funeral was Easter, and the grief was still so fresh. Helen and I dressed in the same lilac-colored two-piece suits and white blouses that we had worn to his funeral which I didn't mind at all. But when I went looking for the shining rags to shine my black patent leather shoes, I got a bittersweet shock. My daddy's shoes were still sitting under the bed where they were always kept. It broke my heart, and I could barely contain myself.

I wanted to ask Mother why Daddy's shoes were not put on him for burial. I picked those shoes up and loved on them for I don't know how long until Mother called, "Sylvia, did you forget we are getting ready for church?" Carefully, I tried to dry the tears from my eyes and his shoes, replacing them exactly as I had found them.

We went to church that Easter Sunday, my first without Daddy, but I had to believe that God truly will wipe all tears away. I never told Mother how I felt finding those shoes under their bed because I didn't want to open up a wound for her. For a long time, I wanted to ask. I suppose that is how they bury people. Perhaps those shoes brought a sense of comfort to her loneliness. How many times had she looked under her bed at his shoes?

When school was out, we'd head to Ohio for the summer with my brothers James (Mary) and Douglas (Betty). Routine things of the summer in Columbus was to ride to the White Castle or to a drive-in movie just to cool off from the long hot, humid days of summer. We would make several trips from my Brother James's house to Mama Gracie and Mr. Ernest's house. (Parents of my sister-in-law Mary).

Mama Minnie—bless her soul (grandmother to Mary and a whole lot more)—could always be found in the kitchen, and you never hit that door at any time that the aroma of some good old meat, vegetable dishes, or sweet cobblers would send your senses to a heavenly place a food heaven. Mama Gracie and Mama Minnie were well known for their ability to cook. Their house was full of children from sun up to sundown.

Their eldest daughter Minnie Ann diligently arrived early in the morning with her crowd. Helen, Nancy, and I ran in and out all day carrying my brother's children with us (Cynthia, Ardis, and eventually Bruce). Bruce had a twin brother (Brian) who had passed at birth. There was never a dull moment in Columbus from June to early August; we would rip and run sometimes going to Detroit and even to Canada with my brothers on their vacations to visit family members.

Mary was our second sister-in-law. We sometimes called her Bootsie. She and James both worked, but they took time to see that we had fun in the summertime. We loved Bootsie's cooking too.

Douglas was the last brother to marry. Betty was short and pleasingly plump; a beautiful woman. She had smooth brown blemish-free skin. Her hair was black and naturally curly. She was a stay-at-home mother. Betty was delightful and easy to talk to. She was pleasant and had encouraging words always. Any good news was always welcomed. She was super proud of her children and their accomplishments. God blessed them with Douglas Jr. (Chucky), Dudley Loran, and Donna Lisa.

We didn't meet a lot of new kids in Columbus because there were a plenty of our own kinfolks to run around with and get into things with.

However, I will have to tell you that I caught the eye of one young fella whom I will call Buddy because I don't know if that was his real name or not. Buddy would manage to be sitting on his porch every morning when I came out to play with my nieces and Helen and Nancy. Usually we would be headed to Momma Gracie's for the day.

One day, Buddy got up the nerve to come all the way across the street from his house and ask me to let him take a picture of me. So I, who was so bashful, posed and allowed him to snap a few pictures. We talked a while, and Buddy put his camera away. He finally convinced us to let him follow along over to Momma Gracie's.

Nancy opened the door when we got there, and as usual, we girls walked in one after another. Nancy's daddy, Mr. Earnest, we thought to be asleep. He was seated in his usual fashion in his usual chair.

Poor Buddy took the opportunity to follow the leader and entered the door right behind me. Well, Skinner (Mr. Earnest), as he was nicknamed, caught sight of an unusual guest in the name of

Buddy. "Hold on, wait just one minute." He straightened up in his chair and began to question poor Buddy as to "who invited you in?"

Buddy was speechless, and we were embarrassed and tickled. After following direction from Skinner, Buddy went back out to the front porch and properly rang the doorbell and was welcomed in by a proud father and overseer of his castle. It was his way of confirming that "every shut-eye ain't sleep."

"Now you are welcome. But you got to know how to come right," he said. "Not just going to go unnoticed. And every good-bye ain't gone either."

From then on, Buddy rang the doorbell properly and entered after being invited. Buddy became part of our gang after that. We went to the movies a few times during the summer, and the time seemed to fly. I didn't think about the picture until a year or two after meeting him.

Finally, I ask to see the picture he took of me. With a great big old smile, he confessed, "There wasn't any film in that camera. That's how I planned on meeting you." We must have been around ten or eleven years old at that time. So men have game even at that young age.

Chapter Twenty-Two
Comes August / Back to School

Come August, everyone's mind returned to Tennessee. For two very important reasons, we had to return to Tennessee. One was for Helen and me to get back to school, and two, the famous Charlotte Picnic. Depending on how the days ran sometime, we made it in time to register on time, and sometimes we were late. But no matter what, "it was a known fact that the Charlotte Picnic was an unofficial holiday in Dickson County.

In less than three months, we would have acquired this Northern accent that was copied from the Northern children we played with that summer. It didn't take long to lose it. I would say right about the time we crossed the Ohio River from Cincinnati, Ohio, to Kentucky, it was about gone. But we would struggle to keep it a few days after we returned home until we got laughed at and realized how ridiculous it sounded.

The inevitable finally happened, and our beloved Promise Land School doors were closing forever. I would be going to the eighth grade that year and would have to ride the bus for the first time to get to Hampton High School in Dickson about ten miles away. My mother worked at Charlotte High School in Charlotte, Tennessee, about three miles away. It never entered my mind that I should or could go to the nearest school which was Charlotte Elementary.

Dickson County School System was still segregated, and to my knowledge, everyone was OK with that. It was part of that old "everyone staying in their place" theory, "separate but equal" jargon. I was safe and happy in my own little world. My parents had been active in both the Promise Land and Hampton High School activities since they had children who went to both places.

My eldest sister entered first grade at Promise Land School. She attended the first grade through eighth grade there and freshman through graduation at Hampton High School. She attended twelve consecutive years without missing a day. Her story was published in the *Dickson Herald*. She was also the first black student in Dickson County to receive a scholarship from Gov. Frank G. Clement Scholarship (attended Tennessee A&I, now TSU). She also received the Dockie Weems Scholarship. Her highest level of education is a master's plus degree from Memphis State. She became a reading specialist and a music instructor during her career. Now she is retired but teaches music and is active with two sororities.

Having learned the most valuable lesson in the Promise Land School from Ms. Ollie Huddleston, I was confident that I would not have any problem transitioning to Hampton. I studied and did the best that I could in school and participated in extracurricular activities. I loved singing in the school chorus, and as soon as the marching band was formed, I began practicing and became the head majorette under Mrs. Goggin and later Prof. Harold Gilbert, instructors of the band. I thought I looked like hot stuff in my majorette outfit.

In my eighth grade year, I met a young man who took a liking to me, and eventually we were inseparable. I was still very skinny and was teased for it I felt very fortunate that he picked me out of all the other full-figured young ladies to be his friend. He was the son of a family that my mother and father had known and respected for years.

Bobby L. Holt, eldest son of Sister Augusta and Rev. Dalton Holt, was also the most popular young man in our school. Both boys and girls wanted to be in his circle of friends. Mother had no objection to our courtship.

He was well built and excelled in sports, both basketball and football, which was the only sports that we had at the school. He was the captain of the football team until he graduated. Being his chosen friend didn't add to my popularity or stop the teasing. Most of the girls probably didn't like me, and because of him, most of the boys were afraid to talk to me. I was still teased for the way God made me too skinny.

My name continued to be Skinny Minnie, Bony Maroni, String Bean, Olive Oil (Popeye's wife), and Mildred Primm—because she was just as skinny as I was. I never thought to ask Mildred if she was being called my name too. I was never much of a fighter either, and the one time I did try to physically take up for myself, I found myself climbing out of a twenty-gallon trash can in the girls' bathroom. It was no fun either. I had loaned a certain classmate a blouse. It was one of my "Sunday blouses." She refused to return it, and she kept wearing it to school.

Finally after conversing with my high school sweetheart, I got the nerve to take it. Well, I tried to! We had decided that the next time she wore it to school, I would just reach out and take back what belonged to me.

The Bible says, "Take back what the devil stole from you." I am glad we didn't get reported to Professor Pendergrass. I would have lost the fight and have been in trouble at school and with Mother. Then after taking into consideration the situation I was in, I decided that it would be in my best interest to stick to my claim of being "too intelligent." Some girls had the habit of borrowing each other's clothes. I never borrowed anyone's clothes. After the trash can episode, I never loaned my clothes again.

About the fortieth year of our high school reunion, a lady came to me and apologized and explained that "we were always jealous of you. That is why we teased you." (Sorry, I don't remember her name.) I thanked her and said, "I wish I had known it then."

Forty years later is better than never. I don't know if Mildred Primm experienced it the way I did. If so, "I hope someone apologized to her before her untimely death." Rest in *peace*, Mildred. They were jealous of *us*. I became known as Miss Intelligent in our senior high school yearbook.

The puppy love of two young teenagers steered up a little commotion among the teachers and our parents and our first Christmas as boyfriend/girlfriend because of the gift that he gave me that year for Christmas. It was my birthstone set in a ring. I was fifteen, and he was seventeen, two years older than me. You would have thought he had asked me to marry him right then.

My mother spoke briefly on the phone to his mother, and they concluded that it was all right since he had asked his mother's permission. She told Mother that he had told her that all he wanted for Christmas was to give Sylvia her birthstone ring. And it was settled.

Two of my teachers called me aside and gave me a very valuable lecture (I think), and that was "Now you are going to have to keep your dress down. You need to hold a walnut between your knees. He is going to be expecting more from you now." An advice like that. With that kind of advice, I didn't know what to expect.

After that year, I gave him the nicest Dollar Store necktie that we could afford. I did not work, and I sure couldn't expect my mother to buy a more expensive gift than that. I am thankful for the best advice they knew, and I can now say I appreciated whatever it was that I was to learn from it. And I might add, that was the extent of my "sex" education.

One thing I did learn later was that Bobby hated every one of those "neckties." But he never complained. Truly, it is better to give than to receive.

I never liked to participate in the practice of drawing names for Christmas because of the mumbling and complaints I heard from the students on the bus as we traveled home from school for the Christmas holidays. It just didn't seem right to draw someone's name and then give that person a gift that they might not like. Besides, they might not even like you for that matter. It was and is my opinion. So when I was in school, it caused a bit of an uproar that I refused to draw names at that time.

But the biggest uproar over Christmas after "the ring" was that a certain young student asked the teacher if there really was a Santa Claus, and the teacher's response was "Well, what did your parents tell you?" When the student responded, "Well, they keep telling me that it is," the rest of the class just laughed. I could not wait to pull the said student aside because I felt like someone needed to do them a favor before they went out looking for the jolly old elf. I got scolded for that. But I have never regretted that I told this student the truth, because we were about to graduate from high school. I hope they appreciated me for that. I made the decision then not to continue that tradition when I had children.

My children enjoyed the elf, Saint Nick but knew from the beginning he was fake and not in the same category as the birth of the Christ Child Jesus.

For the next five years, life centered on school in the fall and vacation in the summer. I enjoyed school chorus basketball and football. Hampton High School Band was just a beginner's band, and it was usual to hear songs that beginners play like "Old MacDonald," "Mary Had a Little Lamb," and "Yankee Doodle Went to Town." We marched just as proud stepping high as if we were the aristocrats of Tennessee State University's marching band (TSU). With our beloved first drum major (Amos L. Sweat) leading the way, we would pick up our legs as high as we could in our royal blue jackets and short barely covering your behind gold skirts. These were our majorette uniforms. We wore white boots with homemade royal blue tassels on the front of them.

We moved to the rhythm of "boom, boom, boom, boom. Boom, boom, boom, boom" in 4/4 time. We struggled to keep up our pace to this relentless rhythm produced by the snares and bass drummers of Hampton High School Marching Band. "Boom, boom, boom, boom. Boom, boom, boom, boom." They went until Amos had us all in position facing the audience of the opposing team. He raised his baton with its own tassel flying. Up and down, up and down while calling out commands and blowing his whistle, he never missed a boom / beat.

First, the band formed the letters *H, H, and S* in single letters representing our school (Hampton High School). Then he called for attention while the band played. We stood there with our hands over our hearts while the band squeaked and honked out the notes of the "Star-Spangled Banner."

Then with a snap of the baton, the majorettes would "throw down."

They performed one of their dances, each individually choreographed by the dancers. Whirling and a few twirling, their batons, they would kick up dust and stomp until the band finished playing its boogie-woogie tune. With our half-time performance over, Drum Major Amos L Sweat had the last dance while yelling out commands. He was tall and skinny with a waistline that reminded you of a toy tin soldier. He wore a tall royal blue hat with a taller white plumb which added to his already tall thin frame. It is hard to describe how he showed out as he stepped high throwing that baton even higher.

While whirling and twirling, he led the entire band single file back to the bleachers. The crowd screamed and yelled. The band resumed its "boom, boom, boom, boom, boom, boom, boom, boom" back to the bleachers.

Since we lived so far from the school, many children went home with friends after school. I always went home with Paulette Corlew and her brother Harold who were a few years behind me in class, but we were friends, country cousins, and band members. It was fun to stay over in the City of Dickson on these occasions. Ms. Bobbie (their mother) usually was not at home when we first got there, but you can be sure that she had the food laid out, and all we had to do was eat and get ready to return to school.

Our school had a basketball team, but I was not into playing sports. Seems like I always ducked when the ball was thrown to me. No matter where I moved, it hit me in the face. I never tried out for that. I did attend the games for lack of something else to do. After the games, sometimes we had dancing in the gym, and I loved to dance with my cousins Thomas and Billy (my partners in crime). Sometimes their girlfriends were jealous. I didn't care as long as the girls didn't want to start a fight. I made sure they knew we were "first cousins."

We made a few trips to other schools for performances by our school's chorus under the leadership of Mrs. Ella B. Pendergrass (wife of our principal). My favorite songs were Negro Spirituals like "Go Down, Moses," "Jacob's Ladder," and "Didn't My Lord Deliver Daniel?" I also loved the "Hallelujah Chorus" from Handel's *Messiah*. She taught us how to appreciate a variety of music and composers. Composers such as Johann Sebastian Bach, Frederic Chopin, Tchaikovsky, and our beloved Mr. Ludwig van Beethoven. Most of these we could barely pronounce their names. Don't you dare say spell it.

Almost ten years later, I decided to further my education at the University of Tennessee. I realized as an adult learner that we had barely touched the subject of music appreciation in high school. When it came time to distinguish if you were listening to Mr. Bach's "Italian Concerto in F Major" or "A Violin Sonata No. 1 in G Minor." I really wished I could have had just a little bit more time to appreciate before the test rolled around. Whew.

It is amazing how woodwinds, strings, and horns sound so much alike under the pressure of a final exam. *And what does a concerto and a sonata have to do with nursing?* I thought. I seriously needed to be studying about cardiac arrest and resuscitation. I was ready to learn the art of caring for the sick and afflicted.

Well, when you are having fun, time seems to fly exceedingly. Fall of 1961, and I was like an only child. My sisters, including Helen, were away in college or married and living away from home.

Chapter Twenty-Three
Dear Alma Mater

August 1961 was an exciting year. My first Tennessee niece Lauretta was born to my sister Wilma and her husband James Edward Talley Sr. It was so exciting because for a while, Mother and I were at home—just the two of us. We were so used to a crowd of people, and it was really hard for me. Luckily, my cousins (Uncle James and Aunt Betty Ruth's children) kept the road hot from our house to theirs. They were our closest neighbors.

So after Wilma and Ed had Lauretta, it was great news that she would come home to recuperate. Wilma and I were always very close, and I would do anything she ask me to. I loved taking care of Lauretta so much that I would wake up during the night to help Wilma change her diaper or rock her back to sleep.

I refused to go visit my brothers that summer. She was born mid-June. That was the end of my summers away from home. I could not bear to leave her. My nephew Gregory was born (a few days after my niece) to my eldest sister Bernice and her husband Hulan Heard. Life for me with these two new babies added to the family was becoming more joyful.

We didn't get to see Gregory as much as we saw Lauretta. I remember we kept him a few days without Bernice. He was only a few months old. He was not sleeping well at all. We didn't have a baby bed, so someone had to sleep next to him mainly so he wouldn't fall out of bed. We realized that he didn't like anyone next to him in bed.

Soon, Bernice, Hulan, and Gregory moved to Memphis where she began her first teaching job with the Memphis Public School System. I was very happy with the addition of my two brothers-in-law plus my niece and nephew. Ed became not only a brother but another father figure to me.

This was the first summer that Helen and I didn't go to Columbus or Chicago for the summer. I was totally in love with these new babies. Lauretta soon became the community baby. We spoiled her and carried her around like she was a delicate little China doll. She had no chance of crying from hunger, being wet, or the lack of being loved.

Summer came and went with the same routine of activities, kicking off until it was time for the Charlotte Picnic and then back to school.

The school term 1961–1962 started as usual. It would lead to graduation and a new chapter in my life. I had made no particular plans for continuing my education after graduation. I don't remember any such activity as a guidance counselor or anyone who gave directions on how to get into college for the most part. I don't know if anyone thought I would go to college.

At seventeen years old, I must have thought I had all the time in the world to think about "stuff like that," so I just continued to flow freely without a thought about tomorrow. It was not that Mother had not encouraged me to do my best, but I just don't remember planning that far ahead. I did know that I wanted to be a wife and mother one day, but that was not something that I had planned or was planning.

After a summer of enjoying my new niece and nephew, school started. Summer wasn't over until the pigs were roasted and the crowd promenaded on the fashion runway of the Charlotte Picnic grounds. My brother James and his family always came home at that time. Lorry (Brother) and his family didn't come for a long time since my father had passed. Douglas had married Betty. She had a hard time with the Tennessee heat waves. So they didn't always come to the festivities. The picnic remained a huge must-not-miss event for the families of Dickson County and surrounding counties.

Hampton High School Trojans (our football team mascot) had started training ahead of time and would start the fall football season with my high school sweetheart Bobby Holt, as captain of the team. That was the extent of what I currently knew about football. Enough for me. I cheered and danced when everyone else did.

The band played a victory tune when it was time and when the scoreboard changed to reflect the score and what team was winning. I can't tell you that I desired to know much more than that. That was enough information to fill my head with. I was out of tune with the world of sports and didn't have enough sense to care. Well, on my way as head majorette of the Hampton High School Marching Band, I expected a wonderful last year in high school.

The school year started off running very smoothly as usual. But suddenly in October, a group of young students from the senior class of Hampton High School felt that good enough could not be let alone. These students, six in all, would petition the board of education to enroll in the two all-white high schools in Dickson County: two for Charlotte High and four for Dickson High School. I am not sure why they waited until October and not go in August, the beginning of the school year. They were refused and returned to Hampton High with business as usual where we all graduated in the spring of 1962.

There was only one male student in the group, and that was my sweetheart of course, Bobby L. Holt. When he was interviewed and was asked why he would want to leave Hampton High at a time when he was captain of the football team (three years in a row) and class president. His answer was simple: "I want to pave the way for my brothers and sisters who will be following behind me, to give them a better chance for a better education."

Although those students were refused, their action did not go unnoticed, and the board of education soon would meet and put in place a plan to integrate the public school system of Dickson County. Peace remained in Dickson.

In my research, the board of education claimed that they had already started looking for an answer to desegregate the school system. It seems like Dickson was following the leader and ready to bring up to date before it could get out of hand like so many other towns had.

Time does seem to fly when it comes to having fun. But when you are young, time seems to go by slower until you seem not to be in a hurry and have all the time in the world.

Our school adviser or counselor never seemed to approach me after the initial talk at the age of fifteen when my high school sweetheart gave me the ring that I wore (and still have today) so proudly on my left hand ring finger. My highest aspiration at that time was to graduate in the spring. That much I knew, but beyond that, "I don't have any plans."

That fall, everything seemed to fall into place with the football team having a winning streak. The basketball teams boys and girls were successful, I think. But I have no real memory of either because of my lack of knowledge of the games. Sports beyond the band was about it for me.

For Christmas, Bobby had given me a record player. I loved to dance, and so a lot of my time was spent listening to Chubby Checker wailing out, "Let's Do the Twist." I played that record over and over again.

Christmas day, I was twisting across the kitchen with a hot pan of water, dancing to the beat. I dropped that boiling hot water just two inches short of the cabinet, and it landed on my left foot. While Chubby continued to howl, I screamed and howled while trying to remove that hot sock off my foot. The top of my left foot took a scalding, and so the rest of the day was spent with my foot wrapped up while my kind brother-in-law Ed (James Talley) drove me all over the county trying to find some ointment to put on my foot. Needless to say, there was not a store to be found open in Dickson County.

I had no doubt that I would graduate, and then what? The events leading up to school closing in the spring started with the prom and athletic banquet. Our class trip was nice since it might have been the first time for some of the students to travel outside of the state of Tennessee. Our class would spend the week of Easter traveling to New York City and Washington DC.

Bobby had a little money to spend. We visited a record shop where we bought some record albums by Ray Charles. One was his Country and Western album. I remember dressing up and walking down the street on Easter Sunday morning feeling so grown up. I don't remember if we had a tour guide or not. I do remember going to a cathedral Easter Sunday. I wore a beautiful yellow dress and a small yellow hat with veil and gloves to match.

We spent a few hours longer in New York because one of our students who got lost just before our departure. He had missed getting on the subway with the rest of the class and of course was reported missing. He was found, and soon we were on our way home back to Hampton High, dear Hampton High.

Spring 1962 marked our final year of school. Our class was the largest class to graduate from Hampton High School since its beginning in the early 1930s.

Chapter Twenty-Four
What's next?

Now what? I was the luckiest girl in the world. Here we are newly graduated from high school, a real accomplishment but not the end. He was my high school sweetheart, and it seemed like we were going to be together no matter what happened. Make no mistake about it; we were in love, and love was all we needed. I thought. It was like superglue stronger than average glue. I was confident our feelings for each other was mutual. I would have followed him to the end of the world with a one-way ticket. He was the smartest young man I knew, smart enough to become whatever he wanted to become.

My only goal was to graduate high school and let the chips fall where they may. On our last few months of school, I had let my feelings for him take over, and of course we began to take our relationship to another level. After all, we were in love, and I knew that we would get married soon or later. And as he said, when I ask him, "What if?" He'd say "It will be ours."

We were in no hurry. I totally trusted his decisions. I believed his love was genuine, and I could trust him with my life. Did I put him on a pedestal? He was more mature than me. We were only two years apart; he was eldest of his siblings. I was youngest in mind.

There are always two sides to a story. I made the mistake of thinking that life didn't need planning. I was content to let others plan for me. No one told me I needed to take charge of my own life. Lucky me. Seems like I always had someone to plan for me. First, my family and then him.

Bobby was actually late graduating high school because of an early childhood habit of playing hooky from school. His sister discovered him hanging out under the house one day while she and their mom were out in the yard hanging out clothes. Apparently, no one from the school system reported this to Mrs. Augusta, and he missed too much time out of school. This placed him in a lower grade than what he should have been in.

I suppose that is why he seemed more mature and was so popular with the other students and teachers. This is the explanation his mother gave me. She explained, "I kept hearing Loretta say, 'Bobby, there's Bobby. Mama, there's Bobby.' She could barely talk. I ignored her for a while. Bobby would come home on time. Right about the time I turned the radio to Young Widow Brown. He would come home from school, I thought. Finally, I paid attention to Loretta and found him playing under the house. He was smart enough to know when my favorite radio show came on, it was safe to come out."

Bobby had worked during his high school years as part-time janitor at the school along with his stepfather, Reverend Holt. Work was nothing new to him. As captain of the football team, he received a scholarship from Knoxville College in Knoxville, Tennessee, a historically black liberal arts college.

That summer after graduation, he packed his bags and went off to Knoxville to work and get ready to embark upon the next chapter of his life, while I continued to just "let the chips fall where they may."

While Bobby was in Knoxville, I had no real plans. My Uncle James and Aunt Betty Ruth planned a trip with Uncle Jesse and Aunt Hattie. They asked me to take care of their children. I don't know if they knew my cooking experience was limited, or they needed to get away so bad they didn't care. However, I agreed to look after the little ones: Jewel C (Mickey), James Theodore (Jimmy), Sharon, Emery Brock, and Robert (Bobby).

Thomas, my partner in crime, was not much help. Hattie Ruth had gone away getting ready for college in Nashville. I don't know what else I cooked, but we had apple trees all around loaded with green apples. Those children wanted fried apples every day. They'd pick, and I would fry green apples every day.

I am so thankful that no one got sick. It must be something to that "apple a day" thing. Right today, my adult little cousins are still bragging about the fun we had that week and the good old fried apples. I know God was also watching me and those children.

During that time, I had developed a serious craving for green apples. There were plenty of green apples still left on the trees between the church and schoolhouse. I liked them raw. I had also began to put on weight, but since I was such a skinny girl anyway, it was not noticed right away.

We didn't know much about the reproductive system or the birds and bees. My sweetheart and I knew enough to know that "we were expecting." And sure enough, it would be ours. He promised to write often while away and continue to make plans for our future.

After getting settled down, he pinned the first and only letter he would write. So excited to hear from him, I first cradled it in my arms close to my heart. My sister, who brought the letter to me, sat with arms folded like a watchman waiting on me to open the letter. I waited as long as I could, hoping for some privacy. I visualized him finding a place for us to live while he was in college.

I started to walk away from the invisible guard shack Wilma was occupying. I gave up; she was going to outlast me. I stopped and tore the letter open. Hot tears were welling up in my eyes, soon to overflow their boundary running down my face. To my amazement, it was a very brief note.

Dear Sylvia,

This place is *hell*. How is Junior?

Love,

Bobby

My sister saw the letter and became very upset over the language he used, emphasizing that no respectable young man would use that kind of language writing to a young lady. That she viewed as very disrespectful. Thus, the battle started to control and protect baby sister from this kind of disrespect.

Bobby was very upset when he found out that she had read the letter in the first place, and the battle for me to grow up quietly began. I never lived that one down. Mother never knew about the letter, or note, I should say. She never acted like she knew anything about my condition. So the key to the letter (How is Junior?) was totally ignored. The fact that I was at that time an unwed pregnant teenager in need of prenatal care flew right out the window.

It was mid-August. I did not receive another letter from him. People had begun to notice and make comments on my weight gain. When someone asked or commented, "You are gaining weight, aren't you?" I simply said, "I hope so," and kept on walking with my head up, nose pointed to the sky. That was my "Miss Intelligent" walk. I never was worried about my condition or my future with him.

Traditionally, black people in Dickson County have planned family reunions, weddings, and other events around the Charlotte Picnic weekend. It is sort of like killing two birds with one stone, for out-of-town guest could make one trip instead of two. No one was going to miss that picnic. It was for sure they would show for any other event around that time frame.

When Bobby returned from Knoxville, his chief complaint was not of Knoxville College at all. Although he had hung out on the farm with his best friend Harold Bell, he was not a farm boy. He was not about to go back to that "pea picking pea patch" ever again in the hot sun. He was a few shades browner than when he had left.

Here, it is Thursday, day before the picnic, and we were busy planning the quickest wedding plan in history.

Rev. J. R. Gray, a former pastor of Saint John Methodist Church, had been notified that we were on our way to Nashville, Tennessee, so that he could perform our wedding.

I pulled out my old prom dress which still fit. Might have been a little snug around the waist, but it fit. It was basically on a white background with large lilac flowers on the top layer of chiffon and taffeta. Bobby picked up Mother and me in Promise Land, and we hurriedly stopped in Charlotte at the courthouse to buy the marriage license. We were followed by his mother, Mrs. Augusta (Sister Holt), Rev. Louis Horner, and his wife Iva Jean (Sister Horner). We drove to Nashville, Tennessee, where Reverend Gray was waiting to pronounce us husband and wife.

Like that with no bouquet to throw or garter to toss, I became Mrs. Bobby Lane Holt. Some people in that situation would call it a shotgun wedding. Ours was motivated by the fact that my family was coming home for the picnic, and it was just best to get this show on the road over and be done before they arrived—a picnic wedding.

Our wedding night was spent sharing space with my brothers and their families at the Edmondson family home in Promise Land.

August 18, 1962, oh happy day. I was elated to be Mrs. Holt, and he was possibly more elated to be out of that hot pea picking pea patch. He was out of a job but not worried. What a tradeoff. Like always, everyone went to the picnic and had a good time with no incidents that I can remember.

Chapter Twenty-Five
A Full Fun House

Moving into the already full house with the Holt family, there was never a dull moment. The baby of my siblings, I was now dealing with my husband's younger brothers and sisters. It was different. Bobby's baby brother Anthony was still a baby (I mean baby) in diapers. I immediately became babysitter for him while Mrs. Augusta worked. That could be another book.

I watched him daily as he threw a fit, watching her get her coat to leave. She left out with bigger tears than his as she made her way to the cab. He'd laugh the minute that cab pulled away, and he was fine all day long until she returned. He acted like he had been crying and neglected the whole time she was gone. Anthony Wayne Holt was no problem once she was gone. He taught me Childcare 101 along with Dr. Spock's latest book on the subject.

My housekeeping and culinary skills were very limited. Bobby's sisters, Loretta, Faye; and his mother, Mrs. Augusta, did most of the cooking. Keeping the house cleaned up was a never-ending battle with the amount of traffic during the waking hours. There was always something to pick up, put up, or mop up. Anthony evidently thought making up a bed was for his pleasure for jumping and tumbling exercises. You couldn't make a bed up with him around. Every time I threw the sheet up to spread out on the bed, he would laugh and try to get under it.

Dalton Eugene had a habit of playing with clothes hangers. There was oftentimes four or five left from his imaginary whatever playing. (Children listed by age). Bobby was the eldest. Next were Loretta, Thomas Louis, Carla Fay, Dalton Eugene, and Anthony Wayne.

At night when the whole clan was asleep, it must have sounded like an orchestra synchronizing their instrument for a recital as each one of us honed our own notes snoring while sleeping.

Bobby soon got a job with Reverend Holt. They left early in the morning going to Nashville to work for Metro Water Department. Since I was pregnant and not good at food preparation, they allowed me to sleep in while Loretta and Mrs. Augusta arose early in the morning to help them get breakfast and pack lunches for the day. I felt sorry for Loretta having to get up so early. But that's how it is when you are the eldest girl.

One morning, she conveniently slide down the wall and fainted. It didn't hurt her, but she was excused to go back to bed. Bobby thought she was acting. "Who do you know that faints like that?" he said. I don't blame her.

I felt sorry for her having to get up so early.

Later when the last child left for school and Mrs. Augusta went to work, the house seemed to take a deep breath and relax until the evening hours when one by one they all returned.

Feeling guilty about leaving Mother alone, I talked to her for long periods on the phone. She still worked at the Charlotte High School.

Promise Land population continued to decrease. Our cousins Tamer Lee and William Primm became her leaning post, and I felt better knowing they often stopped in, with John Lemuel (youngest son) on their heels. James Franklin, Henry, Jerry, and Michael made what we called stair step of their five boys.

December 1962, Mother took her usual trip to Columbus for Christmas with my brothers and their families. It was close to time for my first child to be born. My mother-in-law, I believe, loved me like her own child had assured her that she would look after me when it came time for delivery. So off she went.

On December 29th 1962, Terrell Johann Holt arrived at Bell and Cosby Clinic after a lot of pushing, panting, and screaming I never would have thought of. After a brief stay in the hallway of the clinic, baby and mother were sent home doing well. The whole bill set us back about one hundred twenty-five dollars.

My sister Wilma came home to Promise Land. She and Mother had convinced Bobby that it would be the best place for me to recover while she would care for the baby and me. It was an excellent idea for a month. Wilma and Mother were from the old school and argued that the baby and mother should not go outside until or after six weeks.

Well, Bobby was not having that and gave me an ultimatum to come home with him or else. I listened to many old wives' tales that warranted all kinds of illnesses and setbacks, including death. With fear of offending my family and dying of some old wives' tale disease,

I went back home with him to live with the Holt family. I became proof that those tales were just that—tales.

The real reason eventually emerged. They were concerned about me knowing how to take care of my baby. Right.

Back home with the Holts, I resumed the role of babysitting baby brother Anthony. Anthony and Terrell bonded as babies and remains very close today. Bobby turned out to be a real planner and provider. He continued working in Nashville for the water department. Rising before day in the winter and returning at dark, he and Reverend Holt had plenty of time for father-and-son talks. A time to pass off the older man's wisdom to increase the younger one.

Bobby (without my input) obtained a layaway plan with Meadows Furniture Company where he paid monthly until we had a home of our own to furnish. He purchased three acres of rural land from his stepfather. He never seemed to find time to ask me for my opinion. Not that I would have had one any way. I would follow him to the end of the world, no doubt.

But moving to Worley Furnace was not my idea of some place I wanted to live. Yet I remained silent. Soon, one Saturday morning, we got an alarming message back in Dickson that Worley Furnace was on fire. Bobby was burning the three acres of land he had purchased from Reverend Holt the year before. Fortunately, the fire was contained and no damage to anyone else's property.

Life continued as never a dull moment back at the Holts. Not yet two years old Anthony (Wayne) peeped out the living room window with big fake sobs while his mom (with real tears) boarded the taxi going to work. Soon as the taxi pulled off, he turned and ran to me laughing as if to say, "Got you again." Then it's off to peep in on the baby. Let me remind you that it is only a year between the two of them.

Between Anthony's own personal needs of diaper changes and bottles, he tried to help out with the baby's care. He sometimes got the baby powder. He'd shake it out on the floor, while I'm changing the baby's diaper. He never could keep both shoes on. He'd walk through that powder and you could track him down by his signature left shoe and right bare foot prints on the floor.

Anthony loved to go in the bathroom and pull the toilet tissue off the roll. If he became missing from the room, first place I'd look was the bathroom. Only nineteen years old, I had the energy to do whatever I needed for them. I had to watch them closely. Getting both of them to nap at the same time was only a dream. One of the little Holt boys were on duty at all times.

Anthony, now walking, had a lot of advantage over poor little Terrell. Anthony, a typical toddler, had his own rules built in his head. "It's mine, Mine, mine."

Terrell, who started walking at ten months, was trying to master the art, was at a disadvantage to be knocked down, or have a toy or milk bottle snatched by Anthony at any moment. I was totally exhausted and didn't know how to handle the situation. I knew enough to know that they were both normal, healthy babies. That was a blessing. I didn't have the heart or nerve to speak to my mother-in-law about the situation. She was having enough trouble leaving Anthony every morning.

Terrell was cutting teeth and seemed to enjoy massaging his gums on almost anything. I didn't realize that my problem was soon to be solved. The next time Anthony snatched something from Terrell, to my surprise, Anthony flew like he had been jet propelled. I didn't have to ask what happened. His one-word vocabulary (mind, mind) suddenly increased to "baby bite, baby bite."

Two things you have to learn when you live in an extended family such as ours were respect of others and how to take care of yourself. For months after that, Anthony would not go near that "biting baby." I loved it. I never mentioned this to Mrs. Augusta. Terrell could play in peace without his bottle or toy being snatched.

During the summer, months were both chaotic and fun with all the kids being out of school. Loretta, Faye, and I would share the cleaning, a never-ending battle. Most of the day, we watched TV and tried to exercise. We would all be in the living-room jumping around, mostly dancing.

Most of the cooking was left to Loretta. Basically, we played around all day; and about an hour before Reverend and Bobby were to arrive, both babies were cleaned up, and we girls would take off those shorts and pants and have on our freshly ironed skirts and dresses. Reverend said women should not wear pants. "It's an abomination," he'd say.

I truly loved that daily purifying ritual. We were free to abominate all day long. I don't think he ever knew about the short shorts and pants we sported all day.

With that many people in the house, it was still a fifty percent chance of error in our "Daddy's coming home" preparation. Tommy (Elder Thomas L. Holt today) never seemed to cause any trouble. But if anyone was going to mess up, you could depend on Eugene (Dr. Dalton Eugene Holt Sr. today).

Eugene's episodes would require another book. But one of my favorites was this. At a certain time, Eugene should have been home. No amber alert or cell phones existed, so he is just plain missing. If Bobby and Tommy could not find him, it really was an emergency. While Sister Holt paced the floor and prayed for the safety of her frequently naughty child, the rest of us just remained quiet, knowing this was just another Eugene episode.

Poor Mrs. Augusta, she fell for any kind of explanation those children would give her, and she tried to sell it to Reverend as well. While Reverend cleaned up for supper, the hunt was on for Eugene.

By the time Reverend finished freshening up, the hunt was over, and the *breaking news* was that the missing child had been found safely in a field near the school and his grandmother's (Mama Anna Holt) house where he was reported playing football with some neighborhood buddies. At the age of eight or ten and no cell phone, what else could he do except pull out his best alibi.

On the way home, he had come up with the best of all—developing a juvenile case of amnesia. Bobby and Tommy ushered the dusty tardy little football player into the house as Reverend passed them going to that poor little distressed tree that barely had any limbs left, as most of them had already been plucked for the same party. Sucking his tongue, he made his way to his mother's arms.

A strong tower was soon to be weakened by the power of discipline from the head of household. The older kids chanted, "Boy, Daddy's gone to get a limb. Daddy's gone to get a limb."

Sister Holt cradled her naughty child, rocking him, humming one of her good old prayer meeting (pray that I make it through) songs while she wondered how she could once again convince Reverend that the boy really had forgotten his way home. At eight or ten years old, it was hard to pass up a chance to play with friends.

Mama Anna's house was a straight shot down the same street. He lived to cut a lot more capers, but to tell them all would be his own memoirs. Reverend placed the used or unused switch in the corner for next time. Mrs. Augusta, as soon as Reverend wasn't looking, would have one of those naughty brats to discard "that old switch" rolling her eyes in victory. It looked like that poor tree was never going to get much taller.

Chapter Twenty-Six
My Disability of Minority

In 1964, Bobby was twenty-two, and I was twenty. Such a young man, he was very motivated to care for his family, including his own siblings. He continued to pay on the furniture but abandoned the plans for building in Worley Furnace. His biological father (Nolen Hughes who lived in Nashville) showed him a house near where he lived with his wife (Virgle Lee, and their children, Nora Lee and Pedro or Pete). It was a very nice little red brick house sitting on a huge level lot built around 1955.

It had been almost two years since we moved in with the Holts in Dickson. We got along well for such a crowd, but still it was time. The house was getting too small, just like my clothes, and was busting at the seams. It really was time to move on.

We thought everything was lined up, and we were ready to sign the final papers before taking possession of our home in the City of Nashville, Tennessee. Bobby didn't need a lot of time to make up his mind about something. Without a lot of looking around, we settled on a house in a quiet, well-kept neighborhood. Legal age was twenty-one to sign the documents needed to finalize our purchase. Only seven months shy of my twenty-first birthday and about five months pregnant found us in a bit of a hurry to settle on a permanent place to live.

After the first lawyer failed to represent us (reason unknown), we were left scrambling around early one Saturday morning trying to meet a deadline to have my minority removed. Mother recommended an attorney. We never did get our money back from the first attorney.

We sat patiently in the office of Atty. Weems as he hunt-and-pecked on his old typewriter: Sylvia Holt versus Lizzie Edmondson in a petition for the removal of disability of minority.

We met Atty. Weems at the courthouse in Charlotte, Tennessee (the county seat), arriving a little early than he. Mother was obviously proud of us for the venture that we were about to take on. She took pride in being a landowner herself.

We entered the judge's chamber as he greeted my mother by name. (Sorry for some reason I cannot or should not remember this Your Honor's name). "Why, hello, Lizzie," he said as he cleared his throat and straightened his short stocky self-up in his judgeship chair. "How in the world is Aunt Susie?" He continued smiling while reaching for his handkerchief and wiping the moisture from his fluffy round white face. "Lord I never will forget them good little old biscuits Aunt Susie used to make," he declared.

At his first glimpse of Bobby and me, he straightened up more erect and bowed his head toward us to have a seat. "What's the matter, Lizzie? This gal in trouble?" he said, looking over his wire-rimmed glasses at my rounded little belly. My chest was about to pop as I tried to keep from laughing out loud. Bobby was holding my hand and tickling my palm. I jerked my hand free while I lunged for my seat.

Finally, Your Honor gave someone else a chance to speak. Mother politely sat down and crossed her legs in a ladylike fashion with legs crossed at the ankles. She gave Bobby and me one of her famous "y'all better stop it and behave it or else" glances. Now I have had plenty of those glances in my lifetime. It was time to be serious. You don't even want to know what "or else" meant. I was trying not to laugh at the comment Bobby had made about the judge.

She said, "Well, first, Judge, you know, Mama's been gone (deceased) several years now. And yes, she sure could make good biscuits." She nodded. Adjusting her glasses, she glanced at Bobby and me to be sure we were behaving. After readjusting her glasses and her purse and smoothing out her dress, she extended her hand toward me. "Judge, this is my daughter (emphasis on daughter) Sylvia and her husband Bobby (more emphasis on husband). They are about to purchase a home in Nashville, and Sylvia is …"

More shocked at the news of Grandma Susie's death of about a decade or that these two young giggling Negroes in front of him were about to purchase a home, we couldn't tell. Then about that time our attorney arrived and took charge. So with one pounding of Your Honor's gavel and two calls for "Order in the court. Order in the court," just like that, the petition of Lizzie Edmondson versus Sylvia Holt, Your Honor declared my "Disability of Minority" removed forever.

Bam, bam, went the gavel again. "All rise. Court is adjourned," Your Honor bellowed. Out the door we almost ran giggling on the way. Mother, right on our heels, payed no attention to us. We forgot about the papers we needed. Lucky the lawyer had that.

Mother didn't scold us after we left the courthouse. Bobby had been making some remarks about how my black grandma had become the white judge's aunt. I could not have repeated it here or there with the words he had chosen to use. We just continued to laugh out loud when we were beyond him hearing us. Bobby could make me laugh about anything. Mother just kept on smiling. Soon after that, we signed the papers on our new home in Nashville, Tennessee. Nashville, here we come!

In July 1964, we were ready to make that move to the big city. We packed up our clothes and transported them to the house in Nashville. As easy as pie, all we had to do then was wait on the Meadows Furniture truck to arrive. The house didn't need much preparation. Water, lights, and telephone service were turned on.

Wilma and her husband Ed (James Talley) lived close. Helen and her daughter Stephanie had recently joined her husband Lethal Hughes who was stationed in Germany. Moving into the new house would help because I missed them dearly.

Bernice and her family were in Memphis. Wilma and Lauretta met me at the house to help me with unpacking clothes and arranging furniture when it arrived.

We sat on the front porch watching our children play in the front yard. Right away, I noticed a green snake slithering in the grass. I was disappointed to learn that snakes existed in the city too. I approached my new next-door neighbors, an elderly couple (Mr. and Mrs. Brooks) to help with exterminating that critter. Turned out that they were more afraid of snakes than I was. They instantly became my favorite neighbors. We were neighbors for the next twenty-five years. They were the best.

Miss Sis (Mrs. Brooks) was a stay-at-home grandma. She was helping raise her grandson and granddaughter. Pa Pa (Mr. Brooks) still worked. He soon spoiled my children by bringing them some little trinket or toy every day. By the time all the commotion was over, little green snake was long gone in the hedges. I never saw that snake or his relatives again. We forgot all about it when we saw the delivery truck from Dickson.

Soon the big furniture truck arrived to deliver our furniture. It didn't take long for the men to place the furniture inside the house. I didn't do a lot because of my condition. We arranged furniture and then stood back and admired how well the house was coming together. We did not have a television, so when we needed to sit and take a break, we chose to sit out on the front porch and watch the children play.

Soon after the furniture truck left, I noticed a very refined-looking middle-aged white gentleman dressed in a dark suit and necktie. He was actually coming across the street in the direction of our house. He walked right up to the porch. Smiling, he spoke, "I saw the Meadows Furniture truck just now. I was wondering who was moving in. You folks from Dickson?" he said, reaching out to shake my hand. Well, obviously he was talking to me.

I just smiled and kept watching him, thrilled by his friendliness. Finally, he introduced himself. "I am Lexie Freeman, pastor of the Church here," he said, pointing across the street at the large red brick building on the corner of our street facing the crossing street.

A light went off in my head as I told him, "Yes, I remember listening to you on radio in Dickson." He has been a pastor of a church there in Dickson. He was very kind and friendly, I remember. After a few minutes of friendly conversations, we shook hands again. His last comment as he left the yard was "You all come to church." Did he know what he said? I believe he meant it too. Or was that just a habit? Or did he think it was a white family moving in? I believe he was for real!

We didn't concentrate too much on his visit, nor did I think too much about the church being there. I was used to that. In Promise Land and Dickson, the churches were right across the street. Heck, I have always lived across the street from a church.

So we went back to our furniture arranging and watching our children. I was so happy to be in my own house.

After living in the Holt's household, quietness and privacy was a shock at first. I had to get used to not so many people in the house; the quietness was ire, and I had gotten used to hearing the midnight train that went through downtown Dickson on schedule. It seems like

I woke up at midnight listening for that train. I also had to learn how to cook. That was going to be a problem.

Being the youngest in the family, my folks must have been too tired to teach me how to cook or the real art of cleaning house. The only time I cooked at the Holt's in Dickson, it was spaghetti. You could cut it in squares. Mrs. Augusta thought Loretta had cooked the dinner that day. After she made the comment, "Sister (Loretta), did you forget to rinse this spaghetti?" I shyly admitted that I had helped out with dinner that day. She tried to console me about the mistake. Mistake? Nobody told me you are supposed to rinse it. I just didn't know any better.

With so many mouths to feed, I abandoned any further efforts to try to cook while there. We couldn't afford the food expense or loss on my culinary trials and errors.

Since he was the eldest child, Bobby had better domestic skills than I did. At first, he would clean and cook on the weekends. Maybe because I was pregnant, and again maybe he too was excited to be a homeowner at the age of twenty-two. He might have just wanted a meal he could eat without scraping the burned part off.

Reverend Holt continued to be his transportation to and from work. We did not have a television or car for a while. I learned to ride the city bus to the bank downtown and to HG Hills. If I bought groceries, I would get a taxi cab home. That didn't happen often, but I was simply amused at how those little white ladies looked so offended when I would sit down next to them on the bus.

Welcome to south Nashville, Tennessee, 1964. They would slide as far away as the space allowed, and a few would get up and move to another seat. I pretended not to notice. It was even funny, but I would never laugh at their ignorance. We didn't have public transportation in Dickson. All that was a new experience to me.

Chapter Twenty-Seven
Change Unstoppable

Nashville was one of the first cities in Tennessee to start integration of its schools in September 1957 (same year my father passed). This had been a subject I remembered hearing my mother and older family members talk about making reference to my father. "He would have worried himself to death," they often said over these trying times of the Civil Rights Movement. This seemed to make them feel better that Daddy didn't have to live through these troublesome times.

My father was a peace-loving man, but in my heart, I know he would have done well during the Civil Rights Movement of the sixties. I feel like he was a trailblazer in his own time. Ironically, he had passed in April that year. I don't care what anyone say; that does not take away the deep longing I still felt in my heart.

My children will never know my father. They will never experience the magic of him pulling a quarter from behind their ear or him finding an egg in their pocket. And no matter what they said, I still missed him.

While I was not yet too concerned about war or politics, as I should have been, I grieved the loss of our nation's handsome young President John F. Kennedy in 1963. I remained glued to the television screen for hours watching the events take place from Dallas, Texas, down to his arrival back to Washington DC. I truly felt the pain of knowing his young children would have to grow up without him. No amount of money could take his place. No historical account could take the place of him still being alive.

I compared the First Lady Mrs. Kennedy to my own mother, as I remembered the pain I saw on Mother's face as she kept herself so well composed for the funeral. Who in America or anywhere did not shed tears at the site of little John John and Caroline as they stood with their mother watching the activities of the president's funeral? And yes, our "world is topsy-turvy today" (quoted from a sermon heard from my uncle Jessie J. Bowens).

Bobby did not serve in the military maybe because of being the eldest son and / or being married with children. I had some cousins and friends who went to Vietnam, but to my knowledge, they all returned home physically safe. Maybe a little mentally shaken, but safe they came home. I heard reports of so many who didn't make it back. Not to be funny, I had and still have the greatest respect for our veterans and active military people.

I had survived my first heartbreak in our short marriage of two years. With my heart renewed and full of forgiveness, I was ready to begin a new life in my own home. This was proof of my husband's love for me. I knew that he had not stopped loving me as he tried to comfort and convince me. God gave me a forgiving heart. Only he could deal with his part of the story. It is harder to forget. I was not willing to let anyone or anything take away my joy. Soon our second child would be born. We both were thrilled about our family increasing.

Again, our baby was due in December. Mother left soon going to Ohio where she would spend Christmas with my brothers and their families. This time, she took our almost two-year-old son with her, leaving us not to worry over someone keeping him. With no car or TV, we spent a lot of time talking and imagining the places we would go if we did have a car.

After what seemed like the long way around, Daddy Nolen (Bobby's biological father) finally pulled into the emergency driveway of Vanderbilt Hospital. On December 17th 1964, our second son Andre Duran Holt was born as soon as we got into the delivery room of Vanderbilt Hospital. We barely made it in time. He had what they told us was jaundice and had to spend some time under a type of light for treatments. It was a common occurrence, they assured us. That fact was not enough to console me when I was discharged to go home while my newborn remained in the hospital.

It was the biggest and best Christmas we ever had, bringing Andre home on Christmas Day. Now we are a family of four. Lucky big brother Terrell would have a baby brother when he came home from Ohio. Life became too full for me to dwell on much of anything except taking care of my family. Especially the past, none of us have any power to change it.

Immediately, Terrell took his big brother place. He would stand on a one-gallon can while peeping into the bassinet or baby bed while singing his favorite songs (in his two-year-old voice), "Hi baby, Hi baby. Hi baby. Hi Baby" or "What you doing baby" or "Give me that bottle baby." Add a guitar and drum, he sounded like a two-year-old singing James Brown's music. He was excited to say the least.

I had my hands full with two babies. I was young and energetic. By the end of the day, I was exalted. I learned to cut corners wherever I could. I would wax and shine the floors by setting the babies on a nice wool-shinning rag and a large towel long enough to hold on to while whirling and swirling them all over the hardwood floors. They would giggle and clap their little hands like they were at the state fair.

By the time I was finished, the children were worn out; I was worn out, and the floors sure enough were shining. I soon realized Bobby was impressed by the scent of fresh paste floor wax. I hope this will not make me seem like a cheater.

One time, I just forgot and left the top of the wax. Evidently. Well, what had happened was, uh. When he came in from work, I got a big ole kiss as usual and his compliment on the house being so clean. "Uh. Hon, it smells good in here. You must have been working hard all day," he said while freshly bathed babies climbed all over him. Well, I couldn't dispute his observation or the fact that I had been working hard all day. But he didn't ask, and I shouldn't tell though.

For about half a second, I thought about telling him I hadn't waxed the floor or worked that hard. But who am I to ruin his joy of coming home to a clean house? I tell you no kidding that can of wax served me well and lasted longer too. I mean with only one breadwinner; it was frugal to save wherever I could. So I cut back on a brand floor wax. The smell lasted longer in those half-empty cans left open by mistake. And it did make the house smell fresh. No offense to the wax company. There is no telling how much money we saved on cleaning products alone. That is one to share. Try it; you might like it.

Bobby had been brought up in the Baptist Church and arranged for us to attend Swift's Tabernacle where a former pastor (Rev. E. Scott Howard) of his home church (Worley Furnace) was now pastoring. One of the members (name unknown) volunteered to pick us up on Sundays so that we could attend services. I joined and was water baptized for the first time. (A tradition, not mandatory in my original church)

We attended church as a family for a few months when Bobby, for whatever reason, began to slack up on attending. I really hated putting people out to pick us up for church, and the church was just too far away to walk. I began to think of other ways to remain faithful to God and be able to grow and serve him as I had been trained all my life to go to church.

One Sunday morning, I decided to leave the babies at home and visit the church across the street. The order of worship should be the same as at Saint John in Promise Land where I grew up loving the songs from the hymnals. I really never gave it a second thought. I liked the convenience that it afforded me.

I put on my best Sunday dress, shoes, and purse. I arrived just as service was beginning. Wow. They must have been expecting me. There was one pew placed on the back wall of the church not in line with any other. When I got a chance and no one watching, I peeped over the armrest, trying to see if (FOR COLORED ONLY) might have been lurking around on the end of the pew where the kind usher placed me.

Like a good little visitor, I sat there trying not to notice the blank glances. I didn't need a hymnal, neither was I offered one. I knew all the songs by memory. I imagined soon I would wear one of those robes myself while singing in the choir. With joy in my heart, I sang along as they sung "Come, Thou Almighty King," "Blessed Assurance; Jesus Is Mine," "My Hope Is Built on Nothing Less (Than Jesus Blood and Righteousness)."

I recited the Apostle's Creed, never missing a word. Then finally as the sermon had been delivered, the closing song, and the benediction song, the service was over. As I stood there in front of that lone pew, people began filing out the front door. Some looked, smiled, and spoke; some looked and smiled, and some just looked. I was not surprised, and neither did I care that I was the only black person there.

As I turned to leave the comfort of my pew, one fragile elderly (white) lady placed her hand on my arm and said, "Honey, you come back. And the next time you come, you don't have to sit back here alone. You come and sit with the rest of us." I thanked her for her kindness and concern. I know it was sincerely from her heart. I am sure she was not concerned with who else was watching her making me feel welcome in the "House of the Lord." We did not exchange names, but I will never forget how she made me feel. She could have been an angel for all I know. I am sure she is deceased by this time.

As I think about this lady, I sincerely believe I will see her again (in heaven) where I will know who she is. For only a remnant will be there. "Blest be the ties that bind our hearts in Christian love."

I went home and never mentioned this experience to my husband. I don't know what he would have said. Oh, for clarification, there was no sign on the end of the pew. Two things I really liked about this church: it was close, and they didn't stay all day.

Little did I know that the churches were having their own battle with segregated conferences and their immorality of its black and white congregations? My mother and father diligently attended the conferences of the Church. I don't remember them taking me to these events. I just remember them talking about pastors moving to other locations. We had one pastor to three churches in our area. They would be at the Church in, Dickson Tennessee, every Sunday at eleven o'clock and then alternate Sundays at 1:00 p.m. in Promise Land and Cumberland Furnace. I believe it was called a circuit or sister churches.

Their struggle was just as real in the area of civil rights issues. It was my opinion then and it still is a big issue. Sunday morning is still the most segregated day in America for many reasons. For a cultural awakening in 1964, I didn't realize how much I had been sheltered growing up in the sterile confines of the Promise Land community.

Chapter Twenty-Eight
Flights of the White

In an effort to help out financially, I advertised with the local employment office to offer child care in my home. Right away, I received a call and was set up to keep a beautiful little white girl named Laura (can't remember last name.) She was a few months younger than my eldest son. My youngest was still a baby.

With the help of an old stroller, I was able to spend parts of the day with the three children outside walking to the store or just out playing. There was a small store in the neighborhood that we often went to. The owners were a white family. The lady on the cash register would never fail to ask me questions about Laura but never ask about the boys. She never thought to speak but would just start out, "How old is your little girl?" "When is your little girl's birthday?" and so on until I thought she would finally realize a blonde blue-eyed little girl might not biologically belong to me.

I realized that we were causing quite a stir in the neighborhood. White neighbors looked and asked every question, except "Where did you get that little white girl from?" I just smiled and tended to my own business. I didn't mind all the strange looks we got when this precious little girl called me mama.

And one thing I know is that I loved Laura very much. She raced to the door with my eldest son, both jumping up and down, screaming, "Daddy, Daddy" when my husband came home from work. Laura's mom and I would talk briefly on the phone about her activity or concerns after they got home at night.

After the couple had their second child, I didn't keep her anymore; either it would have been too much, or her mother stayed at home to raise her own children. I still love you, Laura, wherever you are.

Off and on I would keep a neighbor's child, Skip Sawyers, who is still friends with my sons. Elander Madearis was a beautiful little girl. I enjoyed her because I didn't have a little girl of my own. I have lost contact with her family.

For some reason, Bobby never wanted me to work outside the home. He never complained about the fact that I was not a good cook. Our dinner conversation started out with him saying, "What did you burn for dinner today?" I have had to scrape a lot of burnt toast and cut the bottom off the biscuits before serving them. Quite often, I had to change the whole menu after burning a pot of beans or meat too burnt to salvage.

I learned that burnt beans are like people. You can serve them better if you don't stir them up! I loved reading cookbooks and the *World Book Encyclopedia*. *True Romance* magazine was not allowed in our house. We would lay in bed at night reading encyclopedias.

Still, my culinary skills and domestic technology suffered severely. Bobby tried to encourage me by saying, "Hon, stop trying to make the food look good. Just worry about how it tastes." He wanted food that was good, not just look good. I can say that prepackaged and fully cooked were welcomed at my house any time. I discarded the package so that it tasted more like homemade.

Our neighborhood was fast changing before my eyes as I saw white families move out and black families moved in. We were in the middle of what was called white flight. I began to pay closer attention to the news report on television. Disturbing news slowly started catching my attention. Rioting in North Nashville and "sit in" at the lunch counter downtown all seemed so far away. Bus boycott and boycotting the department stores—I just listened as though it didn't concern me or my family. I didn't care a lot about shopping. I didn't ride the public transportation. I just knew that the "world was still topsy-turvy," as my uncle Jessie said.

I finally realized that we had moved into a predominantly white neighborhood. I didn't care. Now I wished I could have been a part of the Civil Rights Movement. With two babies, I knew that was out of sight for me. We still did not have our own transportation, so staying at home is mostly what I did. Occasionally, Bobby's biological father (Nolan Hughes) would pick us up; and the four of us, plus the four of them, would pile into a five-passenger car and ride to Dickson to visit. That was before seatbelts and car seats.

I still missed being able to go to church without bothering someone for a ride. Catching the bus with my two little children was not an option. After a few more times going to the church across the street (CAS) and sitting among the other members, I decided to walk straight up to the altar as the pastor opened the doors of the church one Sunday. The choir sang "Come to Jesus, Come to Jesus" and then "Just as I Am." The pastor stood there solemnly pleading for sinners to come. That handsome black robe trimmed in purple and gold made him look more holy and acceptable.

I briefly remembered the day he had come to visit us as new neighbors. Didn't he say, "You all come to church?" With his head raised and arms extended toward heaven, he continued to plead. I, with no reservation, rose from my seat not as a sinner but as one who felt as though I was among other believers like myself in a church with the same doctrines and beliefs that I had grown up with.

I don't remember ever not being a Christian. At the age of twenty-one, I had known no other way. I was among believers who regularly sent money to support missionaries in other countries like Africa teaching and preaching the good news of the gospel of Jesus Christ. I felt comfortable and knew that not every member would embrace me. But here I am, "just as I am," thinking, "Please accept me for who I am—one young Christian woman who happens to have brown skin who is only seeking a place where I might worship the same God that you claim to be worshiping, a young woman who desires to bring her sons up in the church and in the way God would have them to go." Sure I would be the only black member maybe, but in the name of Jesus, would that be a sin? A young woman whose desire is so sincere and pure? Whose desire sees no color or division in the name of Jesus?

Finally, the choir stopped singing while the organ continued playing softly. The pastor opened his eyes and extended his soft white hand and shook mine in the right hand of fellowship. I expressed my desire to become a part of that congregation and to become active as a volunteer in the children's department. Now let the church say, "Amen."

I don't remember anything unordinary happening on that day. Happy in my own right that I would not have to go far to continue my Christian journey. I intended to one-day sing in the choir and grow spiritually right there. I was happy.

Sometimes I would take the children to church, and at times I left them at home with their father. I noticed that soon after I joined the church across the street, the pastor who I had joined under was replaced almost instantly. The rumor that the church was going to be sold and would move to a new location began to surface. I didn't get into the rumors any more than I had to. I was told that the church was losing members, and it would be necessary to move to another location to continue to serve the people.

My reply was this: "If they are leaving because of me (truth), then those who stay will be the true believers." It takes only one little black girl to move a whole congregation. That is black girl power!

After a few times working in the children's department, I was approached by the Sunday school superintendent. His message was that some of the members were against me working as a volunteer in the children's department. (I am sure if I had been a hired hand, they would have had no problem at all with my black hands touching or working with their children.) Disappointed, I said, "Sure, no problem."

I would remain faithful because this is where God had planted me. Why did I need to go elsewhere? The rumors of the church's "flight" continued. I prayed and asked God to "please guide shall I go or stay." I kept silent about all this to my husband because I knew he would be protective of me and the children. I knew God would take care of us. How could it not be the place for us? How could it be "for white only," not the church? We "believe in the holy … church, the communion of the saints … and of life everlasting …" (from the Apostle's Creed).

As I continued to hear the news each night on the television, I renewed my faith in God and my belief in Jesus Christ (my strong Tower.) I would not let the bombings, cross burning, or stories of lynching make me afraid to continue to worship the Lord our God in the place that he had led me to go. I was not a part of the NAACP or any other organization that you might have heard about in nonviolent demonstrations in the fight for equal rights. It was just me and God. That's enough.

In Christ, all men are equal, I thought. Some of my family and friends started asking me, "You go to a white church, don't you?" I would always reply, "No, as a matter of fact, the building is of red brick."

The church has nothing to do with the color of your skin. I was taught that church is the body of Jesus. We belong to that body, not a building at all. I kept telling myself. It must be the same God. There is only one God who gave his Son Jesus. The Holy Spirit is the same.

I can't tell you what the white members were planning because they never invited me to any of those meetings that must have taken place. Meetings about what the next step would be or how long it would be before more "colored" would show up. I never thought about it then. I am sure now that such a meeting must have occurred before the "disappearance" of the kind pastor who shook my hand that day, the kind pastor who visited us on move in day, he who had welcomed us to the neighborhood.

I longed to see him again, the kind pastor who might have been blamed for me being there in the first place. I was used to pastors being reassigned after the annual conference, but this one was gone before the annual was had. Years later, I did read about him and heard that he was in another position within the conference. I give him my greatest respect for giving me his hand that Sunday. I don't know what or how I would have felt had he refused me. To God be the glory.

I missed the former pastor but remained steadfast and faithful as I could, rooted and grounded until God gives me direction. I tried hard in my heart to listen to the new pastor, but it just wasn't Reverend … I had been taught not to worship the pastor but to worship God. I just felt like the new pastor was preaching what the members wanted to hear and not what they needed to hear. Who am I to complain? I have never believed in running from church to church for whatever reason people do. The Holy Spirit directed me to "be still." I did.

Being a stay-at-home mother, I looked forward to any activity and especially going to church on Sunday. I would get up early to feed my children and dress them first. Then I would get dressed. I didn't have a lot of clothes to pick from. I wore my "Sunday best." The short walk across the street was a pleasure.

We didn't attend Sunday school this Sunday. We arrived just in time for me to leave the baby (Andre) in the nursery. I took Terry (Terrell) into the sanctuary with me. My spirit was hungry for the praise and worship and hearing the word of God. I took my two-and-a half-year-old son's hand and led him beside me into the sanctuary, being careful to pick a seat not intruding on anyone's space. I noticed one seat about midway the sanctuary where only one other person was sitting. There was a middle-aged bald-headed gentleman who was leaning over the back of the pew while talking to someone in front of him. I did not think he was paying any attention to my son and me. He was all the way to the opposite end of the pew.

It was no possible way we could reach out and touch each other. I sat down and lifted my son up and sat him beside me. Immediately the gentleman who was communicating "between the pews" stood up and looked at us with such an evil gesture and spirit. "Well, you can have this whole damn seat, gal," he bellowed while bowing his head and gritting his teeth. "You can have this whole damn seat," he repeated. He stormed out. I don't know which way he went, nor did I care.

I sat there for I don't know how long with hot tears streaming down my cheeks. My heart was telling me to go; my spirit said wait. I knew I had to regain my composure to be able to stand. My precious little son could tell that something was wrong because I could not stop crying. He took his fat little hands and wiped at the tears on my face while I picked him up and held him close to me. For his sake, I had to make a decision.

Finally, I gained enough composure to get up and stand on my feet. I took my son's hand, and we started walking toward the altar. We stopped there briefly as I prayed. "Lord, forgive us our debts as we forgive our debtors. Lord, thank you for loving me. Help me, Abba Father, to understand why I must love my enemy. You commanded us to love one another. As you have commanded I do. I know that God is love. Amen."

I didn't want to leave there with anger in my heart. Neither did I want my children to sense that there was any danger or reason for them to be afraid. The Holy Spirit continued to lead me toward the nursery where my baby son (Andre) was. It was at the eleven o'clock hour, and the choir had begun to march in as the organist played. I had made it to the door of the sanctuary where the choir had begun entering the sanctuary. I stood to the side, quiet as not to interrupt them. As they marched in, some of them must have noticed that I had been crying and was visibly upset. After the choir was in their place, I continued to the nursery to get my baby.

That nursery seemed so far away as my anxiety began to mount. I tried to think positive, but negativity had its way. My heart began to pound so rapidly. I felt like it was coming through my chest at any moment. My mind went as far back as to have visions of young fourteen-year-old Emmett Till's case in Money, Mississippi, one that had taken place a whole decade ago (1955). Then, I was only eleven years old. I can assure you that no one had discussed that case with me.

Later, I had learned that he had been brutally beaten and murdered by some white men (two brothers) for "flirting with the wife" of one of the brothers. I was reminded of the bombing of a church in Birmingham, Alabama (Sixteenth Street Baptist Church) that killed four innocent little girls and wounded several others (September 15, 1963). Was I that naive, and overprotected as a child that I could not relate to the dangers I encountered in the real world?

My mind seemed to roll like a news reel feed as I continued to collect my baby's belongings. I grieved all over again as I remembered the assassination of our beloved President John F. Kennedy. I remembered exactly how I felt that day while watching the events on TV. Did I ask for this assignment, since I was alone in this struggle just to "go into the house of the Lord?"

I had only heard of the NAACP and the SCLC or whatever, and the peaceful demonstrations encouraged by Dr. Martin Luther King Jr. I was aware of the sit-ins at lunch counters and the struggle to desegregate public facilities both in Nashville and other Southern cities. Hadn't I heard about the murders of civil rights workers in recent weeks? The KKK was a real organization (not to be confused with the label on your favorite cereal box), cross burnings were for real (not an Easter celebration), and lynching was a favorite pastime (not a sports event for black men and boys to be swinging from a tree by their necks). I even wondered what Mama Susie meant by "white capping?" I am sure it was not some head attire or Easter bonnet.

All this that had seemed to be worlds away from me suddenly came tumbling down, intruding into my otherwise peaceful, sterile, safety zone of twenty-one years. I could no longer be just a listener of the news because it affected me and my family more than I cared to know. I felt like I just woke up from a good dream. This nightmare was for real. All the what-if's" flooded my mind. It was all right for me to place myself in harm's way.

Lord, I had no right to do this to my children or my husband. He had no idea what was going on at the church across the street. The few steps across the street seemed to take forever. I was glad when they said unto me, "Let us go into the house of the Lord." What is the meaning of that?

The rest of that day, I received calls from different members of the congregation expressing their concern and apologizing for what had happened. I assured them that as for the man in the pew, "he was forgiven by me the moment he spoke." I truly felt sorry for someone who considered himself a Christian, and he could stand up and show such anger and hatred toward another young Christian who only desired to be more like Christ Jesus, just another human created by God the same as he was, who only wanted to serve the same God that he would claim to serve.

I was totally shaken by this event but with no anger—only pity for that poor man when he stands before the Lord. (Blest be the ties that binds our hearts in Christian love.) The Holy Spirit that led me to the church across the street would surely continue to lead me whenever and wherever I needed to go.

Now and then, "what-ifs" consumed my thoughts. What if someone at the church had harmed my children? What if I continued to expose my children to that kind of environment? What if someone would burn a cross in our yard? What if someone would throw a bomb into my windows? Last but most important was when they get older, what if my sons needed spiritual advice?

I realized that my time was up there at the church across the street. I was glad when they said unto me, "Let us go into the house of the Lord." Thus, I made my decision not to expose my children to that kind of hatred. The Christian kind? What God were they serving?

Upon explanation to a few of the inquisitive members, I explained, "I know that everyone does not feel the same as that man "between the pews," but I had a responsibility to my family, especially my underage children to protect them and educate them about the greatest sin in America (beginning with slavery), a divide called racism, as much as possible without instilling the same in them. There is no place for it now or ever in the Kingdom of God. There is no "white church, neither is there a black church." It grieves my heart to think / talk about it. It must grieve the Holy Spirit every time a would-be Christian utters black church or white church. I believe that someone will be held accountable. It is an issue not to be silent about.

It may not be the most popular subject. It is one that needs immediate attention. Racism in our congregations we call church must be silent no more. If churches could lead the way for the world, I believe the United States of America would be a better place spiritually. I believe that the burden lay not on one group but on both the white and black Christian congregations.

Romans 12:5 so we, though many, are one body in Christ, and individually members one of another. (ESV)

Although the church was there until around 1971, I never returned there to worship. They ran like going to put out a forest fire up a hill and without a trace. Some members must have been late getting the message, since I kept explaining my reason for not returning. If my children are to learn racism, let it be anywhere but the church.

By that time, my husband and I had our own cars, plus a motorcycle. I could have joined them wherever they went, but my heart was not in it. That incident would haunt me for a long time and would make me wonder how would-be Christians are perceiving the church.

I finally settled on joining another church, a "black congregation" because my sister went there. I had my own transportation now, so that was not a problem. It might have been easier for me to walk (like Peter) on water than to walk across the street to the church across the street.

Chapter Twenty-Nine
Standing Up, Talking Back

Finally I decided to seek employment against my husband's desires. My children were still small. I felt like there was more to life for me. I had matured in the few years of our marriage, and I knew that there was more in his plans for me.

I took a job at a bakery that barely lasted eight hours. Then I tried a shirt factory. Both places were extremely hot. The factory job lasted a few months. Mother came to babysit Terrell and Andre. Two boys were a lot for her to handle. She said the boys did something (she forgot what). She told them to "behave, or I'm going to get a switch."

As she stepped outside, she heard the storm door click. When she returned, the door was locked. The two boys stood there watching her banging on the door, calling, "Open this door. Open this door, boy. I'm going to whip you if you don't open this door." They stood there shaking their heads, knowing if she can't get in they would never feel that switch.

Seriously, Terrell finally said, "No, Grand Mommy you go'na whip us." She kept banging, and they kept holding off, saying, "No. You go'na whip us." Andre was sticking to big brother on that agreement. Neither one wanted Grand Mommy to use that switch on them. She finally had to discard the switch to get back in the house. The end of Grand Mommy and the switch. Too glad to get back in, she never could remember why she went for that switch in the first place. Because it was too hot not much money and encouragement from hubby, I gave that job up and stayed home for a while longer.

After the two boys started school, I ventured out to find my niche in the job world again. One day I found an ad for nurse aide training progressing to CNT (certified nurse technician). I applied and was accepted. I successfully finished the training. Bobby was still expecting me to give this one up too. *Only a matter of time*, he thought. He teased me about it. I knew I wanted to do the job, but I had to get used to a lot of things I had never seen before. I prayed and cried a lot. New situation, sad situations, helpless situations, seeing people take their last breath—I prayed through it all. My heart was to give the best care with the best knowledge as possible to all mankind. I took a part-time position as a CNT. Learning the difference between empathy and sympathy, finally I was able to feel better about going further in the medical profession.

My husband started bringing home the nursing magazines from the printing company where he worked. I read them from cover to cover. I began to have visions of wearing a cap with stripes indicating the degree of education. I kept working part time, but I became pregnant for the third time. Not knowing I could work while pregnant, I stayed home again.

After the birth of our third son (Kevin Lane Holt March 7th 1971 at Saint Thomas Hospital), I decided to expand my nursing education. When he turned one-year-old, I enrolled in a program for licensed practical nurses. This was the same course my sister Wilma had been turned down for "being overweight." I noticed some white nursing students were much more overweight than my sister had been. This confirmed our suspicion that she experienced discrimination because of her color, not her weight. There were (white) student nurses more overweight than my sister—that was another way to keep our people of color out of the nursing program. She never tried to enroll again. The course was an intense thirteen months straight.

I graduated from the LPN class second highest grade in the class. Only the highest grade, a single young white female student (raised by missionary parents in Africa) was mentioned at graduation. I felt robbed of the recognition of my hard labor, especially since I had a husband, three children, a dog or two, two rabbits, two chickens, and a duck—all of them needing my attention on a regular basis.

I went back to my former employer and started my career on the night shift. I have always been a strong advocate for treating people right. I soon noticed how the black patients were being moved around to keep all blacks in one room. All rooms were semiprivate. The (white) nurse would give report and talk like I was invisible. She would report "moving Mr. J and Mr. T into the same room because the parent of a little white boy threw a fit."

"So you contaminated one room?" I'd ask. "Who did you charge for moving? There was a fee for changing rooms." I thought it unfair to charge patients who didn't ask for that service.

I continued to see the injustices the people of color were expected to endure as patients and on our jobs. I remained outspoken and didn't mind sharing my opinion whenever, wherever, and to whomever.

Evaluation time rolled around for me. My supervisor gave me an excellent on everything. But I couldn't or wouldn't leave well enough alone. I simply made the statement that for a change, there are no complaints on my evaluation. (I usually got some negative reviews.)

And with that said, the evaluating nurse made the statement. "Well, Miss Holt," she said, "someone did say you talked back." Wow, I had not heard that expression since I was a little child. All evidence that I was my mother's child came out of me. My mind traveled back all the way to the stories my grandmother had shared about the white folks, talking about, and "going to white cap somebody."

I aired every complaint back to the first time I notice the inequality and unjust treatment that people seemed to take for granted. That poor nurse suddenly became so teary eyed. All she could do was sniff while wiping her eyes, blaming it on her hair spray. She kept wiping and saying, "I don't know what it is, Miss Holt. It must be the spray." I felt sorry for her because I knew she couldn't admit to the things that I reminded her of. She could not deny it being true. That hair spray must have been pretty strong too. I wondered what brand was it she used. We Negroes needed to invest in it.

I am sure my actions and concerns for the patients must have already been discussed. They evidently didn't know how to process the data collected. I believe a conversation must have come about because of my problem being a Negro and "talking back." Not a good sign. I am sure this nurse must have felt "some kind of way." She could not stop crying any more than I could stop talking. Help me please! (I can't shut up.)

My mind took a timeline view of our struggle way back in the fifties and sixties for equal rights. And here we are in 1973 still talking about my people "talking back." In their mind, *Will we ever grow up? Or will we remain boys and girls forever?* I took that as an insult that allowed me another chance to air my feelings for whatever it was worth. Had we missed something? Or did we just conveniently let it slip our minds?

The reels of my memory began to spin. It flooded with visions of that struggle, much of which I had only heard on TV or read about in the newspaper. Those visions became more real to me. Those four little black girls who lost their lives in a church bombing (Sixteenth Avenue Baptist Church) that was blamed on KKK (Ku Klux Klan) in 1963 in Birmingham, Alabama. Could have been me and my innocent little boys at the church across the street. After all, we were Negroes.

"Getting out of place" was a no-no in the land of the free and home of the brave. That was a phrase I can't deny. I do remember hearing it. But when it came to my hometown, you could just about pitch it to the wind.

We didn't have the convenience of a water fountain. We barely had a bucket of water to share or a toilet for men and one for women. The "White Only/Colored Only" signs didn't exist in my hometown (Promise Land). My parents did such a good job of protecting me from the fears of Jim Crow laws, violence of the KKK, and racism that I was completely immune to news of cross burnings, lynching, sit-ins at lunch counters, and race riots. No matter how near or far, etc., we have had people who experienced these acts of violence while participating in peaceful demonstrations, having police release dogs on them, and turn fire water hoses on them. They risked, and some lost their lives in the fight for freedom.

I wished I could have been a part of this great fight. They sacrificed for all mankind. How soon could we forget Dr. Martin Luther King Jr. who had lost his life standing up for freedom and justice for all? I believe that the least I could do was to stand up for Sylvia! And I did.

I arrived at work one Saturday night only to find that my assignment should have been given to a registered nurse as usual. I was still a new LPN. I didn't feel comfortable in a roll that was beyond my scope of practice. Time and time again, I had discussed this with my supervisor and the RN who should have had my assignment. If I made a mistake, the assignment was out of my scope—period. The supervisor tried to convince me that "they would stand behind me if I made a mistake." I knew that all too well. In times of trouble, it's every man for himself.

I appreciated their confidence in me. But I knew not to go beyond my scope of practice. As soon as I had time, I called my family to let them know I made it to work all right. My mistake is that I had shared the problem with my husband one time too many. This was the last time he would have to hear me complain about my job.

He still had issues about me working anyway. He might have thought this time I would give up and stay home. Right away, he said, "Bring yourself home."

I left that hospital on a Saturday night (March 1973) with my husband's encouragement and threat: "If you are not home in the next thirty minutes, I will be coming to help you out." Well, I knew I didn't want that to happen. I am not sure if he would show up or not. I know I didn't want that to happen. I wouldn't advise anyone to do that now. There is a correct way to leave your employment. What I did is called burning your bridges. In this case, I burned all of them. And I didn't care.

I had just been raised in such a way that I said whatever was on my mind and especially if it had to do with what was right or wrong. A few years later, I ran into a former coworker. She told me that the news went out that I was trying to start a race riot before I left that job. How could I have done that? I didn't have any followers. It was just me.

I evidently didn't have enough sense to be afraid of losing my job or anything else. I just knew that if I was to have any peace in life, it would come at a cost of me speaking up at every opportunity on any platform available to me. So "talk back." I did. A lot. I have to let my light shine!

I believe that what you stand for should be taken seriously. I believe that each of us can make a difference. I was reminded of all the "stuff" that I endured almost fifty years ago as a new nurse in the same hospital where I was scheduled for very serious surgical procedure, October 3, 2015. I was cared for by at least four or five different races of nurses and doctors and other disciplines. When I was discharged, I felt so refreshed as if I had gone through a time capsule because of the fine treatment and care that the nurses, doctors, and any other discipline had delivered. I could not have asked for any more respect or better treatment than that which I received.

I spoke to my son Terrell Sr. about the experience and how it was working there in the late sixties and seventies. I mentioned this here because I felt it is appropriate to say that something positive had to have happened out of my tenure there. If I was wrongly accused, something good came out of it. I am in no way trying to take credit for the total change that I saw. But as my son said, "It must have been the ripple down effect that trickles down over a period of time it can change the course of the whole stream."

I like to think I have been a part of the changes over the years. I was never trying to start a riot, but I was speaking up for justice. My son shared with me that my voice must have counted when and where it was heard. That is why one should never just settle when we know something is wrong and needs to be changed. Silence is a sin. If we all speak up, change is bound to come. Sometimes it looks like nothing is happening. But 2015, "I felt the difference, and "I know there has been changes made." To God be the glory for the things—yes, the things that he has done.

Chapter Thirty
Can't Look Back

Leaving my former employment on Saturday night, I did not remain unemployed for long. Less than three business days, I began my most rewarding tenure at Baptist Hospital. I explained that I was a student at the University of Tennessee Nashville Campus. I did not have time for formal orientation because of my class schedules. With permission, I took the test for medication administration. If I had not passed, I would arrange to take the class that they required all LPNs to take. I was scheduled to start working on Wednesday night. I passed the test in flying colors.

I arrived at Baptist Hospital and took my place in post-anesthesia / surgical intensive care unit. With all the bells and whistles, I immediately fell in love with the high speed, or did I mean fast-paced rhythm that engulfed that room? It was a large L-shaped space with curtains around bed spaces to provide privacy. The long side was for the post-anesthesia patients who were waking up from various surgeries. They had to be monitored closely to prevent any problems arising from their anesthesia / medications.

The short side of the *L* was equipped with real hospital beds and bedside tables that were fully stocked with anything from nasal trumpets / tongue depressors to bed pans and Emerson pumps. Located at the head of each bed space were wall units for administration of oxygen and a unit for air and vacuum for emergency suctioning. IV poles stood at attention like utility poles waiting to hold IV bags of fluid, IV antibiotics, or blood transfusions.

I was assigned to work along beside several of the very skilled certified nurse technicians (CNTs). All the ladies took their jobs seriously. They realized that as an LPN, my job skills were above theirs technically. I showed them all respect due as I learned my way around with Mrs. Musgrove a well-preserved elderly black lady. Anita Cook and Mildred Caldwell taught me the art of working night shift and getting the job done before day shift arrived.

I made friends easily with most of the staff. Those who didn't like me, conveniently I have forgotten their names. I seemed to fit in with everyone from night shift supervisor down to the unit secretary, a short chubby elderly black lady with mixed gray hair who my oldest son thought had the "sexiest voice on the phone." Every night, my boys or my husband would call the unit to be sure I got to work with no problems. Terrell said, "I just love the way she says, 'Ms. Johnson, unit clerk." Finally, he was able to meet the voice he loved.

Despite the fact I had a new job that I loved, I still had a husband who occasionally would tell me of his resentment for "letting you ever get a job in the first place." My independence was bothering him. He felt threatened. He had been my mentor. He had bought me from a mighty long way. He insisted that I learned to drive after buying me that five-speed Corviar. I couldn't even drive and had no license. He insisted on me having my own bank account, both checking and savings. I had no reason not to grow since I was only eighteen when we got married over a decade ago. He had seen me mature from his high school sweetheart girl bride of 1962 into an independent young career-minded lady. I tried to assure him that there was no need for him to fret because everything I did was for the benefit of my family (him and the boys). He was not to blame for my metamorphosis. God was grooming me to do what he wanted me to do.

I had to find time to take the boys to football or track practice sometimes at two different schools. At "pick your child up" time I was transporting a few of the neighborhood children of parents I never knew. For some reason, I became the "soccer mom" of the neighborhood in a one-car carpool. I just smiled and drove very carefully so that everyone arrived home safely.

Occasionally, I run into one of the young men who expects me to remember them when … My response is, "I didn't have time to know your name then. All I was concerned about was getting you all home safely. Smile." I was determined that my family would not miss out on any activity because of my full plate.

I tried to divide my time as much as I could so that I could participate in activities that my husband enjoyed. One of them was deer hunting. We got up early on those days of deer hunting season in preparation to go into the woods in search of deer. He with his 30-0-6 (thirty ought six) and me with a 3-57(three fifty-seven) Magnum mounted around my waist and strapped to my leg. We must have resembled characters out of an old black-and-white western cowboy movie. We dressed in layers in order to stay warm.

On one occasion, we took our three sons hunting. Our main hunting ground was in a pasture belonging to his sister and her husband (Loretta and Jerry Mayberry). Arriving in the pasture, we came upon what looked like dried-up cow poop. What a family outing. It can't get any better.

At the first pile of dry poop, Bobby demonstrated by stepping on this dried-up cow pile; it didn't stick to his shoe. I don't know why this lesson was so important. He continued to demonstrate, seeming more intrigued than the boys were. After the third or fourth demonstration, he took a great slide, almost losing his balance. So the lesson was you can't judge a dried-up cow pile by its appearance. I guess. We had fun.

Our last hunting trip that I remember, it was just the two of us. We had spent quite a bit of time building this architectural structure way up in a large tree at the site of our favorite hunting ground. It stood high up on a hill overlooking a valley below. The landscape immediately took a sharp turn from hillside to hillside being separated only by the creek. I don't know if I realized why we were taking on such a project to erect this thing.

I was so in love with us spending time together. I would have followed him to the end of the world and back. I don't remember how we got the thing erected. Now those of you who are hunters of wild game will understand my predicament.

The clock was set so that we could arise early on Saturday morning. My hunting gear was laid out, except the 3-57 (three fifty-seven magnum), including my gun belt so that at the sound of the clock, I would literally run and jump into warm layers of clothing, grab the 3-57 and my cap. I was ready to rumble, bright eyed and bushy tailed. He would just as easily be ready to go. With coffee in his hand, the 30-0-6 (thirty ought six) in the other, he was ready too. A novel or other school book in my hand, I was ready to follow. "A hunting we must go."

We arrived in the woods a few hours before daybreak in an effort to get in place before the unsuspicious deer started to arouse from their slumber. This time with an advantage, we just might get the prize. I remained ignorant and totally clueless right down the path to that big old tree with the architectural structure, which I learned was a deer stand.

As we approached the tree, Bobby set the 30-0-6 upright against the trunk of the tree. I fully strapped with the 3-57, stood waiting on him to make the next move. He turned to me and said, "Give me your gun."

"Uh, who me?"

"Yeah, you. Who else would I be talking to?" I looked around as if I expected to see someone else beside me.

"Uh, well, why do you want my gun?" I said.

"Hon, you can't climb the tree with your gun on you."

"Oh, uh, well, who said I was going to climb that tree?"

By that time, I had my gun out of the belt, and I handed it to him in slow motion. Trying to get up the nerves to put my foot on the first of those little pieces of wood that we had strategically placed like a ladder leading up to the structure I now know is a deer stand, I lifted my right leg and placed my foot on the first step but couldn't get the left leg to follow. I took one step up and two steps down.

I kept this up for I don't know how long until I finally admitted and apologized for once in my life not having the nerve to follow him to the end of the rainbow. I said, "Hon, I'm sorry I just can't climb that tree." He handed me the 3-57 and said, "Well, you will have to go back to the truck because it is too dangerous, and you could be accidently shot down here on the ground."

Oh, dear me. Or a dear deer, either way you got your dear/deer, I thought. So I gladly took my gun and placed it in my holster. Without looking back, I made my way to the truck. I found my book and blanket. I curled up real cozy and read while waiting on the sound of that 30-0-6.

Finally daylight came, and Bobby returned to the truck empty-handed. I have no proof if he climbed that tree or not. I don't remember discussing it again.

After leaving that site in Hickman County, we went to my mother's property in Dickson County (Promise Land), and the first thing we saw was a herd of deer drinking from the pond in the back field behind her house. It was also rumored that our nephews (Keith, Rex, and Ronnie Mayberry) had caught a fawn (baby deer) by hand.

These were the children of the property owners where we hunted mostly (Jerry and Loretta). Today deer can be seen grazing in my subdivision. Wild turkeys come through my yard daily. Opossums, rabbits and squirrels are plentiful. My hunting days are over.

Bobby liked working on and riding his motorcycle. He was not a mechanic, but he would do little simple things like having small pieces chromed. I would hang out on the back patio reading or studying while he would be tinkering with some part trying to either get it off or put it back on. Usually after watching his trial and error, it was clear to me exactly how to get the job done.

I put my books down and went over to his work space. I stood and watched a few minutes, allowing him to ask for my help and I tried to think how to help him without wounding his "male ego." With my nicest voice, I'd say, "Uh, honey, why don't we try it this way?" No matter how I said it, it was an insult that a woman could know how to do something that a man couldn't do.

Usually I had observed him long enough to understand how to do it. He would get insulted anyway and say a few unpleasant words and send me back into the house. I would go in and sit by the window and read while counting down. By the time I counted to about a one hundred, he would come in and say, "Honey, why don't you come on and show me how you would do this."

Pretending I was not expecting him. "What? Oh hey, sure. Hold on," I'd say, pretending I needed a bathroom break. "I would be glad to show you." Acting like nothing ugly had come through his mouth,

I'd pop that piece on in a few minutes. "Hey, you want to ride around the block?" he'd say with a big old grin. That was his way of saying, "I am so sorry, I shouldn't have spoken to you like I did. I thank you so much for helping me out."

"Nah," I'd usually say, which was my way of saying, "You could have said, 'I'm sorry.' But that's all right. You're sorry."

The boys liked to ride with their father. One day, Andre came to me and said, "Mama, Daddy said to tell you me and him are go ah flip off on the motorcycle." I knew he was trying to say "going to slip off." But, Lord, he said flip. "OK," I said, and immediately I dropped to my knees. I prayed for my husband and child until I heard that motorcycle returning. Amen. Amen.

Despite the discouragement from my family members, I rode with him as much as possible. I really enjoyed riding with one or two other riders. He joined a club. The larger the group, the more apt you were to spend most of your time setting on the side of the road because someone's bike broke down.

Man, why don't they keep that bike up? It was usually the same person—the short guy with the tall heavyset girlfriend. When he stopped at a traffic light, she would put her feet down to balance the bike. Darn, I have forgotten their names. Not important. But anyway, someone needed to tip him that the bike was too small to carry the load imposed upon it. I mean, I'm just saying.

The bikers' club was out of the question for me. He didn't want me to join, nor did I want to. Occasionally, he would ask me to join him at the club house. On one Sunday, he asked me to go "over to the club house." Upon arrival, one of the members met us at the door shaking his head. "Man, they got us. Yes, man, they got us. Yes, man, they got us," he kept saying. No one was there but him. He was very strongly against calling the police.

Upon further inspection, there was no evidence of anyone breaking and entering. The cash register was empty of all cash. I thought that to be strange. Later that afternoon, I was sitting at the table studying. Bobby came in, and I asked him if they found out who stole the cash. He said, "No." I said I know who did it.

I picked up my pencil and pointed it at him. I said the man who made the discovery. "No," he said. He knew I was right.

Fortunately, I have never been in a motorcycle accident. The two times Bobby had an accident, I was home with the children. The last one was most serious. He was with cousins, Eula and Gary Moody. Their son Coveak was riding with him. I don't remember the details. I was told that an ambulance had loaded him up. He aroused and told them, "Let me out of this thing. I'm going home. My wife is a nurse." They could not convince him to let them take him to the ER. I took one look, loaded him into my car, and took him to the emergency room. About two hours later, he was discharged with no broken bones, looking like a mummy. Coveak (Rev. Coveak Moody today) had a broken hand or something. They both survived.

I could not afford the luxury of whining or complaining any more. I wore so many different hats. I would put on my bell-bottom hip huggers and halter top with belly-button showing, pull on my boots and motorcycle helmet when it was time to be a biker chick. I was ready to ride. When it was time for work, I put on my scrubs and nurses cap with stethoscope around my neck. I worked hard to get the job done.

As a student, I would dress casual and dawn my lab coat with books in my arms, purse on my shoulder. I studied hard to pass each exam. When it was time to sing in the choir, I put on my robe and marched in double line down the middle aisle of the sanctuary with the other choir members. I sang for joy.

As a wife and mother, I dressed in anything comfortable while cooking, cleaning, helping with homework; and luckily, I could wear the same as mini zoo keeper to clean out rabbit cages, dog house and feed and water the animals. They ran loose in the backyard while playing with the children or chasing a squirrel. The children helped some, but they are just kids, busy even in the summer while school was out.

Last but not least, I tried to be the best in whatever hat I wore at any given time. I nurtured, consoled, kissed and put bandages on boo-boos, gave back massages and pats on the back, played games, read and cheered for them, and encouraged my family to do their best at all times. I tried hard not to neglect any of my responsibilities. Whatever the task, I did it. I was a church-going, Bible-toting biker chick, a pistol-packing deer hunting (one-car carpool), a soccer mom, a wife, a super nurse, a student nurse, and a mini zoo keeper. I did it all. I did it well. Amen. Thank you, Jesus. I won't look back.

Chapter Thirty-One
A Juggler's Determination

I continued going to school full time while working. The good part about me being at Baptist Hospital was that now I didn't have to worry about money for tuition. One of the staff nurses (Betty White, RN) informed me of this opportunity. From that day on, my education was fully funded by Baptist Hospital. Oh happy day.

Life became more of a juggle than a struggle. I juggled between work and classes. Sometimes I took my lunch break to register for my classes. My children were immersed into college life because there were times I took them to class with me. I left Terrell and Andre in the common area with their books and money for snacks while juggling my books with Kevin, the youngest child. Most of the time he was content to sit beside me in the classroom, keeping himself entertained, scribbling in my books and notebook. But the juggling didn't stop there. With three sons came pets, and I do mean pets. At any given time, we always had a dog, and once there were three.

To add to our collection were Easter oriented animals like two baby chickens, two rabbits, and a duck. With this comes mini zoo care, daily feeding, and vet visits. The (children) owners would take care for a while, and soon the responsibility was mine for whatever reason.

I completely gave up watching TV. With only twenty-four hours in a day, I cut corners anywhere I could. I couldn't afford thirty minutes to watch the ten o'clock news. Eventually, Kevin became my news reporter. The process became routine. As soon as I got to work, he'd call with the latest news from the ten o'clock segment.

As any little boy news reporter, he got it "twisted" Most of the time, leaving me to wonder frequently, "What did he just say they said?" For example, one night, he reported on a much publicized case of a patient who was "brain dead." By the time I received the late breaking news, Kevin Holt-style, it was announced that "the doctor pulled a plug on this patient's brain wave." He knew his mommy was a nurse and would understand and appreciate this medical information.

Once he reported rather urgently, "Mommy, do you wear Rely? Because it can make you die. Some lady got sick and died from wearing Rely." This one was pretty important and deep. His report was right on it. It was concerning a super-absorbent tampon linked to TSS or toxic shock syndrome in the seventies. I was glad to report that I was not wearing the product. Also, I was even more grateful to end the conversation without having to explain to such a young reporter just how do you wear this thing? Some of the other staff nurses looked forward to hearing these news reels as much as I did.

My children helped me as much as possible, but they were kids first. One night, I was running late for work. While getting dressed, I flagged Andre as he was running around playing. "Hey, Andre, go get a hot dog and put it in my purse please. My lunch." I am not sure he understood exactly what I said. However, it was a source of great pleasure when I was hungry later that night. I looked in my purse, and sure enough there, I found an unwrapped hot dog and bread crumbling along with other items we ladies keep in our purses. I smiled. He did exactly what he was told. I learned to ask for the sandwich wrap next time.

    I settled in at Baptist Hospital and never looked back. I found a lot of support from some of the nurses. While some tried to make fun by asking me, "Why did you wait until you got so old to go back to school?" I chose selective hearing deficit and decided not to dignify that stupid question with an answer. I was somewhat disappointed in some of the jealousy that I saw from my own people of color. I was taught so well to hold my head up high and to keep on going that I never engaged in conversation with them about my education unless they wanted information about continuing theirs. Black registered nurses were very few at that time. I was at the point of no return wherein I imagined the green strip on my cap (LPN) turning black for RN.

    I tried as much as I could to take the boys to church. It was hard for me to orchestrate after working all night Saturday night. At times it was almost impossible. After the incident with the bald-headed man and the "whole pew", I had sort of lost my warm fuzzy feeling for church. Since I had so much on my plate, it was easy—I am sorry to say— "to omit the Sabbath day." I tried to keep my self-built up by singing while doing my daily task. I diligently prayed and was truly thankful for the many blessings that had to be nobody but the Lord. I blamed part of this on my experience with the incidents at "church." However, I knew I have to know the Lord for myself.

    Another time I asked for counseling from a pastor that I thought I could trust. This turned out unfavorable and had to be ended because of his inappropriate suggestions. That is why it is so important for Christians to let Jesus be the one you see. Sometime the flesh just isn't good enough.

During my journey, I am sorry to tell you that life was not always a bed of roses as you might not have found in reading this far. Like any married couple, we had our ups and downs a plenty and then some. I don't mind telling you my husband has been an excellent provider, and I live in comfort today because of his wisdom as a young man / husband and father to make good decisions concerning our children and me.

The gulf between us became wider and more troublesome. His insecurity and regrets for letting me get a job had widened and was taking its toll on us. We just couldn't see eye to eye on one subject. Some of his biker friends were giving him their advice. "Man, she is going to leave you when she graduate from college." That was the farthest from my mind because I truly loved this man and would have done whatever I needed to do to set his mind at ease.

I was too busy to entertain the few negative phone calls of so-called female friends trying to make trouble. Misery loves company. I am sure that his biker friends and his one bad habit were packing a powerful punch against the institution of marriage.

I just didn't have time for a lot of foolishness. My life was divided and split up in as many directions as it could possibly be. I kept that attitude and a shield around me that could not be penetrated. Those fiery darts aimed at me slid right off and lay at my feet.

God promised to prepare a table before me in the presence of my enemy. Soon word got around that "Man, you can't make Sylvia mad. You can't say nothing to upset her," and the would-be perpetrators would back up and find someone else to harass for a moment. I believed in attacking my problems at the main source. So gossiping on the phone with "she said, she said" was not a part of my persona, and with that attitude, "I was just too intelligent to get involved with some people." I knew enough not to feed these troublemakers that don't mean anything to me.

During my time in school, old friends fell by the wayside. A few new friends were made, but socializing took last place in my array of things that mattered in my life. Sometimes you have to put things on the back burner.

I successfully did that with less important matters.

As a child and teenager, I heard so much teasing and name-calling that I learned to ignore some of the world's biggest bullies. Even racism is bullying. I remember one night at work, a certain employee who seemed to have something against me would try to "loud talk about me at every opportunity she got." I walked into the supply room, and there she was. She ended her conversation like this: "Yes, child. Some of these women are working and going to school and taking care of these husbands too." Well, I was the only one in the unit working and going to school. I guess she meant me.

I just kept taking care of my business because she obviously was not speaking to me. Later at the end of our shift, I got into my car and started home. While waiting on the red light to turn green, I noticed her waiting at the bus stop. I tell this story here because I feel that bullying is still a big problem today. It is more talked about today. But the moral to this story is that while this person was trying to "throw shade at me," she might have looked at her own situation because at least I didn't have to ride the bus. Again, I say, "God will prepare a table before me in the presence of the enemy." Amen.

"Everyone who is talking about you isn't talking to you." They should be ignored. I wouldn't want to know what they said.

On my way to the destination that I had chosen, nothing seemed to go as planned, but I was determined that nothing was going to turn me around. Failure was not an option. My decision to become a registered nurse depended on the strength of my determination, which would bring me to that destination.

I began to call it out in my mind. I walked and talked like a registered nurse. I read RN magazines I looked at laboratory results and EKG rhythm strips. I looked up medications in the *Physicians' Desk Reference* (PDR). I was first in line to help in or observe medical procedures.

At times when life would throw me a lemon, I had no choice but to make lemonade. And a lot of lemonade I made. My mother would try at times to comfort me by saying, "Honey, you are already an LPN." I would just look at her and try to hold back my anger. This is like picking all the berries, and the biggest juicy one is still on the tree in plain view and within reach. That was like saying, "Why don't you just give up?" But she had no way of knowing the difference I could see in LPN to RN or even why it was so important to me. There were a lot of reasons that I could not give up. The only failure is "the failure to try."

I had the most important audience watching me as I acted out each scene of my drama, alive and on stage. Those most important spectators are none other than my three sons Terrell, Andre and Kevin. If no one but them were to show up nightly, if no one but them were to understand the plot or scheme embedded in this drama, the cost that I have invested will forever be priceless.

It is my desire that their lives will have been impacted in such a way that they will use the wisdom and knowledge gained from watching my life unfold to help them grow into responsible young adults. I hope that they will pass these lessons from generation to generation. I believe that a lesson is better taught when you can set examples. What you say teamed with what you do is an excellent teaching tool.

By the time my children finished high school, there was no question whether they were going to college. They couldn't get me to find any reason why they shouldn't go—proof that an example is a good teaching method. We strongly encourage education. They got their degrees, in Engineering and Human Resources their children are following their examples.

I continued this race, and sometimes it seemed like time stood still. I was fully focused on that green stripe turning black and my name title LPN changing to RN. I had begun to make plans as to how it would change life for my family.

While some of my coworker continued to make slight remarks, I continued to ignore them. I am thankful for one such friend, a young male nurse (Stanley Randolph) who was not only a coworker but also one of my classmates with the same desire to become a registered nurse. We both had the same vision. He was someone that I could depend on if by chance I missed a class or needed help in micro lab. He shared notes and was an excellent motivator and sometimes pounding board. In our downtime, which could not be predicted, our supervisor allowed us to study as much as our time would allow.

My husband seemed to be proud of my accomplishments most of the time, but sometimes Satan has to rise up to test your strength. I am not sure exactly why, but one day I found that he had discarded my books for that semester. I mean in the trash can in the alley. I decided that I would not say anything or even try to retrieve them. I could have purchased more books, but I had something to prove. I kept going to class without books.

God is good all the time. I listened, took notes, and studied intensely in class. By the time I got home, my homework was done. It turned out that I made a better grade than ever in the subjects. It goes to show you what you can accomplish when God is on your side.

In May 1976, I received my degree in nursing from UT (the University of Tennessee Nashville); and in 1977, I successfully became certified in critical care nursing. I immediately treated myself to a new automobile. Nothing fancy, but some folks will be jealous of a hoopty.

I heard through the "grapevine" that my new name was Miss Rich B**** behind my back of course. I didn't give it much thought because I was the one who had sacrificed, no telling how many hours of sleep and time I could have been out partying or just chilling at home. The reward of my hard labor belonged to my family and me. I knew not to play that kind of game. My mission was accomplished and now for the next accomplishment. I had learned to let what anyone say about me not offend me.

The only reason I am sharing these stories is to help the reader to see the value in not trying to address every issue brought to you. Most of the time, you can leave things alone, as my parents used to say, "If you give a fellow enough rope, he'll hang his own neck."

Many problems or misunderstandings can be solved by someone choosing to "be the bigger person." If people would realize that some things don't need to be or as I sometimes say "is not up for discussion," especially if it is your business, it does not need to be discussed unless you are willing to. Many arguments and family feuds can be stopped dead in their tracks by simply making announcements in such a way that there is no question-and-answer session unless the announcer desires it. My theory is that I take my problems to Jesus, and that's enough. After I have dealt with the situation and I feel like anyone else needs to know, then I make an announcement.

If appropriate I am open for discussion, I let it be known. Otherwise, I chose to lead the conversation about any announcement I make. The end.

Since our marriage of two decades, we worked so hard I felt it was past time for us to take a family trip that would, for some, be a lifetime dream. He instead wanted to place a double-wide home on the property that we owned in Dickson County. This would be used as a weekend and summer home.

Our children were at the age that they knew they didn't want to live in the country. Kevin even claimed to be allergic to the country. I agreed to invest in this venture, and I also continued to plan the trip. I started looking for information on vacation packages that would be family friendly.

In the spring of 1980, we acquired a very nice double-wide home and began spending some time together getting it set up. One of the nicest at that time, it had three bedrooms, a large combination of great room and game room with fireplace, a large eat-in kitchen, a formal dining room, and two full bathrooms. A built-in stereo system allowed us to have music through speakers in the ceiling. It truly was a positive experience.

Our two eldest sons were both driving now. We or, should I say, I had this newfound freedom since two sons had their own car. Bobby made sure they learned to drive and provided them with a nice second-hand car. The load for me was lightened since I didn't have to transport them to football practice. Frequently, the boys went with us to the country home. It was a three-acre park like setting. They enjoyed horseback riding.

Our neighbors, the Horner's, were the owners of the horses and were glad to let us exercise them. They also had an assortment of other animals including hound dogs for hunting. Frequently, I was asked to apply some ointment to the hide of the mare or other animal. I was afraid of the horses and cows since childhood. I would stand on the porch while Reverend Horner held the harness, keeping the mare still while I applied the ointment. I dreamed of riding but never got up the nerve.

I enjoyed the peace and quietness the place afforded us. We often talked about how our goal was to own at least three homes, one for each son. I enjoyed cooking more, when I was there. We kept our refrigerator and pantry well stocked there. Often when I was at home in Nashville, I would go to get something out of the pantry or refrigerator only to realize that was in the refrigerator in the country. Life was good. We were so blessed to have these two homes.

We were not rich by any means, but we didn't have any financial problems. The boys were growing up and becoming more and more independent. They were doing well in school and in extracurricular activity. It seems like the more you have, the farther apart you become. We no longer sat on the porch and talked about where we would go if we had a car. Trouble is we all had transportation. Too often, we went our separate ways.

I began to plan a trip to the Bahamas. Terrell was graduating high school in May 1981. I decided that was the time to have that once-in-a-lifetime vacation. It would be a graduation trip for him. I felt like it could be our one and only luxury family vacation—together—or it would start a tradition. I was brought up traveling to see my brothers in the summer. I was able to travel with them during the summer. I wanted my sons to experience traveling. That can be as much a part of children's education as anything.

I planned the trip only to find that my husband was choosing not to go. At first I was heartbroken. Then he suggested that I take my mother instead of him. So I went ahead with the planning. Someone at work saw one of the vacation brochures I was looking at. That became a joke, and soon it got so funny that someone put a picture from a magazine on the bulletin board with my name on it. That would be racial discrimination today. I just smiled and continued my plans. Everyone who is talking about you is not talking to you.

My husband took us to the airport. This was the first flight for all of us, except my mother. We landed in Miami and took a limousine to the Port of Miami where we boarded the SS *Flavia*. As the ship left the port, we listened to the safety regulations and the "what-ifs" and "in the unlikely case this should happen." My mother turned to me and, said, "Oh, this is so beautiful. If anything was to happen, I would be ready to go in." I smiled and said, "You would beat me to one of those life boats."

Three of us were seasick for a few hours. After visiting the ship's clinic, we got stabilized; and for the rest of the trip, we enjoyed free of nausea. We enjoyed most meals on board the ship. We enjoyed sightseeing when the ship was docked. Midnight buffet seemed to be the best of all. It was our first time gambling in the casinos. Not a lot of money was lost in there. We were on a tight budget.

I signed up for the passenger talent show. After practicing with the band, I was ready. That night I was the last one to perform. Saving the best for last? When it was my turn, the master of ceremony announced, "Ladies and gentlemen, we have a young lady here all the way from Music City USA, Mrs. Sylvia Holt from Nashville Tennessee. Folks, let's give her a warm welcome," putting special emphasis on Nashville Tennessee. "Please welcome her to the stage."

I went on stage. Looking at the audience, I smiled while taking the microphone. I stood next to the piano. With microphone in hand and my head held high, I began, from the bottom of my heart, singing in its entirety "I Know Who Holds My Hand." I took a deep breath and continued as I noticed people beginning to wipe at their eyes. Moving a short distance from the piano, I could see my mother and my children's approval. I raised my head again as I stepped forward with right hand raised. I brought it to the ending on center stage. I took a deep breath as I took it to as high a note as possible, holding longer. "And I Know He Holds My Hand." I repeated the ending twice and placed the microphone back in place.

I know those people felt the spirit like I did. My family was all puffed up and smiling. The boys and Mother were proud.

My performance brought me instant fame on board the ship. One (white) lady came up to me screaming, "I knew it. I knew it. I told my sister, when I saw you with all those children. I told her I know that lady is somebody. I knew you were somebody. She has to be somebody with all those children on this trip." She kept screaming as others tried to give their compliments.

The fame overtook me, and the rest of the trip, all eyes were on us. I might add that I don't remember any other black guest on board. We must have stood out like sore thumbs.

That was 1981. I never did find out "who I was." To me, what the lady really meant was "How can a black woman afford to bring all those people on this trip? They have got to have some money? Right? I was excited to be whoever she wanted me to be." No. OK, I don't care. It was fun being famous. I imagined they thought I was a country music star. I sure wasn't going to spoil it for them. Hope they didn't Google for me.

We arrived home in Nashville on July fourth. I barely had enough money to hire a taxi cab from the airport home. It was a trip to remember. Wish hubby had been with us. He chose to ride his bike with the club. *Oh well.* I thought, *back to reality.*

Chapter Thirty-Two
Red Dress / Black Dress

Everyone should have a red dress and a black dress. Yes, a red dress for strength and a black dress for more strength! Hesitantly have I considered how to write this part of my story? Relaying these episodes have been invigorating like a "brisk walk in early morning fresh air." It is hard to tell everything. Neither is it necessary to tell it all.

My struggle with this chapter is how to tell it in a positive way and not to disrespect anyone or the memory of an institution so vital to mankind. I spent hours spanning two decades in prayer, conversation, counseling, writing my thoughts, and exploring options during the time leading to the most profound decision that I had to make. It affected more lives than mine. I had to consider all who were concerned.

My aim is to tell the truth in a way that it does not glamorize the action or decision I had to make. I hope that I might bring inspiration to the reader, but in no way am I sharing this to influence anyone if they are ever faced with the same decision. I wish to convey to the reader that marriage and divorce are equally as important. Marriage should be in sickness and in health, "until death do us part." I believe people should exhaust all efforts and means available to salvage their relationship. The decision only you can make is personal. Without losing my own identity and failing to live up to my God-given potential, I had to make that decision finally. I recommend counseling before both marriage and divorce.

After meeting with the same attorney over ten years, for the last time I let him talk me out of what I knew I had to do. He would ask me, "Is this man taking care of you and those boys? Is he paying the bills? Looking over our access he'd say, "You all are doing good." Yes, but? "Well, I would keep on letting him do just that," he'd say. I left the old attorney and went to find one who did not know me so well. He was too old-fashioned, I decided.

Material things do not bring happiness. My attorney of ten years thought just like someone else very close to me. I had a lot to be thankful for, but part of the marriage equation was missing. A piece was not enough. And the most important piece was missing.

Erasing the past twenty-three years, I hired a new attorney to represent me. One Friday morning, I put on my red knit dress (with a high neckline and a respectful length below my knees) my high-heeled alligator-skin shoes with purse to match. Confident that I would survive, I threw my short mink, stole around my shoulders, and downtown I went. *Click, clack, click, clack,* my heels pounded on the pavement. It was like a murder mystery novel—that sound brought me closer to solving the investigation of the missing pieces.

My attire would hold me up and make me stronger. Bobby had offered to go with me for support, but he announced, "I will go but, Hon …" He was sure I couldn't go through with it. How considerate. I turned him down. No, I don't need any supporting actors. My lovely red dress, with the high neckline and respectful length below my knees, was all I'd needed.

Divorce court doesn't take long if uncontested. Twenty-three years was finally over. Any stray pieces to complete the puzzle of my marriage no longer mattered. I had been Mrs. B. L. Holt longer than I was Sylvia Edmondson. How long would it take to shed the skin you shared with someone since the age of fifteen? How would I know how to be single?

Changing my feelings was the problem. He taught me how to be independent, which he regretted at times, believing that was part of our problem. How can you stop a seed from sprouting after planting it in fertile ground and feeding it all the necessary nutrient to mature? Like a weed, my independence took over and could not be held back. For the first time in my adult life, I was free to make my own decisions—no one to ask about anything.

Being free and feeling free is totally different. The adjustment and waiting to feel free took longer than the finalizing of our divorce. My husband confessed to having one bad habit, often promised that one day he would "make me the best husband" that anyone could have. "I don't drink. It makes me sick. I don't do drugs. Just one bad habit," he'd say. What more could I expect? I forgot how long the waiting period was. I had waited too long. I had to change me. Only I could do that.

I could not be patient and wait on him to become the man he promised. Time runs its course. I wanted him to wait while I became a registered nurse so that we could have a better life together. I thought about all the "could haves and what-ifs" we had. Then we all could celebrate together and reap the benefits of our hard labor.

Saturday morning, he showed up to take me out to breakfast. It was like we started dating all over again. We had a chance to reflect over the past while he apologized for ever causing me pain. It was a purifying moment, I thought, while he reminded me of his promise and of his one bad habit.

We continued this relationship (nothing had really changed) for the next two or three years, until one day our son Terrell came to me and said, "Mama, did you know?" So that's what he was trying to tell me. Apparently, I was the only one having trouble moving on. Someone died. Someone I knew and loved died suddenly. I could not afford the luxury of being grief stricken. I was thankful my son had the wisdom to tell me what his father would not.

Finally I'd found the strength to be free, to feel free. I had no intentions of being the mistress to my ex! He had a wife and she wasn't me. I am sure that neither of us had the desire to be a sister wife. I wished her well in my heart and thanked her for my freedom. How low could my self-esteem be? Not that low. How sad. I, the real determined juggler, had failed at one very important thing. My self-esteem had suffered too long and had gone unnoticed. I, "Little Miss Intelligent," needed a reality check in herself. I had hidden behind her for too long. I realized that I had not failed at all. The only failure is "the failure to try." I had tried. That I knew, I had done.

In review, I did all I could to keep her alive. After resuscitating her so many times she was about to take my breath away. Only I had the power of attorney to discontinue her life support and let her die an honorable death. I will always love you but never miss you. May we never meet again? Rest in peace, little Miss Intelligent. Because of you "A Strong Black Woman" has emerged. Like a breathtakingly beautiful butterfly I had to transform into what God intended for me to be. In no time I was ready to fly away never to return to that second stage caterpillar or any of the four stages in the life cycle of a butterfly.

I felt that my son had pulled the plug on my "brave wave." Yes, my brave wave needed checking up. I was brave in every way, except brave enough to be free. I could not afford to invest any more time in this waiting game some people wanted to play.

Have you ever wondered: does a butterfly realize it used to be a caterpillar, disgustingly crawling around on the ground? If it could, would it speed up the process, anxious to have wings and take flight? Does it ever long for the "good old days of rolling in the dust while taking a risk of being trampled on by some careless person or gobbled up by some greedy bird?" If it could live its life over, would it change anything?

By contrast, does a caterpillar know it will one day become so completely changed to a new creature? The caterpillar waits, crawling around eating leaves until that change has come. God had wrapped this caterpillar in a cocoon in preparation for it to be protected while it goes through the changes needed to reach the final stage.

I believe God had me in the same situation as the caterpillar waiting to be transformed. On the outside it would appear that the caterpillar is at rest in its cocoon. This is a lesson we can apply to ourselves. On the inside God is forever-changing us. At every stage in life, you'd better know who you are in him—God!

She was not dead after all—God had transformed her. I had the perfect little black knit dress for the occasion. It was a celebration of life. I put on my strapless black knit dress (with a low neckline and almost a disrespectful length above my knees). It could have easily been mistaken for a skirt. Up, too much thigh or down, too much cleavage. To pull it up or down was barely respectful on either end.

I believe God is with us in the calm and in the storm. People are the worst of God's creation when it comes to being patient.

Psalm 46:10: "Be still and know that I am God."

My sister Wilma was sometimes overprotective and too nosey but always my strong tower and best friend. I reported to her on all my "Wild Oats" adventures. She had to give her approval on my dress attire, places I went, and partying all night. She had to meet people I hung out with if possible. I would seek her advice sometimes after the fact. She and my brother-in-law must have prayed for me a lot.

One day after discussing a problem and how I had handled it, I heard her say to my brother-in-law, "See there, Ed, I told you, my sister was smart enough to know how to take care of herself." It was obvious they were looking out for me. She approved mostly everything I did because she understood that in time I would settle down.

The devil is a liar. She'd say, "I knew you would be all right." (Besides Lauretta, she and Ed added two sons to the family—James Jr. and Stephen.

My greatest concern was dating again. Since I had married at eighteen, I didn't know much about being single. When a man asked me if I was married, I found it hard to say no. For about the next two to three years, I tried the nightclubs in town.

Smoking, alcohol, and drugs were a definite no-no for me. I refused to keep company with anyone who did. I had grown up in a home where no alcohol was consumed. My ex-husband had not consumed alcohol or drugs. It was easy for me to continue to practice that lifestyle. I chose natural high of feeling good about myself.

I wore that little black dress out. Every time I sent it to the dry cleaners, it came back labeled "skirt." No telling how much money I saved on having a dress mistaken for a skirt. My children became my parents at times questioning my whereabouts. I'm sure they worried about me sometimes. I started taking them to plays at Fisk University. By this time, they were all adults and attending classes at TSU. My eldest son was married. They remained vigilant but calmed down after they realized I was merely having fun.

I loved to dance, and there were times my running buddies and I would stay out dancing all times of night. I enjoyed going to plays. So my calendar was full sometimes—Thursday through Sunday going to plays at TPAC, TSU, Fisk, and Vanderbilt University. I became a great supporter of the arts. Sowing my Wild Oats would seem like Sunday school to some by comparison.

My most fun time was when I went to see Bo Diddly at the Exit End one night. Alone, I parked almost in the front door. Arriving last, there was standing room only. After recent surgery, I couldn't stand for too long.

I went to the first person who looked like an employee and explained my situation. He went backstage and brought out a chair. He took me to a table in front of the stage and asked the occupants (two white men and a lady), "Do you mind sharing this table with her?" Immediately they all said, "Oh no, we'd be glad to have her." Almost immediately, they started wanting to buy me drinks. Of course I turned them down.

The show got started. They began to ask me questions about Mr. Diddly. At first I thought, *I don't know any more about this man than you guys.* Then I realized they thought I was with Mr. Diddly. I got the royal treatment that night. Here I am suddenly famous. I couldn't risk being seen getting into that little red car at the front door.

I decided to hang out a few minutes. I got the great opportunity to share this interesting experience with the entertainer. We both had a great laugh. By that time, most people had left, and I was able to get in my car and leave unnoticed and leave the fame behind.

It seems like I had conditioned myself to rushing around and trying to meet everyone's demands and schedules. I was preconditioned to discussing with someone else when it came to big decisions, like buying a house or car.

One day while stuck in traffic in route to the building site of our new home, I felt a calmness flood over me, and peace overcame me in such a way that I no longer felt the stress of life when I was raising my children and trying to get them to places while trying to fulfill all the other responsibilities. I really could slow down and smell the roses. My only minor child sat in the passenger seat. My only responsibility was to him and myself. I felt good about myself.

Chapter Thirty-Three
Traveling Shoes

So many people put off traveling until "the children get grown." My ex-husband would use that excuse more time than once. I strongly believe the opposite. Great family memories can be made while traveling. I am glad for the trips we took (the boys and I) together. Trips with my sisters and brothers to Lookout Mountain, to my brother's home in Ohio, and to Buffalo and Niagara Falls will always be great memories as we view pictures that captured those memories.

Later we would follow my son Andre and wife Chiquilla to West Virginia, Baltimore, and Pennsylvania as his career moved him to these places. He became a tour guide for us each time we visited him. Because of his love for museums and landmarks, we have been accompanied by him as a family to see Three Rivers Stadium located at the connecting of the Monongahela, Ohio, and Susquehanna Rivers and the Liberty Bell in Philadelphia, the Statue of Liberty, and eating at our favorite restaurant in New York City (Sylvia's in Harlem). We enjoyed riding the subway blending with the New Yorkers as we toured New York City and waited in a drizzling rain to see the ball drop on Time Square on New Year's Eve in 1995.

I have great memories of my adventurous trip with a friend who was a new truck driver at that time. We took about a two-week journey and that in itself could be added to my Wild Oats chapter. I really got to know what life on the road as a truck driver is like. I gained a better understanding of those eighteen-wheelers and learned to respect them by not pulling out in front of them and slowing down. I learned why we needed to give them all the respect due when we visited those mandatory weigh in stations.

One time as I was about to climb down out of the cab, I heard someone announce over their CB radio, "Hey, all you good buddies, there's a lot lizard out on the parking lot." Immediately I crawled back inside wondering, "What kind of animal was that?" I sat there with wide eyes in anticipation of some kind of slimy green monster, with big black eyes bulging out. While waiting on my fellow trucker to return to the truck, I found out that that "Lizard," not a real lizard on four legs, it still might have been as dangerous as I thought. I made every attempt not to be left alone until we left that truck stop.

We covered about fifteen states from Tennessee to California, Oregon, Washington State, and I don't know how many thousands of miles. Listen up, all you two- and four-wheelers (and such). I learned that most truckers are not rude and trying to run you off the road. They have very heavy loads and even more a great responsibility to deliver literally your life to you daily. If it were not for these dedicated men and women who have given up the comforts that we take for granted, we would be in deep trouble without them. So stay out of the way and let the big trucks roll on. They may be delivering something you need or trying to get home to see family after weeks on the road. Thanks to all.

My sisters Wilma, Helen, and I decided to visit a nearby casino in Indiana. It was less than three hours away. We started eating right after filling the gas tank. When we got out of Davison County, we were so excited we laughed and talked until we realized that we were about two or three hours past our destination. We didn't care.

Wilma was my best traveling partner, both at home and abroad. We would start giggling like little children whenever we had a chance to take a trip, usually slipping off from Helen and Bernice. We would laugh and eat all the way to our destination. We were traveling before the convenience of a GPS. Plenty of times, we got lost, but that was just part of the fun. A trip is not a trip if you don't get lost sometimes.

We visited Wilma's daughter Lauretta in Germany while my nephew (Samuel Thomas Sr.) was on military duty. Also, her first grandson Samuel Thomas Jr. (TJ) was only about three or four weeks old. We decided to plan a trip to Europe and to see the new baby TJ. Lauretta planned all our tours ahead of time. All we had to do was get there.

In January 1991, we had one of the biggest snow falls in years. We were not about to let that snow or anything else delay us. Our tours to other countries was already scheduled as soon as we arrived in Germany. We presented to BNA (Nashville airport) at the appointed time only to find that our flight was delayed. They told us that our connecting flight would leave Atlanta before our plane landed. They suggested we return home and fly out in two days. No. No. No. We would not bulge. We waited on the delayed plane, and sure enough when we arrived in Atlanta, our beloved Lufthansa flight was gone. We spent the night in a hotel without luggage.

We were happy to be on our way. The next day, we flew from Atlanta to Cincinnati and then to Frankfurt, Germany, where we boarded a smaller plane to where my niece was living.

We were barely in Germany before we were on a bus headed out to another country. We visited ten countries including the United Kingdom. The jet lag was unreal. When we were not sightseeing, we were sleeping or asking, "What time is it?"

We had a wonderful time. We ate Wiener schnitzel while in Germany, and real waffles in Belgium. We visited Amsterdam (while sneaking pictures) in the Red District. We viewed the mountains and castles in Switzerland. One of the funniest things about being in a foreign country was knowing a little of the language enough to use the money and other necessities like going in the right bathroom. I was in charge of the money.

One night while taking a break at a restaurant in the Black Forest, we both needed a bathroom break. We had so many packages from shopping that day we decided to take turns since the bathroom was on the lower level of the building. Wilma ran down the steps and returned too quickly. Dancing around, she announced, "Girl, I forgot which one is for girls." Well, we both made it in the "nick of time." One thing I really did appreciate while in Europe was the cleanliness of the bathroom facilities.

When we were on a ship returning from London (an overnight journey), most people were seasick because of the turbulent water. It was so choppy that you could be standing on one side of the room, and unless you held on, you would literally slide to the other side. That ship was rocking. There were a few people who didn't seem to be bothered by the choppy waters. Wilma and I were among the few who spent the night on the dance floor of the ship's nightclub. We danced while sliding side to side before "the electric slide" was popular.

One of the only times, I should say the only time we were left to babysit TJ, I can only say that while Lauretta was gone all day. We never moved while she was gone. We slept, and the baby slept like he had jet lag too. Thank the Lord he didn't need anything, and we didn't offer him anything. Not even a bottle or dry diaper was offered. It seemed like he knew it was best for him to be cool and all that; he didn't even whimper.

Chapter Thirty-Four
Business Ventures: What about James Sr.?

You asked me about James? Sure I'm glad you did. I met James while purchasing a one room air filter for my infant granddaughter's room. He was sent to me by a friend. He had, "just the right filter." Air and water filters was his business at the time. Our friendship continued because of similar interest and background. I was led into this human spider web because of a nice little motorcycle, I thought belonged to him. I really had not gotten over having been a biker chick in the not-too-distance past. He learned through my friend that I might like to ride the motorcycle sometimes. He also had learned that I was dating someone much younger than him. A cougar, I was. He pretended not to be interested in a relationship. In the meantime, we started hanging out and having fun.

I liked the idea that no club was involved in the motorcycle riding. It turned out he was a newly divorced business owner (living in his office), a homeless Christian man. Being his own boss and was available to ride and travel whenever I was, became attractive. I liked having someone with that kind of freedom. I said freedom, not cash.

Soon I met his mother, Mrs. Bessie Hurt and his brother Thomas. Eventually I met his five adult children.

Right away, he told his mother about this younger man I was dating. She said, "Well, son, don't you think you could beat that young man's time?" Finally, I had met someone who was interested in the things I enjoyed. We enjoyed spending weekends at Mama Bessie's where she was strict about sleeping arrangements. I loved this lady. My second mother. Turns out that, when the younger man caught up with my game he was ready to throw in the towel. He was not having that. After one deep breath, a hug and a hardy laugh, we decided to remain, "just friends." I had no time to waste. I was just having fun!

James and I eventually decided to start a business selling school supplies. I had no experience in business. He did the leg work of marketing and selling school supplies. We became members of the Chamber of Commerce and the National School Supply and Equipment Association (NSSEA). In this organization, we traveled all over the United States attending conferences or hauling child care supplies. I went to the local meeting of the Chamber of Commerce and was active in visiting the Public School System biannually.

It would take another book to tell all the many adventures we had from running into forest fires, tumble weeds and dust storms in the deserts from California, Arizona and Texas to trying to drive in a whiteout in Minnesota.

We acquired a little motor home that was used for my nursing conferences as well as the school supply business. We set up several child care centers. Many times after a conference, James started driving and would not wake me up until we were in the middle of a body of water like the James River in Virginia following a nursing conference. Usually he'd say, "Baby, you better come up here and look," To watch the sunrise or sunset while overlooking the Atlantic or Pacific Ocean was awesome. We enjoyed a different lifestyle as part-time RVer's. James made sure I learned to drive the "Big truck and RV." Stating, "Anything that you own; you should know how to operate it." That was good advice.

After a nursing conference, we stayed overnight at Cades Cove in the Smokey's. It was very calm and peaceful when we woke up the next morning. We were almost snowbound. Few roads were open because of the snow. We were able to drive out, but it wasn't easy. What a surprise! We were not used to snow in April.

We started fishing and hanging out on a houseboat on the local lakes.

We met people who lived in their houseboats year round. It was a cool lifestyle. I enjoyed it part time.

James was performing as a disc jockey (DJ) when I first met him. He was the best, but it was hard for him to cut it off, and he would end up getting on my nerves long after the show was over. He is still quite loquacious, but I have learned to turn him off or change the station.

We were compatible in many ways. He was willing to do things that I liked (Broadway plays in New York City, traveling etc.). I was willing to ride the motorcycle with him. Finally he confessed that the motorcycle belonged to his son. He eventually bought one that was larger and more suitable for the two of us to ride. I was ready for adventures outside my usual box. Things he liked were hayrides, helicopter rides over the Great Smoky Mountains and Grand Canyon, motorcycles / car races, and rodeos. We have climbed mountains, explored caves and too many things to mention here.

During the time we traveled to business conferences, we never networked together. Rarely would you see the two of us together. Once James was surprised to see me in a fenced-in area. He was standing at the fence. Tapping me on the shoulder, he asks "Hey. What are you doing in there?"

"What does it look like I'm doing? Getting ready to race." I was down on all fours holding an armadillo getting ready to race against five others. We had to follow behind them on our knees, encouraging them to keep going. We were in Texas; I won a certificate and a can of Road Kill.

Another time, I surprised him on stage singing "My Endless Love." He was a bit outdone. He realized I was unpredictable. We went to Saint Thomas, U.S. Virgin Island, to a conference, one I enjoyed most. We met a lot of interesting people including the governor.

This is my memoir, not James's. We have a lot of real cool memories.

I have to tell this. We had a large box truck. James put it in the shop for repair. He asked me to carry him to pick it up. Listen up, all you men. He was criticizing my driving. Upon opening his big mouth the third time, he said, "Baby, just pull over. Let me out." I did as I was told. He began to walk around the back of my car as I pulled off.

When we saw each other again, James was pretty tired and sweaty from walking in the hot sun. He pointed his finger at me and said, "Baby, if I ever talk about your driving or ask you to let me out, kick me where I sit down. I thought you were going to let me drive?"

I looked at him and said, "I did let you drive. I let you out to drive the truck."

"But we were a long way from the shop," he said.

"I know, but you the one ask to get out. Should have waited."

We are still traveling companions and BFFs. He doesn't complain about my driving anymore. I elected not to continue these business ventures since I feel like it is too demanding. I have worked hard enough, and owning a business requires 24/7, 365 days a year. He relocated and continued as a clever businessman today.

The funniest thing that happened was when he decided to teach me how to shoot. We were spending the weekend with Mama Bessie. James loaded the rifle. We headed out a short distance from the house. He set a can on a stump. Handing me the gun, he said, "Baby, see if you can hit that."

Taking the gun, I played dumb. I held it up and said, "Uh, which eye do I look out of?"

He started to take the gun. "Hold on. Hold on," I said, motioning him to stand back. I raised that rifle and bam. One shot, I split the can in half. He set a piece up again. "Now hit that," he directed. I was getting tickled and couldn't hold back. I hit every time he told me to. I was laughing so loud.

Scratching his head, James took the gun, and we started back to the house, passing Tom who was in the shed. "What in the world was going on? What was so funny?" he asked. James just kept going. I was too tickle to talk.

Finally I asked, "James, I thought I told you my husband and I used to hunt. I bought most of his guns and rifles as presents. He always made sure I knew how to shoot. He'd say, "You might have to shoot me one day." James was shell-shocked from that day. He still does not talk about "what happened in the woods," that day. I think that is "male ego."

Chapter Thirty-Five
Spirit and Family

I joined Faith Is the Victory Church around 1992 because it was closer to me, and I enjoyed the teaching. At first when I would worship there, tears would stream down my face, and I could not control them. I felt that was God's way of cleansing my spirit that had been wounded in times past.

Soon after joining this congregation, I enrolled in the Bible school. At that time, my sweet mother had been in a nursing home suffering from Alzheimer's disease. She had lost her memory and didn't know who I was. When I visited her, I sang her favorite songs and then prayed with her (asking her permission). I prayed, asking God that when he did take her home, I would be able to speak at her funeral.

Less than a month after starting Bible school class, God called her home. I spoke to my Pastor, Dr. Charles Cowen before the funeral and told him my desire. He prayed with me. The day of the funeral, I gave the family tribute; and afterward, my friend James Hurt and I sang a duet. My brothers and sisters had doubted that I would be able to do it. They looked directly at me the whole time smiling. You could see the peace my speaking and singing brought to them in a time of grief. To God be the glory.

After four years of attending Life Christian Bible Institute, I graduated as a member of the Charter Class of 2010. During that time of my ministry practicum, I was active in the nursery / preschool ministry at my church, and I sung with the chancel choir at John Wesley United Methodist Church where my sister, Mrs. S. Bernice Heard, was director. I have appeared in two Easter Drama Performances.

After working at Baptist Hospital for twenty-five years, I retired at the age of fifty-five. My former employer and coworkers gave me a retirement party that was fitting for the occasion. My goal was not to retire but to work at something different.

For about two years, I worked with my businesses (a temporary staffing business, the school supply business and a barbecue restaurant in partnership with George Patterson and his wife Colleen. Imagine me the one who still struggles to prepare a meal, owning an "Eatery."

One day I was visiting our restaurant. (Justine's Southern BBQ) I was basically doing a walk through, when I heard someone say "Excuse me Miss, do you mind fixing me a fish sandwich?" Turning to look I saw a very distinguished looking elderly gentleman with an enormous smile. I thought, *he must be flirting*. Smiling back, I said in my sweetest and most excusatory voice.

"Yes, I do mind. Sir, I'm sorry I can't."

Shocked he said, "You do mind? You can't? Well aren't you the owner?"

Hearing the commotion George landed on me like an angel and took over the conversation.

"Trust me. You don't want Mrs. Holt to fix you a fish sandwich. She's the owner, not the cook." Bowing his head, he continued. "Now what can I do for you sir?"

Thankful that George had rescued me once more, I made my exit from the building. That gentleman became a frequent customer. He never ask me to serve him again; not even a canned soda.

Top of the Line VIP Staffing immersed me into the Spanish speaking culture and a second language. I taught Alcohol Awareness classes for servers and business owners. I learned enough of the language to be able to teach in Spanish using videos in both languages.

Often I made mistakes in speaking Spanish which allowed the students in the class to have fun correcting the instructor. By 2001 Top of the Line VIP Staffing had offices in Atlanta Georgia and Nashville. However, the events of 9/11 paid its toll on many small businesses including ours.

During that time, I gave a speech to a fraternity at Austin Peay State University on the subject of alcohol and how it relates to college students. When I began to give some statics about accidents caused by alcohol and intoxication, I noticed one young man in the group who obviously was about to "bust out laughing." I thought. What, have I said something wrong? I kept on until the end of my lecture. After a standing ovation I opened up for discussion.

The young man who was still laughing, came to me. He said, "Mrs. Holt, what you described was exactly what happened on another campus where I was a student. Our fraternity had a party and we served alcohol. We had bicycles located throughout the campus free for students to ride. The day after the party, wracked bicycles were all over the campus. Not even one could be ridden." I had given information about bicycle accidents related to alcohol. The young man continued. "I was thinking about that party. We must have added to the numbers of that statistics in one party."

I worked part time in the clinic of a correctional center. I enjoyed every minute but felt like God had me there only for a season. I noticed right away that the nurses' language was as foul as the inmates'. Used to more professionalism, I could not tolerate that kind of language.

After an unwelcome few weeks being there, I decided that someone must address the problem, or I would have to leave. God, being my leader, had not given the clearance (to leave) I was seeking. I spoke to my boss and asked to have a meeting with the staff. I did most of the talking, and it did not go well with them. I met strong resistance. I made an agreement with the nurses that every time I hear someone swear, I would say, "Praise the Lord or Jesus." One nurse told me, "We are in the f***king jail." I said, "I know, honey. We are in it but not of it. We should not conform to what we hear around us but try to uplift people." It is possible even in the jail.

As nurses, we are here to give medical care, not to punish anyone. I have cared for people accused of some of the most horrific crimes. It is hard. I had to be nonjudgmental and care for them like I would anyone. I am not the judge. Keeping my agreement that "calling on Jesus each time they swore, things had to change and Satan had to flee."

I started taking my portable PA system, microphone and a few sound tracks on Sundays. I learned some of the nurses could sing very well. Sundays were a little bit slower. We started singing inside that jail and lifting our voices to God in praise. One nurse came to me during one of our praise sessions and stated, "Miss. Sylvia, I don't know what has come over me. I feel something all over me. I have never felt this way before." She kept rubbing her arms with tears in her eyes. I explained it is the anointing of the Holy Spirit even in this jail.

Those nurses who had the foulest of mouths and resisted my call meeting the most began to call out to me at the end of the day; they repented. Many times I left before the rest of the staff. One by one, they began to show their love for me by calling out to me on my way out. "I love you, Miss. Sylvia. I'll see you tomorrow. We love you." Praise God I felt like Paul and Silas must have felt when those prison gates swung open. Praise God from whom all blessings flow.

The whole atmosphere in that jail clinic changed. I stayed there until around 2003 when God gave me clearance to move on. My boss asked me, "How much can we pay you to stay with us?" I smiled and told him, "Nothing, sir. I thank you, but I have received clearance. Confirmation from above. My time is up."

I am thankful for many good experiences there. I could not leave without permission. I know it was an assignment from God. I know what he can do.

May 2003 I started a very rewarding journey at the Veteran's Affairs Hospital in Nashville Tennessee. My experience there has been like no other place I have worked. The appreciation I received from caring for the men and women who have served our country is indescribable.

On December 31th 2015 (long past my retirement age), I made a decision to retire again. My career caring for veterans ended formally after twelve and a half years. I will continue to pray diligently for our men and women on active duty and our veterans. A lifetime learner, I don't know at the moment what the next venture will be. I refuse to be idle.

My Tribute
Keep History Alive in the Museums

Whether we make an effort to move on or stand still, history will be made simply by the passing of time. I thank God for those people who chose to be movers and shakers in the past, the present, and the future. What would the Civil Rights Movement have been like without the brave men and women who fought for justice? These leaders dedicated their lives to ending slavery, segregation, and unfair treatment.

I want to pay a special tribute and to thank all these great people. Not all those who fought have ended up in our history books and documentaries or with their names on streets signs. We know that there are many behind the scenes who have gone unnoticed and unheard of. There are many great men and women who stood in the background and placed themselves in harm's way so that someone else could say mission is accomplished. A building when it is completed, we see the brick and mortar on the outside, but the frame and footing that holds it to be erect cannot be seen. These are the people I want to talk about in my tribute to the progress that we as a nation have experienced.

If I were to call names today, such as Mary McLeod Bethune, a black / colored woman who was born to former slaves, most of you would agree that we have at least heard of her. The fifteenth of seventeen children, she was the first child in the family to be born not a slave. Her interest in education led her to become known as a leader in opening opportunities for children of color to get an education. She became a special advisor of minority affairs to Pres. Franklin Delano Roosevelt and was cofounder of Bethune-Cookman College.

Come closer to home and let me remind you of the great men and women who single-handedly in many cases managed our little one-room school houses that spread out around the rural areas of Dickson County, Tennessee. People such as Miss. Mae Etta Dansby, Mr. J.O. Dickson, Mrs. Fannie Horner, Mrs. Tommy Gilbert, Mr. Ersley Van Leer, and Miss Ollie Huddleston, the last teacher to teach at the Promise Land School near Charlotte Tennessee. These dear souls were not only principals, but they were teachers of every subject and grade, first through eighth grade, including special education because even then they believed in the idea of Inclusion and "no child should be left behind." They were guidance counselors, coaches and heads of the athletics department, and school nurses all in one.

These ladies and gentlemen were the custodians, chief of the Department of Sanitation and Environmental Services. In other words, they made the fire and kept it roaring, called the roll, and kept on going. With no running water, they made sure that everyone washed their hands after going to an outside toilet and before eating lunch. School was fun; it was safe, and no one called 911. Their only assistants were the older students.

Our dear Miss Ollie also had to walk at least a mile or two from the highway to get to the school after catching a ride with the mail carrier. These teachers were brilliant because they didn't have the best tools for teaching. They were creative and did their best with what they had.

A word on bringing a gun to school. If you did, you would have been aiming at that rattlesnake and copperhead hanging around in the back field! That's why the big stick hung out next to the front door.

With our elementary foundation laid, the brilliant and creative principals and teachers of Hampton High School would continue to hone and to mold and make us at the only high school in the county for secondary education of the colored population in Dickson County and some of the surrounding counties until 1965.

Then if I were to mention a lady by the name of Rosa Parks, we know that she was a colored seamstress who was arrested for refusing to give up her seat on the bus to whites in Montgomery Alabama. Her actions brought seventeen thousand colored residents together which led to over a yearlong, "bus boycott." She became known as Mother of the Civil Rights Movement.

We didn't have public transportation in Dickson County. I want to pay respect to those bus drivers of the Dickson County School System, both black and white, because there were poor white people and black people who needed to go to school. I thank God for those who got up early in the morning to get little white boys and girls and little black boys and girls to school safely (even in times of a segregated system) and back home. They recognized the importance of education, and I would say a job well done. Our thanks to Mr. B.

Driver, Mr. Bill Gilbert, Mr. Spicer, and I am sure there are other names that should be on the list.

I am truly thankful for the late Rev. Dr. Martin Luther King Jr. We simply do not have time to give credit to this extraordinary leader. He is best known for his nonviolence approach. He organized demonstrations, marches, boycotts, strikes, and voters' registrations and eventually lost his life for the cause. He spent time in jail where he wrote some of his most famous speeches from behind bars. For example, his letter from the Birmingham Jail. One of my favorite of his speeches is the "I Have a Dream" speech.

I want to honor those great leaders of Dickson County who also had dreams. People such as Prof. A.J. Hardy and Prof. Larry Pendergrass. We owe the utmost respect to teachers such as Miss Imogene Springer; she was an excellent physical education teacher and pianist. Mrs. Susie Nesbitt for her home economics and life in general insights and her gentle way of ushering young girls into homemaking and society.

Mrs. Beverly Gilbert-Williams (business education teacher) who still blesses me today when I am writing on my computer using the home-row keys. Thanks to Mrs. Janie Nesbitt for driving to Dickson five days a week; often she might have a few students to pick up on the way.

Thanks to Mrs. Ella B. Pendergrass for introducing me to the music of Johann Sebastian Bach and a love of the arts (so much that I named my firstborn for the famous composer). And I might add, she taught me a few words of French too.

I thank God for Mrs. Goggins and Prof. Harold Gilbert for their leadership in the music department of marching bands. Mr. D. B. Fuller who taught our young men in the Trades department. Thank you Mr. Reed Evans who led the Hampton High School Trojans on a journey in football that gave us dignity as a high school and opportunities to have fun screaming and dancing whether winning or losing.

To Mr. Donald Corlew; you did your best to teach us algebra and trigonometry too. It's just that by the time I enrolled in college at the age of thirty and with three children of my own, I had a hard time recalling. "Just what was it that you had taught me?" But I made it. I have a degree in nursing from the University of Tennessee where most of my classmates were younger and whiter than me. My first chemistry and biology labs were on that campus. I'm proud to be a "Big Orange."

The Little Rock Nine were the first black teenagers to attend an all-white Central High School in Little Rock Arkansas, in 1957. These remarkable young African-American students challenged segregation in the Deep South and won. But it was not easy. On the first day of school, the governor of Arkansas ordered the state's National Guard to block the black students from entering the school. President Eisenhower finally had to send the federal troops to protect the students.

Let me remind some and introduce to others that in 1961, a group of young students from Hampton High School (under the leadership of Prof. Larry Pendergrass, Rev. Dalton Holt, Mr. Thomas Nesbitt, and other leaders whom I do not remember) attempted to enroll in two all-white high schools in Dickson County. These students became known as the Courageous Six. These students were all seniors and due to graduate the next year. Thank you to those young women (Joann Lanier, Josephine Robertson, the late Peggy Jean Evans, Patricia Driver, Roberta Russ, and the only young man in the group, the late Bobby L. Holt). Although they were denied this privilege, it was a catalyst for change in the county that would end peacefully. Beginning with the elementary grades first, by 1965, all grades were integrated.

During that time, different groups organized, and soon the lunch counters and restaurants became integrated. Therefore, I want to thank those men and women, both black and white, of the county of Dickson Tennessee, during that time. We didn't make national news. Who would have been interested in a peaceful transformation?

I am thankful for a few black business owners who provided services to the African-American citizens prior to that time. I may not remember all names. They owned barber shops, beauty shops, restaurants and dance halls. These business men and women contributed a great deal to Dickson County. Names I remember are Mr. Theodore Nesbitt, Mr. Sam Hannah, Mr. Ralph Holt, Mrs. Vera Van Leer, Mrs. Daisy Moody and Mr. Hurley Clark. Mr. Hubert Thompson a blind gentleman and Mrs. Mollie sold Watkins products door to door.

We must take our hats off to a few good cooks by the names of Sister Augusta Holt and Mrs. Polly Evans who walked out of a restaurant because their own black sons and daughters were refused service there. I am thankful for those leaders, both black and white, who recognized that it was a time for change and that it could be a peaceful one.

In October 1957, my research found that four schools in Dickson County were approved by the courts to receive $400,000 toward improvement. Hampton High School only got $40,000, which amounted to four new classrooms. So I tell you, I am thankful for those leaders who recognized the inequality in our school's buildings and grounds and that the second-hand books were not good enough. They recognized that old Jim Crow thinking of separate but equal was unacceptable, and it was wrong. Someone recognized all children, black or white, needed a real chemistry and biology labs so that they could grow up to be not only teachers but also lawyers, doctors, nurses, engineers, and politicians.

I am proud to bring my children, grandchildren, and friends here to see our legacy on display in the historic Promise Land Community and the Clement Railroad Museum. The Holbrook Hotel is home to the CRHM and birth place of former Governor Frank G. Clement. He was considered a moderate on civil rights who courageously sent the National Guards and State police officers to Clinton Tennessee in 1956 to break up crowds protesting the integration of schools. I am sure that did not set well with many people at that time. Tennessee and Dickson County, was way ahead of many southern states and communities. I am proud to show off the history of our past. Dickson County, a family of people who stood up for righteousness.

Our parents cannot be forgotten for bringing us up in a loving way. We had, most of all, love from our families and their belief in "love thy neighbor as thyself." I am thankful that we as a nation have come from a long, long way. But we still have a long way to go. I encourage you to support these organizations and spread the news. Our children and their children can be proud for generations to come of the roots of their existence on display at the Clement Railroad Museum in Dickson Tennessee, and the efforts of the Promise Land Community Heritage Association for its preservation of a historically black community.

Like Dr. Martin Luther King Jr., I to have a dream. My dream is that someday we will forget about the color of our skin and look deep inside ourselves and see who God created in us, that we will look closer and be thankful for our differences that makes us more alike. My dream is that I leave this world a better place for my children, grandchildren, and generations to come. We should refuse to judge each other by the color of our skin. Satan has deceived the entire human race by using the color of our skin to divide and conquer. It is still at work for him today. How can we believe 1 John 4:20 if we can't love one another? How on earth can we love God?

My dream is that one day, as our flag of red, white, and blue streams from sea to shining sea, we will realize that "the earth is the Lord's," then we can be proud to sing, "God Bless America."

As we continue our struggle for justice, let us pray for every nation and its leaders around the world. We cannot afford to be divided in our fight for justice. Let us be proud of what we know about our ancestors and be proud to be Americans no matter what race. Let us purpose in our hearts a forgiving nature as God so generously has forgiven us.

And in closing, I proclaim that the journey has not been easy for me; and the struggle, for many of us, has been "more than a Sabbath Day's journey from the Promise Land."

The end.

REBELLIOUS

R - Rebellious to me is to realize that I have my own mind.

E - Educating myself about the reality of life and time.

B - Bombarding my mind with my own desire and thoughts.

E - Eventually being able to sort out and process.

L - Language of my own heart, my own desire.

L - Language in my own voice.

I - It matters what I think. What I desire. How I create my;

O - Own heart and thoughts of right and wrong.

U - Unselfishly, I live my life, living below my means

S - So someone else can be nourished to accomplish their own dreams.

Rebellious. Yes, that is what I mean. Rebellious should be everyone's dream.

Educate your mind. Be brave enough to let it be known that you have a voice.

Life is too short here on earth to live in someone else's world.

So live out loud. Yes, make a noise. It's OK to shout. Let your voice be heard.

Within and without. That's what it's all about.

Everyone has one. An opinion. Because you own it does not make it wrong or right.

It just means that you are alive in your own right.

Rebellious from the day I was born. Rebellious is my right.

Rebellious should never lead to trouble. It is what makes us a piece of this great big puzzle.

The world in its integrity. No two pieces are or should be alike. But they all fit together.

And that's what makes it right.

Sylvia Edmondson-Holt

Mrs. Lizzie Edmondson and Mrs. Essie Gilbert. Circa, 1985.

Jaime Holt Diego in New York City for New Year's Eve. 2015.

Sylvia Edmondson-Holt

Promise Land School closing 1957. Front: Hattie Edmondson, Birdie Robertson, Back Helen Edmondson Hughes, Lorenzy Robertson, and Sylvia Edmondson-Holt.

Retirement Party, 1999 after twenty-five years (at Baptist Hospital) Critical Care Registered Nurse. Terrell Holt Jr. Jaime Holt. Second row: Kevin Holt, Toshebia Cato-Holt, Sylvia Edmondson-Holt, and Terrell Holt Sr. Back: Shawn Cato.

No. 10. A business trip to Virgin Islands. Sylvia Edmondson-Holt and James Hurt, 2002.

On piano: S. Bernice Heard. Front row: Sylvia Edmondson-Holt, Mary Edmondson, Helen Hughes, Beverly Williams, John Primm, and Hubert Robertson. Back: Wilma Talley. First Sunday in June Homecoming. Circa 1979.

Bobby and Sylvia Edmondson-Holt, 1986.

Ivy Maria Diego prays with Great-Grandma Sylvia Edmondson-Holt, 2016.

Brothers, L-R: James, O.C., W.C. Thomas, and Theodore Edmondson. Knelling Jewel and Robert Gilbert. CIRCA 1945.

Theodore Edmondson on guitar and S. Bernice Edmondson Heard on piano at the Edmondson home in Promise Land. Circa 1954.

Andre and Terrell Holt Sr. practicing karate. 1973.

My family after Wilma's funeral. Seated, L-R: Sheila Heard, Cynthia Edmondson, Helen Hughes, James Talley Sr., Lauretta Talley-Thomas, Lory Edmondson, and Bruce Edmondson. Second row: Alexis Heard, Samuel Thomas Jr. Second row right: Stephanie Blackwell, Lashonda Talley with baby, Ardis Edmondson-Holt, Fydencia Edmondson with daughter Tiniya. Back row: Gregory Heard, Danita Cromwell, Steven Talley, James Edmondson, S. Bernice Heard, Sylvia Edmondson-Holt, Jaime Holt-Diego, Kevin Holt, James Talley Jr., and David Holt.

Top three Edmondson sisters go blackberry picking. L-R: Sylvia Edmondson-Holt, Helen Edmondson Hughes, and Wilma Edmondson Talley.

Seated: Andrea A. Lawful-Sanders, Chiquilla Holt. Standing: Gold medal recipient Candice Holt, Roslyn Smith, and Camille Holt 2014.

Front god-grandmother: Mrs. Ruth Howard. L-R: Chiquilla, Camille, Candice, Grandmother Sylvia Edmondson-Holt, and Andre Holt. Congressional Gold Medal awards (Candice and Camille), Washington DC 2014.

Bobby Lane Holt, Kevin Lane Holt, and Jaime Lane Holt, 1990.

Terrell Holt Jr. and Mikayla Holt in New York City, New Year's Day, 2016.

Sylvia Edmondson-Holt, 2000.

L-R Chiquilla Knox Holt, Mrs. Rebecca Owens, Sylvia Edmondson-Holt and Andre Holt 1989 A wedding party.

Michael E Crutcher, Sr. (www.spiritoffrederickdouglass.com) Frederick Douglas historical presentations was at the Promise Land Festival June 2016. Pictured with author Sylvia Edmondson-Holt.

Pictured in front of the Promise Land School. L-R Mrs. Mansfield (Mrs. Lincoln) Author Sylvia Edmondson-Holt and John Mansfield (President Lincoln) at the festival June 2016. For engagements A. Lincoln e-mail: johnaslincoln@live.com Phone 615-269-4303.

Cousin Vernon Holt of, The Dynamic Dixie Travelers (Praising God in Songs) with Author Sylvia Edmondson-Holt at the Promise Land Festival June 2016(For booking call 615-227-8922).

L-R Terrell Holt Jr. Great Grand Mommy Lizzie Edmondson and Briana Heard. Circa 1989.

Ivy Larue Dobson and Sister Jaime Holt Diego at the rodeo. Circa 1995.

Dominic Dobson, Jaime Holt Diego and (Top) Ivy Larue Dobson 2011.

Wilma Edmondson Talley and Sylvia Edmondson-Holt at Three Rivers Stadium in Pittsburg Pa. Circa 1989.

Sitting James Talley and Wilma Edmondson Talley, Helen Edmondson Hughes and back is Sylvia Edmondson-Holt. At a Hampton High School reunion. Circa 1992.

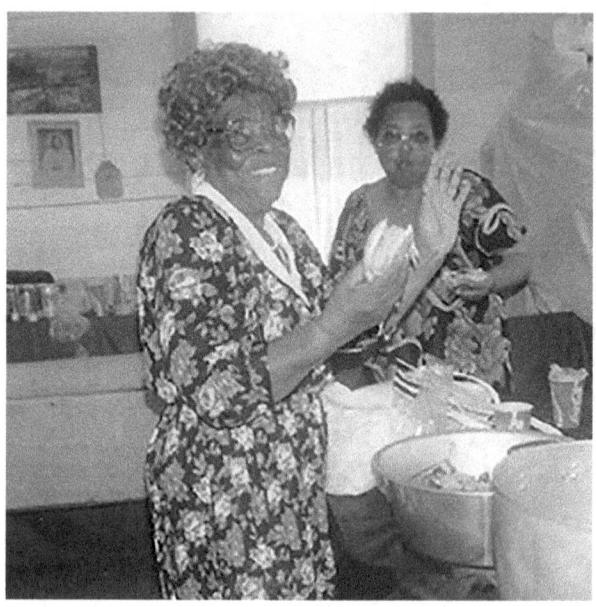

Front Aunts Essie V. Gilbert and Betty Ruth Edmondson at the Promise Land School. Serving dinner at a Frist Sunday in June celebration. Circa 1970's. Aunt Essie turned 100 years old 2016.

L-R Front Ronnie Mayberry, Kevin Holt, Second row Andre Holt, Keith Mayberry, Rex Mayberry Back Terrell Holt and Uncle Anthony Holt. At the home of grandparents Rev Dalton Holt and Sister Augusta Holt Christmas Circa 1974.

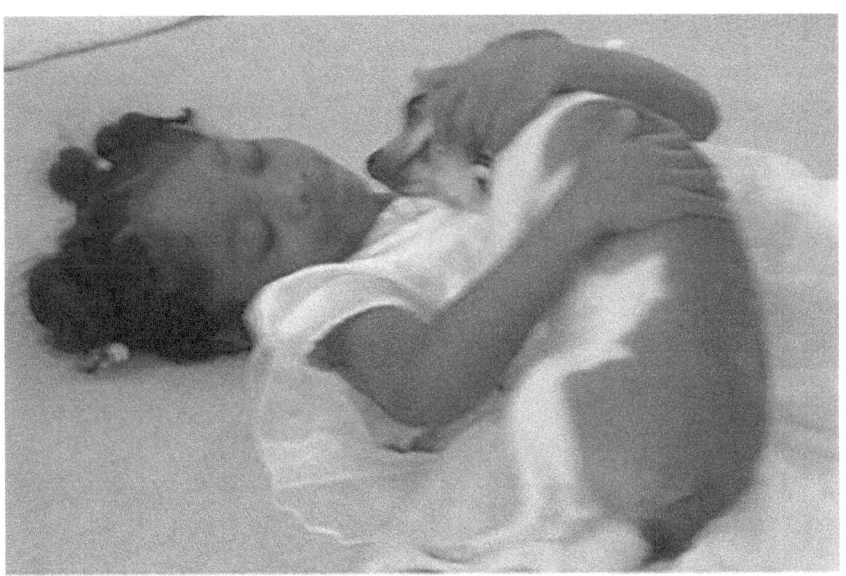

Mikayla Maria Holt at grandmother's home with Scratchy. Circa 2014.

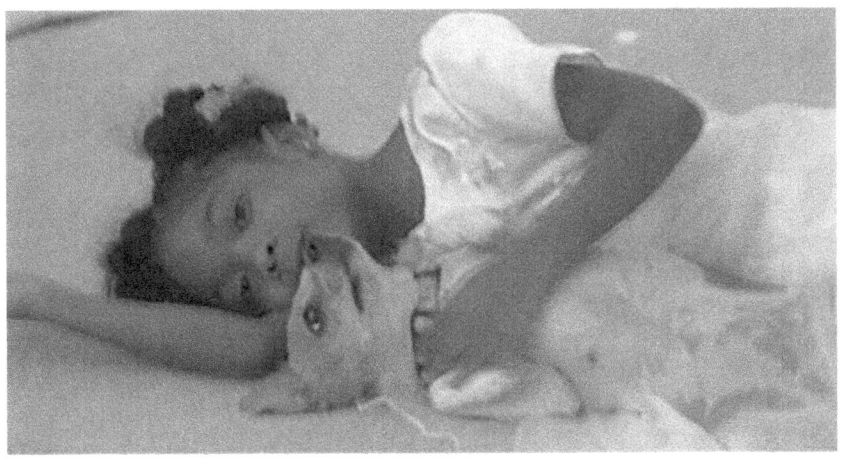

Mikayla Maria Holt and Scratchy, Circa 2014.

Sylvia Edmondson-Holt. Retirement from Baptist Hospital 1999.

Sylvia Edmondson-Holt with Kevin and Terrell Holt after graduation from Nursing School (The University of Tennessee) 1977.

Jaime Holt Diego Circa 1990. Jaime and daddy Kiven Holt rides in Barbie car.

Sylvia Edmondson-Holt

Candice and Camille Holt with Duke in the middle.
Duke licked Camille. Um not bad. Circa 1998 at grandmommy's home in Tennessee.

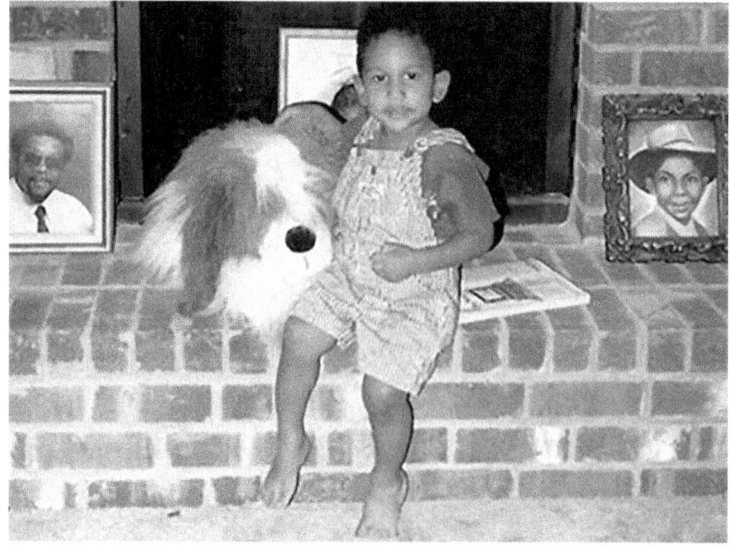

Terrell Johann Holt Jr.

Sylvia Edmondson-Holt

Kevin Holt in Worley Furnace TN.

Compliments of McCreary Studio (Est. 1939) 102 W. College St. Dickson Tn. 37056 (Ph. 615-812-0036)

Theodore Edmondson and the Promise Land Singers. At piano S. Bernice Heard. Standing L-R Mrs. Lizzie Edmondson (Manager) Beverley Gilbert Williams, Bro. Edmondson, Mary Nesbitt Edmondson and Wilma Edmondson Talley circa 1953 Could be heard on WSOK (now WVOL).

Mrs. Lizzie Edmondson and First Lady Mrs. Hattie Gilbert Bowen.
A Promise Land homecoming.

Rev. Jessie J. Bowen native and former pastor pictured on the Promise Land
Memorial Wall at Saint John Church

Sylvia Edmondson-Holt

Front L-R Jewel Gilbert, Thomas Edmondson. Second row standing Ruby Gilbert Robertson and Hattie Gilbert Bowen. And Robert Gilbert. Back row Theodore Edmondson, James Edmondson, O.C. Edmondson and Peonie Edmondson. Circa 1940s

A view inside Saint John Church in Promise Land TN. 2016

Sylvia Edmondson-Holt

Sylvia Edmondson-Holt at program Honoring Theodore Edmondson and the Promise Land singers Circa 2014

Sylvia Edmondson-Holt continues to entertain the audience as she shows of the mink stole worn by her mother, the late Mrs. Lizzie Edmondson. 2014

Standing Mrs. Betty Ruth Edmondson and her son Jewel Edmondson. Seated Sylvia Edmondson-Holt and Lauretta Talley-Thomas. Circa 1990. At John Wesley UMC Nashville, TN.

Mrs. Essie Van Leer Gilbert celebrated 100 years old (2016) and has lived in Promise Land her whole life. She is sitting in the historical Promise Land School 2015.

Inside the main room of the historical Promise Land School as it is today. 2016

Kevin Holt and great aunt Rev. Sis. Annie Sadler circa 1980. Sis Sadler pastored a church in Louisville KY

Kevin and father Bobby Holt 1973

Graduation party for Terrell Holt Sr. 1981
Seated, Loretta Holt Mayberry. Standing L-R
Grandmother Lizzie Edmondson, Terrell, Kevin and Wilma Edmondson
Talley

L-R Anthony Holt, Carla Faye Holt-Houston and Terrell Holt Sr. Celebrating Graduations from Real Estate classes.

Chaplain John Morris, Sylvia Edmondson-Holt and Ronnie Clark. A Birthday at work with coworkers. Circa 1990s.

Sylvia Edmondson-Holt

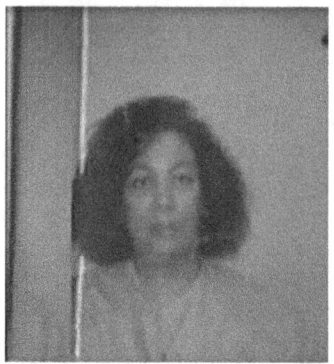

Sylvia Edmondson-Holt at work

Front; Mikayla Holt. Back Olivia and Aliyah Holt leaving a historical tour of our roots at Clement Railroad Museum 2012

A tour of Cumberland Furnace TN, the Holt girls are leaving an original slave cabin circa mid 1800's

Left is Grandmother Miss Susie Van Leer with the Niblette brothers and at right pictured alone. Early 1900.

Circa 1944
Helen M. Edmondson Hughes, ninth child born to Theodore and Lizzie Edmondson

Sylvia Edmondson-Holt circa 1944 pondering this journey called life. In Grandma Josie's rocking chair.

Sylvia Edmondson-Holt

These gentlemen who accompany me in this picture are my three sons. They have been spectators since their birth as my life unfolds live and on stage. They have been my biggest fans, supporting actors and sometimes stages directors all in one. Early in their life I tried to teach them that # one I love them more than… life. They know that I work hard, am goal directed, love to have fun and am "perfect" even though I have made a few mistakes. I receive new roles and the scenes continue to change in my life. Together we try to understand the plot embedded in each dialogue. Sometimes it is difficult to comprehend but one thing we know is that Love remains our main focus, and the spotlight is on JESUS. Amen.

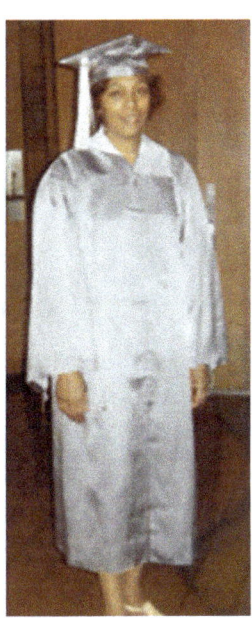

Sylvia Edmondson-Holt Left LPN graduation 1973. Middle: Kevin Holt with mother's cap on. Right graduation from the University of Tennessee Nursing School. Circa 1977.

Bottom left on tractor Sylvia Edmondson-Holt: right grilling Sylvia with brother-in-law: left Lathel Hughes and husband Bobby L. Holt at home in Nashville circa 1971.

Trucking adventure Circa 1989 in Washington state. Sylvia Edmondson-Holt and Graham Bell.
Pictured above Dr. Ardis Edmondson-Holt and Sylvia Edmondson-Holt in Promise Land 1971.

Andre and Kevin Holt with Fiber and Peter rabbits on the ground in Nashville. Circa 1976
Pictured left Andre Holt with Lassie and Brutus in Nashville. Circa 1974

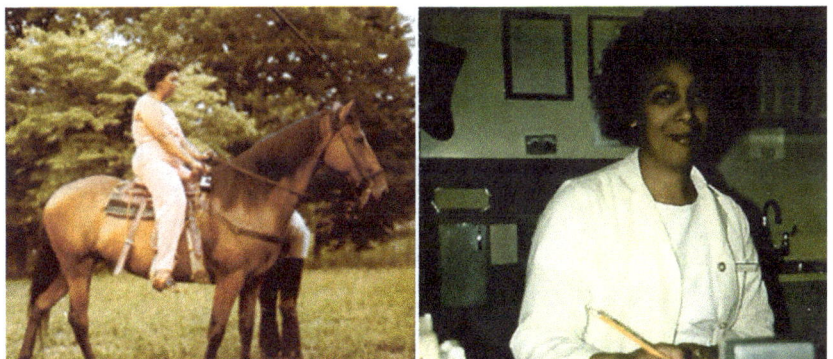

She wears many hats. Top left (Horseback) Sylvia Edmondson-Holt in Worley Furnice Dickson Tennessee. Circa 1981. Top right at Baptist Hospital PASR. Circa 1975

After church. L-R: Ronnie, Rex, and Keith Mayberry. Second row: Jerry Mayberry, Rev. Dalton Holt, Sis. Augusta Holt, Carla Fay Holt-Houston baby Tony, and Loretta Holt Mayberry. Circa 1977.

Spring Break in Atlanta, Georgia. Center: Sylvia Edmondson-Holt. Second row: Olivia and Aliyah Holt. Back row: Domingo, Ivy, and Juan Diego, 2016.

Saint John M.E. Church, Sunday school, June 1961. Pictured below are: (Front kneeling) Robert Gilbert holding Lauretta Talley. Front row (L-R): Essie Gilbert, George Mosley, Rita Gilbert, Bobby Edmondson, and Brock Edmondson. Second row (L-R): Della Gilbert Bryant, Jimmy Edmondson, Bill Gilbert, Jerry Primm, John Primm, Sharon Edmondson Harrington, Linda Gilbert Watson, Ruth Robertson, Beverly Gilbert Williams. Back row (L-R): Michael Primm, William Henry Primm, Serina Gilbert, Helen Edmondson Hughes, Lizzie Edmondson, Hattie Edmondson, Sylvia Edmondson-Holt, and Thomas Edmondson.

Kevin (four years old) with Bobby Holt, 1975.

The Edmondson sisters and brothers (L-R): Helen Hughes, Douglas Edmondson, S. Bernice Heard, Sylvia Edmondson-Holt, and James Edmondson, March 2016.

Bobby Holt, 1974.

L-R Olivia, Aliyah Holt and Grand Mommy Sylvia Edmondson-Holt. 2016
(Ohio twins summer vacation in Tennessee)

Promise Land School and Church located on Essie V. Gilbert Blvd (Promise Land Road) People are gathering for a service. Circa 2010.

Kevin Holt dances with mother Sylvia Edmondson-Holt at a Top of the Line Christmas party. Circa 1996.

Sylvia Edmondson-Holt front with Dee Appleton beside her at a Democratic Women's Club Meeting. Circa 1996

Graduation from Life Christian Bible Institute (At Faith is the Victory Church) Front Aliyah and Olivia Holt. Back Camille, Sylvia Edmondson-Holt and Candice Holt. 2007

Sylvia Edmondson-Holt with Pastor Dr. Charles Cowan, Faith is the Victory Church Nashville Tennessee. Graduation from Life Christian Bible Institute Charter Class of 2010 with a degree in Theology.

Wilma Talley, Lorry Edmondson and Bernice Heard. (From left to right)

Graduation 2015. Olivia Holt, Camille, Sylvia Edmondson-Holt and Candice. (From left to right)

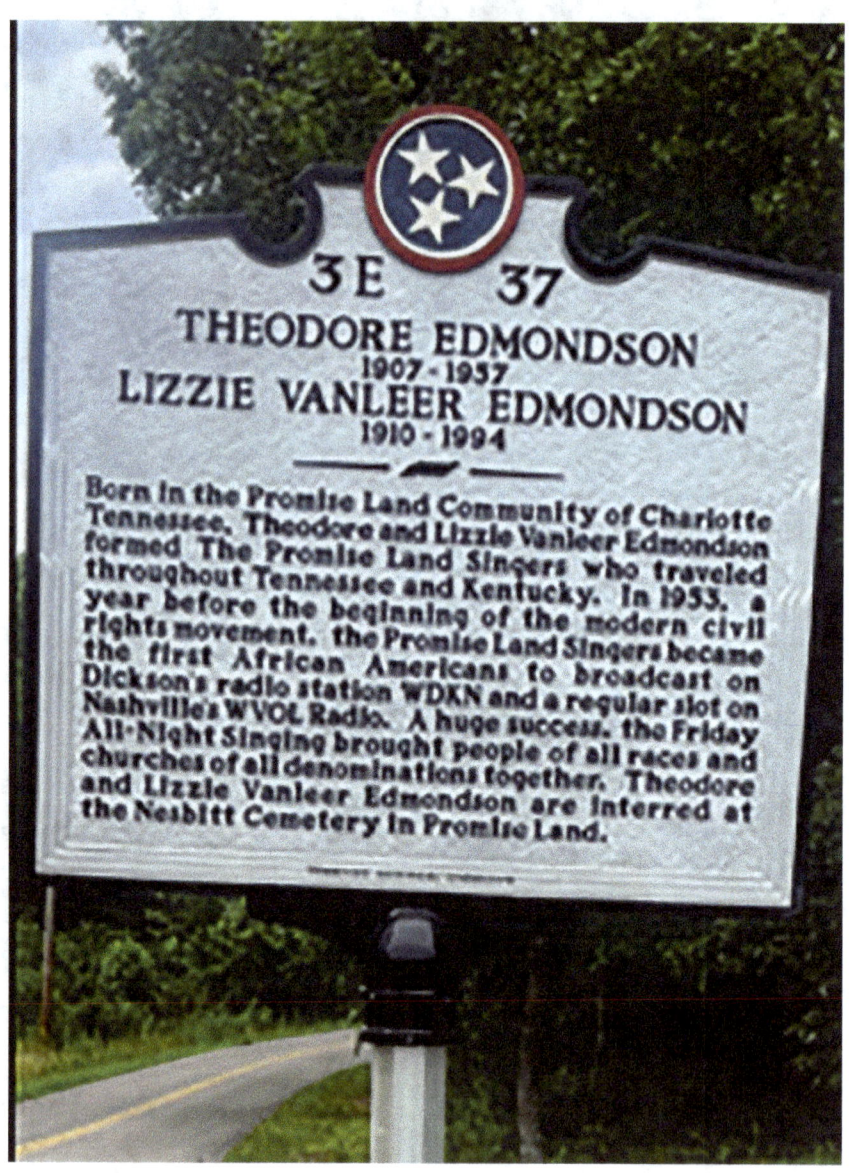

Historical Marker for My Parents on the Property in Promise Land

Alexis, Donavon, Jaime, Briana and Sylvia Edmondson-Holt
(From left to right)

Kevin Holt with dog Nikki

Sylvia Edmondson-Holt and Samuel Thomas in Germany.

Sylvia Edmondson-Holt at the Governor's Mansion during a meeting of Democratic Women's Club circa 1992.

Sylvia Edmondson-Holt

When in Europe Sylvia Edmondson-Holt

My Mother

My Mother Brings Sunshine to our heart. She the most understanding Mother. She Loves us so much, we Know it By the way she takes care of us. When I Think of My Mother I Think of Happness and joy. But the Most THING of All We Love Her Me my Brothers and ALL

We
Love
You
Mom

Sylvia Edmondson-Holt Mother's Day
(Poem written by Terrell Holt Circa 1973)

```
PHONE 242-1325



          REV. JESSE J. BOWEN



                    2713 MEHARRY BLVD.
                    NASHVILLE, TENN. 37208
```

```
RT. 2 BOX 45                CHARLOTTE,
                               TENN


       BRO. THEODORE EDMONDSON
               AND HIS
         PROMISE LAND SINGERS
         CAN BE HEARD SUNDAYS' ON  W S O K


MGR.                     MRS. T. EDMONDSON
```

An original business card of Bro. Edmondson
and the Promise Land Singers

THE PARTY IN NEW YORK CITY. The word was out. CALLING ALL SUPERHEROES, it said. Sophia's 5th Birthday and Elijah's 3rd Birthday

COME CELEBRATE SUNDAY

JANUARY 26th 2025

The Superheroes piled into the venue at noon until two. After tossing and screaming, jumping and screaming, and all the snacks one could eat the Super heroes headed home. But the party didn't stop there. All the gifts were delivered to the hero's home.

Grandpa Terrell Sr., grandmother Sheebe, Aunties, Uncles and big and little cousins came from four different states to celebrate the Birthday Heroes. The party continued well into the night with presents being opened. The Heroes continued to exhibit all that super power until Great Grand mommy Sylvia thought even she might take flight with Wonder Woman. Fortunately for her the real Wonder Woman (Sophia) and the real Green Lantern (Elijah) were there to save the day. There was so much love flowing throughout the house and we soaked it up like a real family reunion. We are looking forward to the next family events.

Since 2016 our family has been blessed with Iliana Diego 5 years old and Sophia Holt 5 years old and Elijah Holt 3 years old. The Ohio twins Olivia and Aaliyah are in the Navy and also in college for Engineering and Pharmacy.

Sylvia Edmondson-Holt

Terrell Holt Sr is with grandson Elijah Holt 3 years and granddaughter Sophia Holt 5 years old. They are going to the party NYC.

NYC Birthday Party: Left to right Terrell Holt Jr. Josh Jones and Kahmbrel Lewis: Front Sophia Holt (Wonder Woman) and Elijah Holt at the after party the Birthday Party

Father Terrell J Holt Jr holding Sophia and grandmother Sheebe Holt holding Elijah 2025

Sylvia Edmondson-Holt

NYC Birthday Party for Sophia and Elijah Center

Elijah Holt the hero Green Lantern after the birthday Party.

Auntie Carla is playing with Elijah at the after party. 2025

Toshebia Holt Carla Cato back Undrea and Dee Matthew - 2025 Super Heroes Birthday in NYC.

Mikayla Marie Holt my youngest granddaughter is enjoying her 17th birthday

Left to right Candice, mother Chiquilla and twin sister to Candice is Camille front Sylvia Edmondson-Holt

Sylvia Edmondson-Holt

Iliana Diego and the Cat Jeniperr Lo'paws

Juan, Jaime , Ivy and Iliana Diego 2024
The Birthday Party in New York City for
Sophia Noelle 5 years and Elijah Mateo Holt 3 years old

Kevin Holt with twin daughters Olivia and Aaliyah Holt Christmas 2024

Iliana Diego center performing at Christmas Recital for Malone Dance Academy

Ivy Maria Diego is now 12 years old with her sister Iliana Lane Diego. They are ready for the Christmas Recital for Malone Dance Academy.

Iliana Lane 5th Birthday

Toshebia Holt and Terrell Holt Jr.

Abby Christmas Recital.

Twins Candice and Camille Holt with grand-mommy in Washington DC after receiving Congressional Gold Medals.

Congressional Gold Medal Awards in Washington DC June 2014 Candice and grand-mother Sylvia Edmondson-Holt.

Sylvia Edmondson-Holt

Douglas Edmondson plays with great-great-niece Ivy Diego

Lorry Edmondson enjoying a visit to Promise Land.
He is exploring an old house that might have been built by our Father.

Sylvia Edmondson-Holt

Wilma Edmondson Talley modeling at a church event.

Lorry Edmondson and Bernice Edmondson enjoying "Between the Pews." First Edition Our sister in law Mary in the background.

NYC Party (From the right Mikayla Marie, Candice and Camille Holt and the two girls is Abby and sister Illianna)

Sylvia's Sons: Kevin, Andre, and Terell Sr.

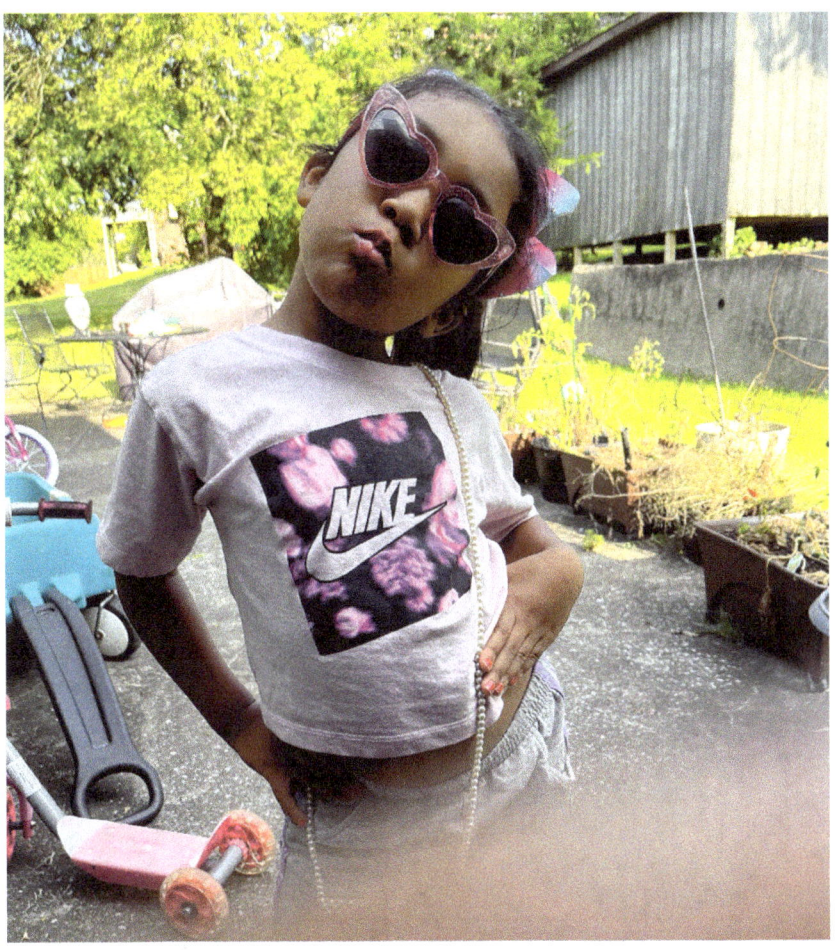

Iliana Diego enjoying a day playing at Great Granmommy's patio 2024

Sylvia Edmondson-Holt

Sylvia Edmondson-Holt

Illiana enjoying in Promise Land.

Iliana is working on the container garden on the patio 2024.

Look at that big fat pepper Ivy picked

Sylvia Edmondson-Holt

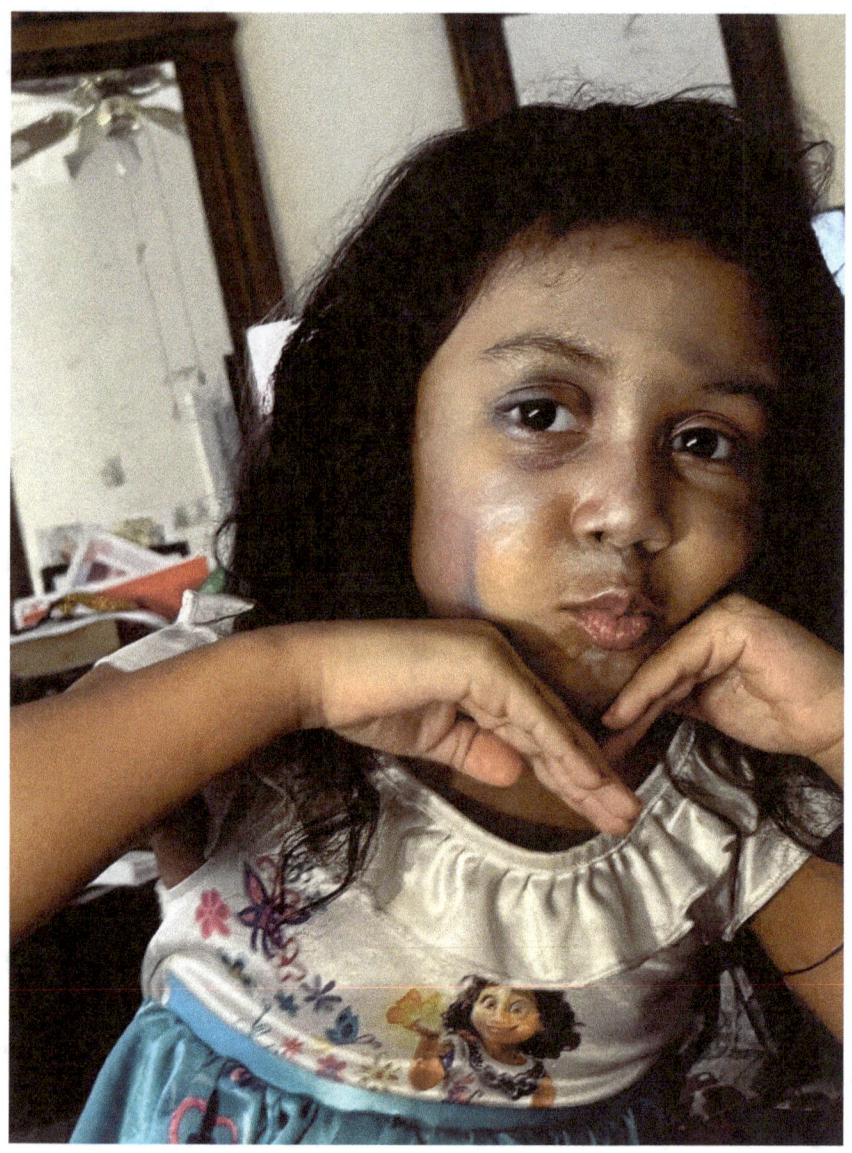

Iliana loves putting on make-up 2024

Iliana loves her container garden

Sylvia Edmondson-Holt

Iliana loves, going to the beach Panama Beach, Florida

In loving Memory of Rosie Ludwid. Rosie we miss you and no one could cook like you. Rest in peace 2023 (Grandmother to our twins Candice and Camille Holt)

Sylvia Edmondson-Holt

Sylvia Edmondson Holt spending a day in Promise Land

Terrell Holt Jr escorts Jaime in the Little Miss AKA pageant

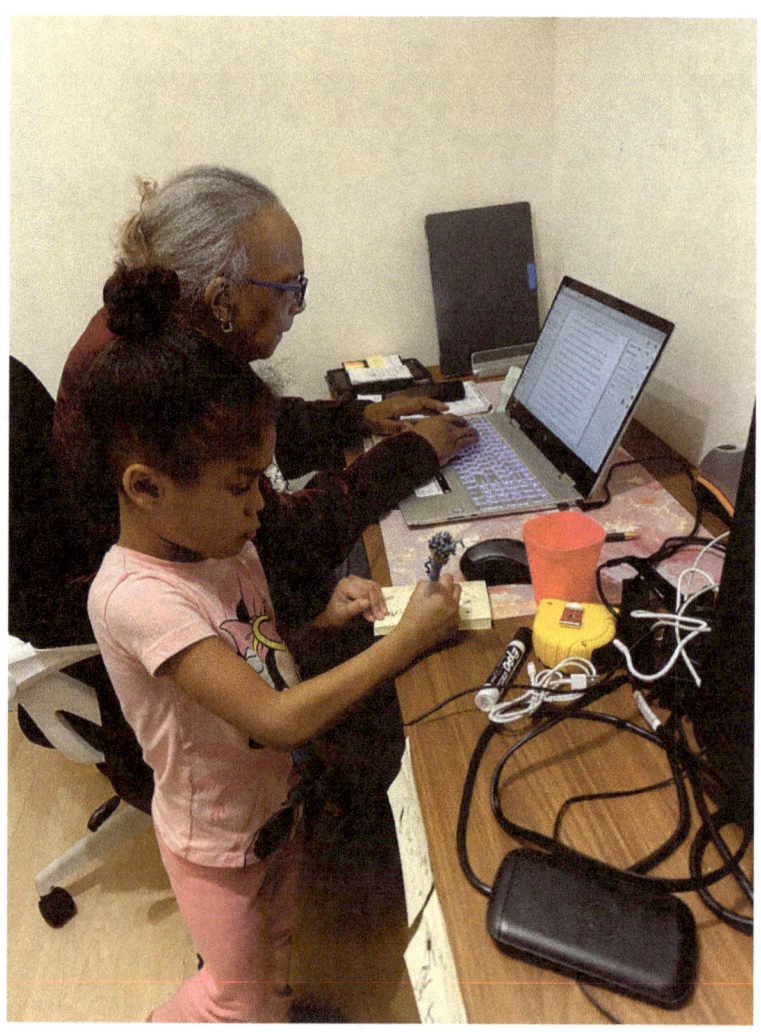

Mommy Sylvia and Sophia having little work.

www.ingramcontent.com/pod-product-compliance
Lightning Source LLC
LaVergne TN
LVHW012245070526
838201LV00090B/122